LIFE BEGINS AT 90

A Three-in-One Book
telling the stories of
Norman and Joyce Lambert Giller MBE
and The Music Man Project

A 21st CENTURY LOVE STORY

NGB

A Norman Giller Books publication
First published 2025
Daws Heath, Essex

Website: www.normangillerbooks.com
© Norman Giller 2025

Music Man Project words and photos
© David P. Stanley 2025
Website: www.themusicmanproject.com

A CPI catalogue record is available for this book from the British Library

ISBN 978-0-9567711-1-7

Typesetting and origination by NMG Enterprises

Printed and bound in the United Kingdom
by CPI Group (UK) Ltd, Croydon CRO 4YY

Special thanks to David Stanley BEM for the co-operation of The Music Man Project, to Alison Lambert for her safety-net checking, and to No 1 son Michael Alan Giller for his specialist input. All illustrations are from the authors' private collection and/or The Music Man Project, with thanks to Michael Lambert for his photographic expertise.

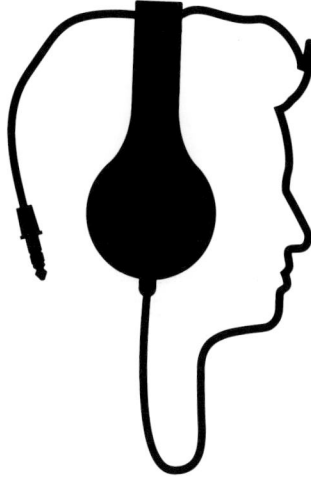

Music Man Project

For every copy of this book sold after overheads have been cleared, author/publisher Norman Giller will make a donation to the marvellous Music Man Project. For details how to add to their funds please email: musicmanprojectsouthend@gmail.com

About The Music Man Project

The Music Man Project is an award-winning, world record breaking service for people with learning disabilities, providing music tuition leading to performance. Run by volunteers under the supervision of multi-talented David Stanley BEM, the charity gives grants for accessible education, promotes equal access, carries out research and raises awareness. See our gallery of special Philanthropists on Page 198-203. Thank you for buying this book and helping a great cause.

Charity number: 1188041.

In loving memory of
Sir David Amess
(1952-2021)

Taken from us, but always there as an inspiration.

LIFE BEGINS AT 90

A Three-in-One Book
telling the stories of
Norman and Joyce Lambert Giller MBE
and The Music Man Project

A 21st CENTURY LOVE STORY

CONTENTS

Chapter One:
The Matchmaking Game

THANK you for joining us for this journey through our fairly eventful lives. We are going to start near the end, with a wedding. Our wedding.

As the writer in the family, I will carry the main load of our story, acting as a sort of orchestra conductor, with Joyce as the chief soloist. *She will be talking in fluent italics.*

Joyce had been widowed for 45 years after her first husband, also Norman, died of lung congestion in 1979. I lost my lovely first wife, Eileen, to a kidney disease in 2006 after an idyllic 45 year marriage.

Our 'children' – son-in-law John East, my daughter Lisa and Joyce's youngest son Michael Lambert and his wife, Alison – were long-time friends, and they secretly plotted to have us meet at a Sunday lunch at Belfairs Golf Club in Essex on December 8, 2019.

I had been thinking more in terms of a dolly bird to put spice into my old age, but reluctantly went along with the sly, blindingly obvious match-making scheme. I was certainly not thinking of an older model. *Joyce will not mind me saying that in her late 80s, she could be considered fairly ancient.* I was five and a bit years her junior.

Anyway, their ploy worked and it was 'interest' at first sight. Joyce and I quietly arranged to meet for breakfast the next week at the Beach Hut at Westcliff-on-Sea, equidistant our Essex homes without interference from our well-meaning 'kids.'

This Estuary-side café became a regular rendezvous and gradually our friendship started to reveal a romantic twist, hand holding and taking long, slow walks along the seafront. We continually counted our blessings that at our advanced ages we were both fit and healthy enough to put in the miles with lots of smiles.

Then along came Covid-19.

We followed the no-gathering rules (listening, Boris?) and kept the flame of interest alive with daily messaging on line. This hugely amused our grandchildren and great grandkids, watching we old wrinklies struggle with modern communication techniques that are commonplace to them.

I had started out in the writing game with clunky, clattering typewriters and carbon paper 70-plus years earlier, and along the way had been chief football writer for the *Daily Express*, a member of the *This Is Your Life* scriptwriting team for 14 years, and a boxing PR for the likes of Muhammad Ali, Sir Henry Cooper, Joe Bugner and Frank Bruno. I had also for nine years written magazine and newspaper columns in harness with comedian Eric Morecambe and four books and a TV show with Scouse scallywag Ricky Tomlinson.

Keeping such hilarious. company while earning a few bob guaranteed laughs along the way. And I'd had published 120 books, 20 in collaboration with my best mate, football and broadcasting legend Jimmy Greaves. I had been a busy boy and had gained a reputation as a renowned sports historian (I can bore for Britain on the subject).

Now here I was messaging via my iPhone a lovely little old lady with whom I shared an East London background but had little else in common. Joyce was a former Southend Tory councillor, while I was left of centre, and she had just minimal interest in sport that had been at the heart of my journalistic life. On paper, it should never have worked. But this was Romeo and Juliet with an ancient angle.

"Romeo, Romeo, wherefor art thou, Romeo ...?"
"Just putting me long johns on and will be with yer in a jiffy."

We first declared our love for each other while huddling up in freezing temperatures during a 14-hour walk to pay our respects to the late Queen Elizabeth in September, 2022.

Though poles apart politically, we both wanted to show our thanks to Her Majesty for always doing her duty and displaying old-fashioned discipline and dignity that appealed to the generation that Joyce and I represented.

After cruelly losing her first husband after 23 years of marriage, she concentrated on running her car batteries shop business in Essex with her two sons and getting heavily involved in the local community.

When I first got to know her she was serving in a volunteer capacity on five committees, and was 'chair' of the revered Iveagh Conservative club, based in Leigh-on-Sea. She had been made a Freeman of the City of London in recognition of her unselfish work on behalf of her fellow citizens.

At the time Joyce and I got together, I was helping local Tory MP Sir David Amess with his campaign to get Southend long-awaited City status.

I had written a song, the chorus of which Sir David secretly and mischievously planned to sing at PMQs in the House:

'*Good old Southend on Sea*
Such a lovely place to be
So much to do, so much to see
At good old Southend on Sea.'

Okay, not exactly Milton or Masefield but it struck a chord with the man who had the seaside town stamped through him like a stick of Southend rock.

I mentioned in passing to Sir David that I was surprised Joyce had not been acknowledged in the Honours List, considering the way she continually put others first, and was always there to help anybody with problems and the number of local committees to which she gave her time and energy.

Action man Sir David immediately set the ball rolling and we nominated Joyce for Royal recognition, with the support of then Southend Mayor Stephen Habermel.

Suddenly, a thunderbolt from hell. Sir David was senselessly stabbed to death in a crazy terrorist attack while giving a constituency surgery on a tragic day in the autumn of 2021. Just hours before his awful death, Sir David – a fellow East Ender – telephoned me to see how the Joyce campaign was going. More by luck than judgement, she did not, as usual, help out at the surgery where he was murdered.

Sir David's successor as Southend West MP, Anna Firth, took up the baton to get Joyce the recognition she deserved. Meantime, thanks largely to the generosity of benefactor Dr Vijay Patel, a statue was raised in Sir David's memory. It was erected on Westcliff Beach, which was the site I selected for my proposal of marriage, blinded by love and not taking the gusty weather conditions into account.

I asked a passing stranger to video the moment I popped the question on my iPhone and then led Joyce to Sir David's statue.

As I went down on one knee in traditional style to ask for Joyce's hand, the gale-force wind was raging at increasing knots. She has not got the best of hearing and I shouted, 'I want us to spend our sunset years together, Will you marry me?'

Joyce leant forward and I repeated the proposal. It was right out of a Monty Python sketch.

'I thought you'd been blown over,' Joyce told me later. 'Because of the wind I couldn't hear what you were saying but your lips moved beautifully, so I bent forward and kissed you.'

I took that as a 'yes' and six weeks later, after going through all the official paper rigmarole, we were married in a quiet ceremony at the sumptuous Roslin Beach Hotel in Thorpe Bay, with our sons and daughters as witnesses. The ceremony in front of just our closest relatives included a 20-minute PowerPoint presentation by me of our love story, and then my traditional sing-a-long-a-Norm rendering of old Cockney songs that had been passed down to me by my Dad, an East End pub pianist for more than 40 years standing (and often staggering).

Love of older music, the standard classics, and ballet and opera masterpieces, helped bond us and we're regular visitors to the Royal Opera House in Covent Garden and to Ronnie Scott's Jazz Club (a little trivia for you: Ronnie Scott went to the same East End grammar school as me when his name was Ronnie Schatt. Goodness knows why he changed it!).

More than five years younger than Joyce, I told her I was prepared to be her Toy Boy but not her Tory Boy. We've agreed that laughter will play a major part in whatever time we've got left as we walk together into the setting sun.

Moral of our story is that it is never too late to fall in love.

We had a brief honeymoon in our home town of London, staying in the bridal suite at Chelsea Harbour Hotel, taking the Uber boat along the Thames to see three cracking West End Shows – *SIX*, about Henry the Eighth's six wives, for the third time *Operation Mince Meat*, comfortably the most entertaining of British musicals, and then the Daddy of them all for a fifth time, *Les Miserables*.

Highlight for us was a visit to the Battersea Power Station, that used to be a shell of a building but is now an anthem to Art Deco design. You must take Lift 109, the stunning glass elevator that hurtles you to the top of one of Battersea's iconic chimneys with breath-taking views down the Thames and across London and the South of England. You will thank us for recommending it.

Setting up home in John and Lisa's coach house in the grounds of their beautiful dwelling in Daws Heath, Essex, we celebrated Joyce's 90th birthday on November 23 (two days after the actual event), with 70 guests and a good old East End knees up, again at the Roslin Beach Hotel, where we had tied the knot five weeks earlier.

It was all organised and paid for by Joyce's two sons Steven and Michael and their wives, Alison and Lucy. We felt blessed.

Two weeks after her 90th birthday, Joyce was stunned and thrilled to receive a letter from the Cabinet Office inviting her to be an MBE in the King's 2025 New Year's Honours List.

I could sense Sir David smiling in the heavens.

Chapter Two:
The Palmer Girls

WE are now in London in the 1930s, a turbulent decade into which Joyce Hannah Palmer was born on Wednesday 21 November, 1934. She started life with older sister Eileen on the top floor of an elegant, rented four-storey Victorian block of flats at 92 Cressy House in Stepney, right in the heart of London's East End.

Joyce arrived the exact day that Cole Porter's exhilarating musical *Anything Goes* opened on Broadway, a smash-hit show including songs that would becomes standards like *You're the Top*, *It's De-Lovely* and *I Get A Kick Out of You*. Joyce has always got a kick out of life.

The world was just emerging from the Great Depression after the Wall Street crash of 1929, and while Joyce was still in her cot Hitler was proclaiming himself Führer of Germany following the death of President Paul von Hindenburg. Nobody knew it then, but the seeds of war had been sown.

When she was two in 1936 Britain had three monarchs. George the V died, Edward V111 abdicated and George the Sixth was crowned. In that same eventful year, the Spanish Civil War started, there was the haunting Jarrow Hunger March, Hitler turned the Berlin Olympics into a propaganda platform for the Nazis, and BBCtv went public for the first time.

Over to Joyce:

"There was lots of poverty in the East End when I was a girl, but I'll not try to pretend that I knew what it was to go hungry. My Mum and Dad would make sure we had food on the table and there was always a generous uncle to push a twopenny piece into my grateful little hand.

"Mum – Flossie Arundell before she became a Palmer – had five brothers, all living around the corner in a small terraced house in Redman's Road and they spoilt me and my older sister Eileen rotten. Three other sisters, Ann, Sheila and Lorna, arrived later, during and after the war.

"Dad had a steady, if low-paid job in the City, working in a warehouse, in charge of sorting the ton loads of paper that the clerks and stockbrokers generated in those pre-computer days.

"Early on I got the nickname of the Bag Baby, because one of my Mum's brothers caused great amusement by hanging me in a shopping bag on the hook of the back door. I apparently used to laugh as I hung there, and it gave a whole new meaning to 'hanging around.'

"My Granny Palmer's house in nearby Charles Street was always tumbling with people and was an exciting place for Eileen and me to visit from our flat around the corner. Auntie Min, Dad's oldest sister on the Palmer side, was a formidable force in my early life and I have often been told I most resemble her, both with my looks and ceaseless energy. She and her husband (Uncle Ben Macdonald) ran a small factory in Arbour Square, specialising in tailoring men's trousers and it was from Auntie Min I first learned the skills of working a Singer sewing machine, my trusted companion for most of my 90 years on earth.

"And it was Min and Uncle Ben, who first led the exodus of my huge family to Southend in the late pre-war years. Dad had six sisters. Minnie, Rose, Florence, Grace, Margaret and Beatrice. Then there were Eileen, me, and our younger sisters Ann, Sheila and Lorna. So the Palmer girls ruled, and my poor Daddy always lived in a world filled with females!

"But I'm jumping ahead of myself, and Norman is nagging me to keep the story in the 1930s My uncles on Mum's side were all keen followers of Oswald Mosley, the Enoch Powell/Nigel Farage of his day, and my Granny Arundell (we didn't use christian names for grandparents in those days) used to make buckets of whitewash for them to paint slogans on the dock walls.

"They were very strong in their opinion that Britain should be for the British and so they joined the Mosley marches in black shirts made for them by my gran. So I was exposed very early to their views that British people should come first in getting Government housing and any hand-outs that are going. It doesn't make me racist. I don't judge people by the colour of their skin but by their deeds and actions. I am just very proud to be British and I don't mind saying it out loud. Charity begins at home.

"I, of course, was unaware of all the fighting and feuding going on with the Mosley marches and was enjoying an idyllic childhood. I used to hold my older sister Eileen's hand and we would walk together to the local primary school at nearby Dempsey Street. There was no need for knowledge

of the Highway Code because the only cars we saw were the occasional black Wolsley saloons used by the police. It was more likely that we had to be careful of the carthorses pulling the milk, coal or barrels of beer.

"I have a clear memory of my first experience of being in a motor car. It was a highly polished Standard 8 that my Uncle Ben drove, and he would take me and my sister Eileen on regular visits to his factory in Arbour Square. All I need is a smell of leather and I am back sitting in the car as Uncle Ben steered his way through streets that were busy and bustling with people going about their business.

"The red-brick flats where I grew up for a council rent of 25 bob a week (£1.05) were stylish and designed by a Victorian architect with imagination, not like those eye-sore buildings that later dominated the London skyline and were just blocks of concrete. If I can digress a little here and tell the story of a TV researcher contacting me when news of our marriage broke in 2024. She asked where I had been born and when I told her it was in Cressy House there was suddenly the sound of silence on the other end of the line. 'That's astonishing,' she eventually said, catching her breath. 'I lived in that same block of flats for five years when first arriving in London. And they are still beautiful to the eye.' What are the odds, when you consider how many blocks of flats there are in London? But back to my story ...

"I can recall clearly the 'quiet hour' each afternoon at the Dempsey Street primary school, when we used to lie down and doze in the afternoon. To this day, I cannot remember anything so peaceful and relaxing, the sun coming through the huge windows and dancing on the iron bedsteads on which we were laying. There were very few obese children, and kids with mental problems were unheard of, and fast-food had not entered our vocabulary. If anybody felt down in those days they were simply told to pull themselves together. Child psychiatrists were as rare as hen's teeth.

"From school, Eileen and I would stroll either to my Aunt Flo's small furrier shop in Charles Street or to our Granny Arundell's house at Cherry Place in Redman's Road. Aunt Flo was quite a character. She had a baby, Joe, out of wedlock – a 'love child' they called it back then – and he followed his mum into the fur trade. He was brought up as more of a brother than cousin to me, and was answerable to my Dad as the man in his life. Rather than being a disciplinarian, Dad used to spoil him as if he was somebody *very special. He looked on him as the son he never had.*

"Aunt Flo was considered something of a toff because she was the only one in our area who had a telephone, and I think I recall the number was Stepney Green 4251. Everybody else had to queue at the one red GPO telephone box 200 yards away in Commercial Road. If someone was monopilising the phone, you had to walk down to Whitechapel Station to find half a dozen telephone boxes.

"The women in my family were always the entrepreneurial ones, none more so than dear Granny Arundell. She was a remarkable lady, unable to read or write yet a whiz with mental arithmetic, and she had loads of good-sense sayings, such as: 'Educate a girl and you'll educate a family'. She understood interest rates and became a money lender. With five strapping sons, she did not have to worry about people knocking her. It was Granny Arundell who used to say, 'Never send a man to work on an empty belly.'

"We were brought up as Roman Catholics and Procession Sundays were always special, when we used to put on 'Sunday best' pristine white dresses and feel like little princesses. The East End would come to a halt and people used to line the route of the Procession from St Mary's and St Michael's Catholic church in the Commercial Road, looking on in respectful silence broken only by the sound of the marching band or sometimes the bagpipes of the famous Dagenham Girl Pipers.

"My Mum used to supplement Dad's low income by working in an East End factory, making the fancy hat and chocolate boxes for the big West London stores. My aunts would take me 'up West' for a treat at least once a month, and my first visit to the theatre was to see Peter Pan at the London Palladium and they dropped the Flanagan and Allen hit song of the time, Any Umbrellas, into the show and brought the house down.

"The Singer Sewing machine was our best friend, and most of my aunts could quickly run up a dress or do a quick repair. My Aunt Grace, I recall, would crochet socks and give them to Eileen and me as regular presents, and my darling Uncle Ben would buy us shiny new shoes. Rags and second-hand clothes were never part of my childhood.

"We always had food to eat, often cooked on a huge, black range oven by Granny Arundell, with her five hungry sons – my uncles – dominating a table that had extensions which when pulled out filled much of the kitchen.

Our favourite dishes were Granny's beautifully prepared stews that sent an aroma all the way down Redman's Road and making just about everybody feel famished. I can also recall bread and butter pudding, bread pudding, pease pudding with salt beef and carrots, mussels, caraway seed cakes, jellied eels, stewed eels with parsley sauce and loads of fruit when in season like apples, strawberries and tangerines. The 'Hungry Thirties' did not apply to the Palmers or the Arundells.

"For our weekend entertainment we used to go to Saturday morning pictures at the Troxy cinema in Commercial Road, where there would be lots of boy-orientated western films starring the likes of Hopalong Cassidy, Roy Rogers and Tom Mix, plus to keep we girls happy Mickey Mouse and Donald Duck cartoons. To see the biggest star of the era we used to queue to watch films featuring child prodigy Shirley Temple. When the lights went down and our attention was centred on the big screen we were alone with our imaginations and all was at peace with the world.

"The Troxy, built the year before I was born and noted for its Art Deco design, later became a training centre for the London Opera Company and was designated a Grade II building.

"On the Sundays in the summer our destination was often King Edward Memorial Park in Shadwell, where we would be entertained by a travelling Punch and Judy Show, and there was an Italian man on a three-wheeler bicycle selling ice cream cones, and later in the day the muffin man and a winkles, shrimps and cockles stallholder competed for our tastebuds. These memories are making me feel hungry!

"We also made regular visits to Victoria Park after Granny Arundell had moved to Bethnal Green, and I particularly recall when we watched my Dad taking part in fire brigade drills. I was so proud of him and kept telling onlookers, 'That's my Dad.'

"In those days we could play in the street without fear of being knocked down, and we used to have skipping ropes, tennis balls to bounce against the wall, hoops and marbles and we used to chalk hop-scotch grids on the pavement. A favourite game was 'It', when you just had to touch somebody you were chasing. So simple, yet so satisfying. The cheekier boys used to play 'knock down ginger', knocking on doors and then hiding while people opened their doors to nobody. Stupid but hilarious.

"*Our amusement at home included what was a life-long love of card games, including rummy and sevens before moving on to more complicated games like whist and canasta. I later tried bridge but for me that was too serious and dampened the social side of cards. People who see me shuffle a pack of cards like a magician often accuse me, jokingly, of being a card sharp.*

"*Music has always been an important part of my recreational life and this dates back to when we had a wind-up gramophone on which my favourite record was a big band arrangement by the Artie Shaw orchestra of Cole Porter's* Begin the Beguine *on a heavy 78 RPM His Masters' Voice Bakelite disc. Another favourite of mine was* I Scream, You Scream, Everybody Likes Ice Cream, *and this featured on a transparent orange-coloured record that my cousin Gil Tipper, a sailor, brought home from the United States. Later in life there was nobody to touch the Queens of jazz, Ella Fitzgerald and Sarah Vaughan.*

"*No television, of course. Only the very rich could afford the brand new sets to watch black and white programmes that drew audiences of a few hundred. The wireless ruled the airwaves and British stars of radio, stage and the cinema screen included Gracie Fields, George Formby, Will Hay, Jessie Matthews, Sandy Powell, Robb Wilton, Stainless Stephen, Tommy Handley and Jessie Matthews. J. Arthur Rank was the big British film producer of the day, who I only recently discovered made his fortune producing self-raising flour.*

"*Misery came into my life for the first time when my Granny Palmer died in that eventful year of 1936. I was too young to appreciate what was going on, but I recall lots of weeping and as was the tradition in those days, Granny's open coffin lay for a week in the Charles Street lounge, with family and friends calling in to pay their respects. My Gran was laid to rest in a family plot at Leytonstone Cemetery. The manager of the burial ground later informed us that Dad had bought the family plot for a fee of £14, more than two weeks' wages back then. 'My grandfather was buried in a pauper's grave,' Dad told me. 'I wasn't going to let that happen to my mother.'*

"*A couple of years later, we moved from our flat in Cressy Court to Gran's terraced house 300 yards away at 34 Charles Street. We had three bedrooms and a small garden to play in, and Eileen and I slept downstairs in* one double bed in a small room adjoining the lounge. There was an outside loo, and we used to take turns washing ourselves in a tin bath, continually topped up with jugs of hot water from a firewood-heated copper boiler. My Mum set the standards of 'cleanliness being next to Godliness'.

"In those 1930s they had no antibiotics to cure diseases and infections, and there was no vaccine to stop measles or flu spreading. A painful memory is of falling into into a bucket of boiling water with which my mum was preparing to clean the floor, and I was rushed to hospital for treatment that had to be paid for. The NHS was still nine years away."

The most special time of year was Christmas and the hair stood up on the back of my neck in excitement and anticipation as soon as the first carol singers appeared in the streets, and all the shops had their windows dressed with Christmas trees and bunting. Our lounge rooms at Cressy House and later Charles Street were decorated with huge circles of pasted paper chains that we made from the coloured cut-offs that Daddy brought home from his warehouse job in the City. There were also large Chinese lanterns that were enormously colourful and gave a special hue to the room.

"Sounds like a Victorian Christmas scene, and that was exactly what it was, with the streets warmed and brightened by gaslit lampposts. You could almost feel the presence of Tiny Tim and Ebenezer Scrooge. The lamplighters used to make pennies on the side by acting as early-morning alarms, banging on doors to wake up sleeping tenants in time to go to work.

"Back then, my sister Eileen and I had total belief in Father Christmas, and he never ever let us down. Our toys included dolls, board games and, one year, a post office made of cardboard that laid the foundation for my money-counting skills in later years! In the stockings that we hung at the bottom of our bed we found a tangerine, a walnut and the rare treat of chocolate sweets. Heaven.

"It has gone down in history as the era of the Great Depression, but this little girl and her sister were protected from the worst of it by a caring Mum and Dad and uncles and aunts who refused to surrender to the misery surrounding us. I can honestly claim to have had a wonderful childhood. Make do and mend was the order of the day and all the women in our family were experts at sewing, knitting and machining. The 'Rag Trade' has always been a big part of my life, and to this day I have been a regular window *shopper. If dreams had come true I would have been a window dresser at one of the major West End stores. There are few things I liked better when growing up than ogling the gowns that adorned the shops and trying to think how I could have improved their positioning and decoration. Anybody who knows me well will confirm that I am fastidious about my dress sense, It all comes down to my Aunts and their insistence on things being well ordered and properly presented.*

"There was no such thing as the luxury of summer holidays, and the nearest we got to it was crossing the Thames via the Rotherhithe Tunnel and travelling by jam-packed lorry down through South London to Kent to join the thousands of Cockneys earning pocket money picking hops for the local brewers. The hop fields had a scent all of their own, and as we struggled to sleep in wooden shacks the aroma was almost overpowering.

"While we children played in the fields, our parents worked at filling bins with the hops they had collected from the hop vines. They would clear row after row and then move on to the next field, getting paid vital pennies according to the weight of their bins.

"We used to spend the nights around a large log fire and sing old musical songs and people would take turns to sing solos or give a monologue. There was a great community spirit and everybody was respectful and pulling together to get the hops collected.

"Life was gently paced and wonderful for Eileen and I and we had no idea of the horrors that lay ahead.

"Each evening Mum and Dad would sit and listen to the BBC Home Service news bulletin, and I vividly remember Dad shushing us once as we all listened in silence to our Prime Minister Neville Chamberlain telling us we were at war with Germany.

"It was September 3 1939. I was six and petrified because Dad had told us he would not be around so often. He had volunteered to join the Fire Service, and for the next six years I was pushed from pillar to post as the world erupted into an insane war."

Chapter Three:
The Kid from Cable Street

THIS is where I enter the story, some 400 yards away as the crow flies at number four Ring House in Shadwell, a block of flats owned by Stepney Borough Council and which ran from notorious Cable Street to The Highway, a busy thoroughfare that served the docks and the Tower Hamlets area. Like Joyce, I had started life at the back of the queue. The only way from here was up. The two of us had been born in one of the poorest boroughs in the land.

Some geography for you. Cable Street ran parallel to the River Thames through the East End of London, snaking for just under two miles from Limehouse to near Tower Bridge and the edge of the City's financial empire. It is infamous for having been a haunt of Jack the Ripper, the inspiration for Dickens at his darkest, and once the last refuge for paupers, pickpockets, prostitutes and their pimps.

It was also infamous when I arrived for being where Fascism got a bloody nose in that brutal Battle of Cable Street in 1936, with my Dad and Joyce's uncles on opposite sides as the Jew-baiting Oswald Moseley led his Blackshirts on their violently disrupted march in terrifying impersonation of Hitler's Nazis.

Cable Street. This is where I was born on 18 April 1940, just as the 'apprehensive appeaser' Neville Chamberlain was about to hand the Prime Ministerial reins over to the war-hungry, inspirational Winston Churchill. It was a Jewish stronghold, with many refugees who had fled the evil influence of Hitler and his unhinged, Nazi cohorts.

Little did I know that 400 yards as the crow flies across the Commercial and Mile End Roads, Joyce and the Palmer sisters were growing up

For me, life started as a home birth at 4 Ring House, Tower Hamlets, a cramped two-bedroom ground floor flat in the heart of Docklands when they were a thriving magnet for ships from across the world. Ring House was a 1920s-built four-storey block of 106 Stepney Council flats stretching 100 yards from Cable Street – the end where I was born – to The Highway, which is the main artery to what used to be the Docks.

The flats, within discus-throwing distance of what is now the Shadwell Basin maritime leisure complex, still stand but have been modernised beyond recognition from the wartime days when I was growing up next door to my Granny and Granddad Giller.

Granny (Frances) Giller, a gold medallist at Irish dancing, was the family legend who had eight children, losing three of them in childbirth and ruling the surviving five and her dominated docker husband with a strict discipline born of the Roman Catholic Church doctrine. The daughter of an immigrant labourer from County Cork who spent time in the workhouse, she – right into her mid-80s – would show off her jig.

Granny Giller's most prized possession, worn on a chain around her neck alongside a shining crucifix, was a gold medal with the inscription, "Awarded to Frances Waite, Under-18 Champion, Irish Dance Festival 1878." Her only son, my Dad, used to lead everybody a dance.

My mother's father, Tom Sims, was a Kent-born Thames lighterman, who worked the barges and tugs from Wapping wharf, and became a Freeman of the Thames after 50 years' service on the river. He suffered severe Bell's palsy as a teenager that left him with a half paralysed face and a mouth that ran lopsided down to his chin, and with a bloodshot left eye that never closed. It sounds horrific, but I never once thought it odd, and he won himself a pretty bride, Martha, who presented him with two sons and four daughters. (Three generations later, my granddaughter Kate and husband Callum produced a great grand daughter who without knowledge of my grandmother's name, christened her Martha. It was perfect, because I have never come across a lady as gentle, generous and kind as my Nanny Sims).

It is from Granny Giller and Granddad Sims that I inherited my energy gene. Both lived into their late 80s and were dynamos, never satisfied unless physically or mentally challenged. Show me a man who has written more than100 books, and I will show you somebody who cannot switch off.

When I was growing up at No 4 Ring House in the immediate post-war years my playground was bombed ruins, there were just three black families in our vicinity (the Barrows, the Lardners and the Lynches, including singer Kenny), hardly a single Asian to be seen but a multitude of Jews, many of them Holocaust survivors and with nothing but the clothes on their backs.

They were driven by hunger and desperation to be more enterprising than the mainly dock-working, indigenous East Enders, and we bought our bread and beigels from Sugarman the baker, our eggs from Gratofsky the grocer, and nobody could mend shoes better than Lipman, the cobbler up the road at Brick Lane. We also shopped and bartered at the sprawling Jews' Market in Hessel Street, which was eventually to be taken over by the Bangladeshi community.

The world map was largely imperialistic pink, with India still the jewel in the crown of the British Empire but preparing for Gandhi-led Independence, while in South Africa they were laying the foundations to the poison of Apartheid.

Weeks after my arrival in 1940 and while I was still a babe in arms, our trapped British Expeditionary Force was being miraculously rescued from Dunkirk and, soon after, the Luftwaffe started knocking the hell out of Cable Street because of its close proximity to the London Docks.

By the time the London Blitz was at its terrifying peak I had been whisked off with my Mum, Winifred, and two older brothers, five-year-old George and three-year-old Alan, to join the mass evacuation from a city bombed to its knees. From the terrors of London we found a comparative paradise, taken in by the charming, loving Dart family on a picturesque dairy and sheep farm in North Devonshire, equidistant Bideford and the beaches of Instow.

We were made so welcome by the Darts and their neighbouring farmers, the Steers, that my Mum later used to refer affectionately to that dark period as 'the best years of my life.'

I returned to the farm for long hot summers during every one of my post-war school holidays. In 2010 my eldest brother, George, and I revisited the village church to jointly deliver a eulogy to Molly Steer, oldest of the Dart daughters and one of the final remaining members of our generation of farming friends. End of an era and lasting thanks to the Darts and Steers.

For baby me, those five war years were heaven on earth. Along with my Mum, there were six women on the farm: Granny Dart, farmer's wife Mrs Florence Dart, farmer's daughters Molly and Joan, and land girl Doris (who later married Tom, the oldest of three Dart sons). They used to take turns cuddling me to get out of housework chores, and so I must have been one of the most spoiled, cosseted babies in history. No wonder that being cuddled by women has continued to be a favourite passion of mine. Thank you, Joyce!

I think of my generation, anybody born between 1930 and the end of the war, as the Last of the Victorians. We were sung to by grannies born in the 19th century, educated and disciplined by teachers who had been educated and disciplined by Victorians, listened to wireless broadcasts by plum-voiced presenters with Victorian backgrounds and values, and were brought up by parents who passed on the standards of respect and reverence they had learned from their Victorian-born parents.

We were taught to respect our teachers and anybody in authority, and while at first something of a cowed generation we learned the advantages of discipline and attention to detail, and had the pluck, the imagination and the confidence to break free of the shackles and launch the magical, life-changing decade of the 1960s.

Back in those early 1940s, farm life for we Cockney ragamuffin Gillers was idyllic, and when I first started talking it was with the west country burr of Granny Dart mixed with the Wapping accent of my mother. Both my older brothers went to the small local village school just three hundred yards from the farmhouse, and I joined them for one day, when I shamed myself by peeing on the classroom floor while singing around the piano. I ran crying back to the farm as fast as my five-year-old legs would carry me, and the belittling memory has never gone away.

The only reminder that a war was going on is that Farmer Dart was a brigadier in the Home Guard, and there was an ack-ack gun in the farmyard alongside a searchlight that used to pick out warplanes in the night sky, but they were usually American bombers that were based in North Devon preparing for the D-Day Landings. A sight that remains in my memory is of craning my neck and looking to the sky to see it black with wave upon wave of huge bombers carrying their destructive cargo on raids on occupied Europe. We could also hear the chilling air raid sirens from Barnstaple and

Bideford, usually when Plymouth was taking a pounding on the south coast.

Brigadier Dart supervised Dad's Army-style parades on the large farmhouse lawn that looked out over a lush, green valley that had a stream running through like a silver thread.

Last time I looked, a concrete bypass had replaced the stream.

During the war – while we were running free across the lush fields of Devonshire – Dad, Corporal George Giller, was away fighting the Germans in Yorkshire, where he was in the catering corps. He was helping an Army march on its stomach.

The war was an irritating interruption to his fleet-of-foot life as a bookie's runner by day and pub pianist by night. He was actuary-class at stand-up maths and could work out in his head an each-way sixpenny yankee bet (six each-way doubles, four each-way trebles and an accumulator) almost as quickly as he could sink a pint or three. He could also play by ear just about every popular song composed from Marie Lloyd's music hall days up to the modern-day hits of Gracie Fields, Bing Crosby and the new heartthrob, Frank Sinatra.

His four sisters – he was the only boy, and the youngest – clubbed together to buy him an upright piano for a wedding present in 1934, and our Ring House flat was the weekend party HQ for anybody in the mood for a knees-up. My party piece is that I can sing lots of the old Cockney songs, and I can name every Summer Olympics venue plus who were USA President, Prime Minister, British monarch and world heavyweight champion at the time. I am not invited to many parties.

At 32 when war was declared and the father of three sons, Dad was spared overseas duty. He was a good-quality footballer who played wartime League soccer as an amateur for Nottingham Forest and Doncaster Rovers, and every time he asked for a transfer because he wanted to see some action he was shifted to another regiment in Yorkshire. We used to joke he had won the Yorkshire Star.

He had a boxer pal in the Army called Alf Brown, who was a future Southern Area heavyweight champion. Alf, a huge, cheerful character from Catford, struggled to get sparring partners, and to help him keep in shape welterweight Dad used to go into a pub and start an argument with the biggest bloke he could find, invite him outside and let Alf take over to finish the job. We thought Dad was making up the story, but Alf confirmed the details when we visited him on a rare family trip to the foreign territory of South London after the war. It was worth a film: *Carry On Boxing*.

Dad was a complete stranger to me during the war, somebody dressed in khaki I saw just half a dozen times when he visited the farm while on leave. For me, Farmer Dart was the father figure.

My earliest, hazy memories of my Dad are of him on his knees sparring with my older brothers and encouraging me to hit him. His early birthday present to each of his sons was a pair of boxing gloves, and from our youngest days we were taught to defend ourselves.

I also recall him losing his temper with us after big brother George had knocked over a bottle of ink on the roll top desk in Farmer Dart's office, which was forbidden territory. I was four and the sight and sound of this unknown man in soldier's uniform yelling in anger has stayed with me all these years.

Another early memory of my Dad is of him killing a good friend of mine. Three huge bomb shelters dominated the grounds of Ring House, and immediately after the war I secretly kept a special pet fed and watered down inside one of them, leaning on my experience as a farm boy. Then my father discovered that it was not a rabbit as I had reported but a king-size rat which I called Winston. Dad killed it with a viciously aimed shovel to the back of the neck, and this distraught little six-year-old cried for hours.

Yes, welcome to the rat race.

Chapter Four:
Bombs, Shelters and the Blitz

JOYCE'S war was far more harrowing than mine, safe and spoiled down on the farm in Devonshire. People of a nervous disposition may want to skip these raw memories from my little East End girl …

"When war was declared, my Mum was expecting our sister Ann, third of the Palmer girls. Mum was due to go to the East London lying-in home in Stepney for the birth but because the maternity hospital was so close to the bomb-target of the Docks the delivery was switched to the historic Hill House in Theydon Mount near Epping in Essex. We think of Ann as more Arundell than Palmer in looks and manner.. She has always been very regal and being born in that mansion near Epping really suited her status. While Eileen and I were slight and typical Palmers, Ann had the proud and upright bearing and physicality of our Mum.

"While Mum was away bringing Ann into the world, Eileen and I were left with Granny Arundell. When it was announced that all children would be evacuated from London, my Gran's back went up and she proclaimed: 'No way. My girls stay with me. I am not allowing them to go into some stranger's house.

"The stand-off was solved by Gran coming with us on the evacuee train from Whitechapel Station. The three of us – stubborn Granny Arundell, Eileen and I – were deposited in a detached, tree-surrounded house in Egham in Surrey. This was posh stockbroker territory but Gran quickly decided it was not right for her precious charges. There was wet washing everywhere and the house could have done with a good spring clean.

"She sniffed the air and declared: 'This is a damp house. I'm not having my girls catch pneumonia.'

"The lady of the house took an instant dislike to this troublesome trio from the East End and had a stand-up row with Gran when Eileen and I were accused of knocking walnuts off some of the huge trees in her garden. It was autumn and the trees were automatically shedding their fruit. We were completely innocent.

"We had been there for about two weeks when Uncle Lenny, Gran's second eldest son, arrived to give his Mum the news that he was being shipped overseas. I can see him clearly on my memory screen, so handsome in his smart khaki shorts and shirt. Like all the Arundell men, he had a trim moustache and a proud, upright stance that is a family trait.

"After a private talk with his Mum, he invited Eileen and I to go for a walk with him along the towpath that bordered the nearby River Thames. Uncle Lenny, obviously wound up by Gran, quietly quizzed us about how we liked being evacuated.

"We couldn't wait to spill the beans and told told him the whole story of the wet washing, the damp walls and being told off about the walnuts.

"'When will we be going home?' Eileen asked. He said, 'Don't worry darling. Soon.'

"Three days later Lenny returned to Egham, driving a van. He put our belongings in the back and then headed home to Charles Street in the East End with a grinning Granny Arundell and Eileen and me in tow. Don't mess with the Arundells!

"We were reunited with our Mummy, and she had with her our beautiful baby sister Ann, who had distinctive black curly hair and a smile on which you could warm your hands. Eat your heart out, Adolf Hitler.

"My Aunt Florrie had moved further up Charles Street to a small shop that, along with her sister, Aunt Mag, she turned into a furriers in the days when there were not animal-rights protesters to make a nuisance of themselves.

"Daddy by then was in the fire service and became one of the unsung heroes. It was heartbreaking to see him come home every evening completely exhausted, his face covered in soot and muck and his uniform soaked, and heaven knows what horrific sights he had seen. Of course, there was no such thing as waterproof clothing and his black serge uniform just clung to him. His shoes and socks would

be soaking wet where the water from the hoses he was helping to hold would slip and hit the firemen as they desperately fought the blazes.

"Dad would sit in the chair in front of our fire, dazed and just staring into space while Mummy helped him take off his webbing belt and, carefully, the axe that it contained. We would take turns loosening his shirt round his neck, and then using a damp cloth to wipe him clean. He could not undress, because he needed to be ready in case another siren sounded.

I know the soldiers at the front and the sailors at sea and the brave pilots in the air were getting it bad, but the courageous work of the fire servicemen too often goes unrecognised. Believe me, they were all heroes, including my lovely Dad. One of the most memorable days I recall from the war years was when Dad featured in the centre spread of the Sunday Pictorial. He appeared in a large photo aiming his hose at a blaze, with the caption: 'Fireman John Palmer puts out the London blazes while his daughters Eileen, Joyce and Ann are evacuated in Harpenden' That took pride of place in the family cuttings book.

"I was six when the war started and nearing twelve when it finished. These are vital, formative years in any child's life and I'm afraid my education suffered badly. We had a small Anderson shelter in the garden, but when the London Blitz started I was hurried to and from a large public shelter at Bishop's Way in Bethnal Green, passing the Blind Beggar pub as we dashed for safety. Yes, the same Blind Beggar where the Krays twins went a murder too far 20 years later.

"We slept on wooden bunk beds built for us by Uncle Dick, and Uncle Ben was a tailor who made bright green siren suits for we Palmer girls. We must have looked as if we were three of the ten green bottles hanging on the wall. Our shelter was overcrowded and heavy with the stench of sweat and body odour, but everybody adopted a make-the-most-of-it attitude and accepted the appalling conditions with a smile and a shrug.

"All these years later I can still recall an echo of a regular shout from airraid wardens: 'Put that light out!' These were the black-out days and heaven help anybody who allowed a single chink of light to show through their drawn curtains. Everywhere we went we had to remember to take our gas mask. Mine was made in the likeness of Mickey Mouse, but I promise there was nothing funny when putting it on and trying to ignore the suffocating smell of rubber.

"Hitler's bombers were making a mess of the East End, and we would come blinking out of the shelter to find more landmarks flattened, and my dear old Dad, an unsung hero, was back on fire duty.

"They did their best to get some basic English and maths into my head and schoolteachers used to set up classrooms inside the shelters. I saw first hand the 'Spirit of the Blitz' and joined in singing the old songs, with people lining up to get a tune out of an old upright piano in the shelter. They were at one and the same time terrible and uplifting moments in all our lives. It was then I first became aware of the importance of community character and enterprise.

"The bombing became so bad that it was decided we Palmer girls had to be got out of London, and this time we were evacuated to a cousin's house in Harpenden, Hertfordshire, where we lived with our Aunt Lily Palmer. Later Eileen, Ann and I moved with our Mum to a small farm near Batford on the way to Luton, where she was employed in a munitions factory producing weapons of war.

"I remember us arriving at the farm late at night and being told that Eileen and I would be sleeping upstairs. I could not see any stairs, then the farmer's wife, a Mrs Smith, pulled open a sliding door to reveal a hidden flight of steps winding towards the roof. Eileen and I spent the night in the attic where the farmer stored all his apples. It was a lovely scent in our nostrils to drift off to and made a change from the heat, human sweat and fear of the shelter.

"In the morning we had porridge made with fresh milk from the cows, eggs laid by the chickens and juice squeezed from the newly picked apples. We had landed in paradise.

"We went out into the garden and saw climbing up the side of the farmhouse a mauve coloured Wisteria. This set my imagination racing and I pumped Mrs Smith for all I was worth about the history of the plant. It awakened in me a lifetime's love of gardening, and I got great satisfaction growing my very own row of cornflowers in a beautiful shade of blue.

"As I am casting my mind back my senses are filled with a special smell that accompanied the shoeing of horses by the local blacksmith, who worked at the farriers adjoining the farmer's cottage that we were transferred to in Batford. We were as free as birds as we paddled in the nearby River Lea, and it was all a million miles from the Blitz on London. The Cockney Palmer girls were having the time of their lives.

"During the 1930s, dear Uncle Lenny had won a prize at school for good behaviour. It was a book called Jason and the Golden Fleece, and I sharpened my reading skills by devouring it at least three, maybe four times. I have been hooked on books ever since and read at every spare moment. The local libraries became my favourite haunt and I always had – and still have – my nose in a book.

"One day in 1944 there was the dreaded knock at the door by a telegram boy. Granny Arundell, who had been bombed out of her house, now lived in a small flat in Bethnal Green and she had to have the telegram read to her. It revealed that her beloved son, Lenny, was 'missing in action.' This was followed by the inevitable news that he had been killed during the invasion of Italy.

"Eileen and I were back in London with Granny when she got the news of Lenny's death and she sobbed for days. I was eleven and the events of the war had made me an emotional wreck, and seeing my beloved Granny so upset cost me many nights sleep. Today I would have been sent to a team of psychiatrists, but I was simply told to 'pull myself together' and life went on.

"Those last few months of the war were a nightmare because of the flying bombs, the V1 rockets, that Hitler unleashed. We called them Doodlebugs and we used to catch our breath at they came overhead. Their engines would suddenly cut out and there was an ominous silence followed by a terrifying explosion as they suddenly fell on unprotected targets.

"We would come out of the shelter, shielding our eyes from the sudden daylight and see where the rockets had landed. Several houses either side of Commercial Road were hit and I knew of a couple of families who lost loved ones. You would see mothers walking round with red eyes from crying as they reacted to news of losing sons.

Terrible, terrible times and it got worse when the Germans unleashed an even more terrifying weapon, the V2 rocket. This was close to a modern ballistic missile, much bigger than the doodlebug and they landed without warning on undefended East End homes.

"Just as we were thinking the war would never end, the Germans surrendered, and VE Day, I remember, was marked with a good old Cockney knees up and people found old flags in their attics and cellars and everywhere was a splash of red, white and blue.

"But the celebrations were muted in the Arundell household because we had lost dear Uncle Lenny in the invasion of Italy and his younger brother, Ted, was still a prisoner of war in Japan.

"We went with Granny Arundell to the Troxy cinema to see newsreel of the VE Day celebrations, with thousands thronging the Mall to cheer the King and Queen on the Buckingham Palace balcony. This 12-year-old East End girl did not dream that one day I would be visiting that very Palace to receive an MBE

"We watched the VE Day celebrations with pride and awe, but suddenly the newsreel was featuring a report from Japan showing the continuing war. As shots of the Prisoners of War came on the screen Granny Arundell started weeping and pushed the heads of we Palmer girls down to try to prevent us seeing the film.

"When Uncle Ted finally came home after the Atom Bomb had been dropped to force VJ Day in the August, he was a skeleton of a man. Call me any names you want to but I've never ever forgiven the Japanese for what they did to my Uncle Ted.

"The Arundells, Mum's family, had paid an awful price and our dear Granny was inconsolable. She had lost her second eldest son Lenny and lovely Uncle Ted was a shadow of the man who lit up any party before the Japanese brutalised the spirit out of him.

"War, bloody war."

Chapter Five:
East End Ruins As A Playground

WITH Joyce learning to deal with the horrors of war, what a shock to this five-year-old's eyes when we returned to bomb-blitzed London following the 1945 German surrender. All I knew in Devonshire were winding country lanes, rolling hills, tree-lined fields, rich, green meadows, hedges bursting with bird song and the distinctive sounds and aroma of cows, horses, pigs, sheep and working dogs, and the unmistakable growl of a tractor engine. This was all replaced with wrecked houses, exhaust-filled, traffic-jammed roads, long lines of cranes at the nearby docks looking like giant iron dinosaurs, thousands of chimneys belching smoke, the ear-piercing ringing of police alarm bells as black Wolseley flying squad cars chased the petty thieves, and the air continually filled with a stinking smog that left clothes grimy and faces grey. No wonder London was known as The Smoke.

Right up until the early 1950s gaslight illuminated the East End streets, and my earliest memories are shrouded in a yellow haze. These were still days of trolley buses and trams, only one in thirty thousand homes with a new-fangled television, and refrigerators as rare as bananas and bars of chocolate – another planet.

There was row upon row of skeletal bombed houses in Cable Street and The Highway, and the far end of the Ring House buildings were roped off because of a direct hit on the top balcony. This was eventually repaired, and in 1947 Mum, Dad, new brother Kenneth and older brothers Alan, George and I moved 100 yards to 89 Ring House.

This was a refurbished, repaired top-floor flat, with a large living room and stairs leading to two bedrooms, the front one for Mum and Dad, with Kenneth in a cot, the rear one in which George, Alan and I shared a double bed. Today the estate agents call it a maisonette or an apartment. For us, it was a flat, plain and very simple.

Centre piece of the living room was a tiled mantelpiece, with a railed guard in front of a fireplace that would never have passed today's health and safety standards. In winter we took turns setting fire to chopped wood on a bed of rolled-up paper, then drawing a draught down the chimney by holding a double page of the broadsheet Socialist-supporting *Daily Herald* over the open fireplace. We often had to stamp out the *Herald* pages as they went up in flames in our hands. Finally, we would use a hand shovel to put half a dozen lumps of nutty slack coal on to the wood, and it would take all of an hour to get the room warmed up in those pre-central heating days.

There was no lift to the top balcony, but a regular gallop up and down 64 stone stairs, with your senses assaulted on the way by cooking smells wafting from dozens of kitchens. My little legs were a blur as I raced up and down those eight flights of stairs, and it explains why when I arrived in Fleet Street the following decade my 5ft 10in frame weighed nine stone wet through. Obesity was a word in the dictionary, and I am convinced we half-starved, ration-book kids were far fitter and healthier than today's fast food generation.

On the wall at the bottom of the first flight of stairs in what were tuberculosis-epidemic days, there was a white metal plate with the instruction in huge black lettering: 'DO NOT SPIT, By Order of Stepney Borough Council.' For some of our boisterous neighbours it presented an irresistible target for a spit.

From the bedroom and living room windows of our Ring House home we looked directly out on to the Wapping Walls surrounding the docks and, in the distance, half a mile away, the Tower of London and Tower Bridge. Our rent was 27 shillings a week (£1.35). For the same Thames-side view today the Yuppies pay upwards of half a million pounds for their flats.

At meal times, Mum used to stand on the corner of the top balcony screaming each of our names as if a crier on a minaret summoning us to prayer. "Georgie ... Alan ... Norman ... Kenny ..." Our farmer friend Frank Steer, on a late 1940s visit to our flat during the annual Smithfield Meat Show, listened with amusement as Mum went through the calling-in routine. The next week a whistle arrived in the post from Frank that Mum started to use as her signal to bring us home, much to the consternation of the local police section house in an era when the police whistle was the common sound to alert and alarm.

Big brother George, five years older than me, got satisfaction out of bossing me around, and it was Alan who used to protect me from his bullying. Two years older, he was my best mate and did more than anybody to guide me through those growing up days when you are finding your way in life.

There was something about Alan that set him apart from the rest of us. He was the brightest at school, a high-quality chorister, the best at sports, the most sensible and always seeming much older than his years.

Yes, there was something special about Alan.

My Dad's Dad, like all first sons of the Giller family, called George William, passed on in 1946 from a form of cancer, and I have a fading memory of seeing him lying in an open coffin in my Aunt Mary's front room, a macabre tradition to allow relatives, neighbours and friends to pay their last respects, as Joyce had experienced when her grandma died in 1936.

Something more chilling that I recall is of Nanny Giller, his wife of 50 years, screaming because she was barred from attending granddad's funeral as she was considered too emotional.

Nanny Giller lived into her 90s, and she never ever forgave her family preventing her going to her husband's funeral. It's a cruel old world.

With all foods rationed, Mum could never stretch the family budget to include sweets, but we enterprising kids found our way around that. For several years after the war American warships used to moor near Shadwell Basin, and we'd line up at the dock gates and shout "Any gum, chum?" to US navy sailors on shore leave. They rarely said no, often including a bar of chocolate in their public relation hand-outs. Good old Uncle Sam.

The older boys also used to get handed American cigarettes in an era when it seemed everybody smoked everywhere. Along with my next-door mate Billy Hart, we used to pick up discarded dog-ends from the gutter and smoke them while sitting in the bombed-out houses, acting like grown-ups. Stupid boys.

These were days when the Government actually encouraged people to smoke because of the tobacco tax they were collecting, allowing alluring poster advertisements and incentives such as football-player cards and trading stamps. Woodbines, Player's Weights and Turf were the favourite smokes for we working-class families, while my Dad virtually chain-smoked the heavily nicotined Senior Service, dismissing the newly introduced tipped and menthol cigarettes as being "for pansies."

My Granddad Sims always had a hooked pipe hanging from his mouth, balancing the stiffness of the paralysed side of his face.

If you had said then that one day smoking would be banned in pubs and in many public places they would have thought you had lost your marbles.

Thanks mainly to my Dad's heavy smoking, I built up a collection of hundreds of cigarette cards featuring my footballing and cricketing heroes, and used to spend every playground break time at Chapman Street primary school playing 'swapsie'. "I'll give you a Stanley Matthews for a Duquemin and a Ramsey," would be a typical negotiation. "Plus a Bedser and a Godfrey Evans for a Denis Compton," the biggest of all the sporting heroes for we star-struck schoolboys Who'd have guessed that this East End ragamuffin would one day be working in Fleet Street in the same office as his idol?

In early 1948 I came home with a leaflet from my Chapman Street primary school advertising "the Country Holiday Fund for disadvantaged children." Mum persuaded me to go away for a free two weeks to Wakefield in Yorkshire, where I joined eight East End kids I had never met before in a rambling house on the edge of the coal-mining district. It was the holiday from hell. Our axe-faced landlady started off by warning us in a heavy Yorkshire accent we could barely understand that if any of us misbehaved we would get her husband's belt. Starving dogs would have turned down the food she served, and she had us in bed by seven o'clock every evening.

I used to lie there dreaming of ways to escape from our three-to-a-bed rooms, drifting off to the background noise of homesick kids crying. The local Yorkie boys did not take kindly to us invading their patch, and every day we would get involved in fistfights and throwing lumps of coal at each other. One of the braver members of our gang complained about the food to the lady we nicknamed Frosty Knickers, and she responded by tipping his food into the dustbin and sending him to bed hungry. I would imagine the woman got paid for putting us up. She should have got fined and flogged.

Back home later that year I was sitting looking out of the living room window of our flat when a lorry carrying a small mountain of sand suddenly shot its load. It remains part of my nightmares all these years later that I watched as the sand buried and suffocated a young police cadet cycling behind the lorry on his way to work at the nearby police section house.

A week later, a lorry stolen from the docks shed its load of untethered planks as it careered down Cable Street, which was then two-way. The wood toppled on a grandmother and granddaughter from Ring House as they were walking to the local grocery shop. Both were killed.

Sorry to share those two horrific stories, but they remain burned in my memory and are an unforgettable part of my story. To this day I cannot drive past a sand lorry or one carrying wood without revisiting that terrible week.

Mum and Dad had what was known in those days as a mixed marriage, Dad a Roman Catholic and Mum Church of England. When Mum decided to bring her sons up as Protestants two Roman Catholic nuns were sent to try to 'save' us. They made the mistake of telling Dad that he would go to hell if his children were not brought up as Catholics. He gave them and the follow-up priest such an x-rated mouthful that he was excommunicated, and all the Giller boys were brought up Church of England, and each of us in turn became head choirboy at nearby St Paul's Church in The Highway.

Our lives revolved around St Paul's, and all these years on from what is now a dithering, agnostic viewpoint I recognise the importance of the foundation my heavy church involvement gave me.

St Paul's sits on the north bank of the Thames in Shadwell, and has a rich history going back to Oliver Cromwell's rule as Lord Protector in the mid-17th Century. It is traditionally known as the Church of Ship Captains, and all births and deaths at sea of British citizens were registered there. Explorer Captain James Cook was a regular worshipper, and he had his son baptised at St Paul's, where John Wesley was a regular preacher before founding Methodism. All we Giller brothers were altar servers as well as choristers, and we used to get threepence for attending the morning family Communion and then the Evensong service, plus twopence for choir practice.

I used to also pick up half-a-crown (12.5p) for singing solo at weddings. We used to get paid monthly and would be weighed down with coppers as we raided the Cable Street sweet shop run by Russian Jews, the Muscoviches

While I was singing the praises of the Lord, Joyce and the Palmer *family* had upped sticks and moved 30 miles to the Thames Estuary town of Southend-on-Sea ...

Chapter Six:
So Nice to Be Beside the Seaside

JOYCE now takes up the story, and we join her as the war is about to end in the spring of 1945. Britain was on its knees and particularly the East End of London, with widespread destruction of buildings and infrastructure. Yet there was a sense of collective relief, a cocktail of exhaustion and elation after years of hardship …

"The war nearly killed Daddy. All the soakings he got while working as a fireman with poor equipment and totally unsuitable uniform left him vulnerable to any disease going and he was at death's door with first pneumonia and then painful quinsy, an abscess that attacks the throat.

"He was a shadow of the man who'd joined the fire brigade six years earlier, but was not considered eligible for any sort of pension. When he was invalided out of the fire service he was given a lump sum payment of £60, and there was a lot of quiet resentment that the firemen who had gallantly battled through the Blitz were not given demob suits.

Returning servicemen tended to think the fire fighters had got off lightly and looked down on them. I promise they were the bravest of the brave.

"So there we were, the East End a bombed mess and Sheila had arrived to make it four Palmer sisters and Lorna was on her way. John Palmer was not completely invalided!

"It was Daddy who had the brainwave of asking his eldest sister, my Auntie Min, what were the chances of us moving down to join them in Southend, where she and her cheerful husband, Uncle Ben, had set up home just before the war.

"In those days you could not just up and go to wherever you liked. It meant organising a permit for us to move down to the town on the Thames Estuary, believe me a bold move at the time.

"Thanks to my Dad's valiant service with the fire brigade, he was given priority to make the move and so it was that Mum and Dad and we four Palmer girls – Sheila a babe in arms – packed all our belongings and got on a train at Stepney East station and made the 75-minute journey to Southend.

Our sparse furniture followed on down the A13 by lorry.

It was the start of a new life.

"This was now late in 1945 and the Army was still occupying Southend, where hundreds of soldiers and sailors had been stationed while training for war duties. There was barbed wire stretching across all the beaches to repel a Nazi invasion that never came, and row upon row of intimidating concrete anti-tank defences known as Dragon's Teeth gave an unfriendly welcome to the Southend where I was to spend the rest of my life..

"The Estuary was still being cleared of mines that the Luftwaffe had dropped during their attacks on ships heading for London, one of the world's busiest ports back then.

"It's a proud part of Southend history that scores of Essex boats played a part in the 'Miracle of Dunkirk,' Operation Dynamo, when 300,000 soldiers of the British Expeditionary Force were plucked from French beaches and brought home in that famous evacuation, a retreat cleverly painted as a triumph by Churchill. Throwing the story forward 70 years, I was privileged to be a Trustee of the industrious committee that got the Endeavour fishing boat – one of the Dunkirk rescue ships – seaworthy for the Queen's Diamond Jubilee parade down the Thames in 2012. Dame Helen Mirren was our patron and we were so pleased and proud to have such an historic occasion marked with an echo of wartime Southend.

"When we Palmer Girls arrived from the bomb-scarred East End the Estuary was just coming off a war footing. Southend was bulging with military personnel awaiting their demob, and there were no houses for us to rent, so at Auntie Min and Uncle Ben's kind invitation we moved in with them to their semi-detached house at 106 Victoria Road. We had been down for a couple of holidays before the war, and so slipped comfortably into a routine of we Palmer sisters sleeping on bedsteads in the summer house at the bottom of the garden.

"I have clear memories of going with Auntie Min and Mum to the Warrior Square office of Dowsett Estate Agency and being told there was not a hope of renting a place because so many soldiers, sailors and airmen were still billeted in the town. The kindly estate agent promised that the moment he knew there was accommodation available he would let us know, and true to his word we were able to put down proper roots right in the heart of Southend at 2 Chelmsford Avenue, a semi-detached house with five bedrooms and a garden that had apple and pear trees and a large lawn.

"The blitzed East End seemed a planet away. Our rent was 32s 6d (70.5p) a week at a time when the average weekly wage was around £6. Things in those ration book days were tight but we loved our new surroundings.

"It became a real family home when Granny Arundell moved down to live with us, which freed Mum to go out working as a char lady at the local school and in shops and offices, anything to help make ends meet.

"Eventually Daddy got his strength and health back and started commuting to his old paper-organising job in the City. The Palmers were back on their feet.

"Anybody arriving in this 1940s Southend from today would think they had landed in a foreign land. Keddies' department store, with imaginatively dressed shop windows based on the Selfridges design in London's West End was king of the High Street, plus Dixons and the sprawling Garons, which had butchers, bakers, greengrocers, banqueting suites and even their own cinema. Of course there was not yet Debenham's or The Royals.

"We had a saying, 'Southend was founded by DIRT.' That was shorthand for four wealthy and entrepreneurial Southend-based families who virtually built the town in Victorian and then Edwardian times: the Dowsetts, Ingrams, Ramuz and Tolhursts forming the acronym DIRT. They are all names that meant a lot locally and which anybody growing up in Southend knew well. Along with the Rossis, Tomassis, Tweedy Smiths and the Absaloms, they were the families that lay the business foundation to the town and with which I became familiar when moving down in the immediate post-war months.

"The High Street was always busy and bustling and the array of small shops flourished despite the ration book restrictions. They had great character and atmosphere compared with today's concrete jungle. I know I shouldn't live in the past, but things were definitely more appealing and attractive then, despite it being an Age of Austerity.

"The seafront started to attract day-trippers again after the deprivation of the war and I used to tingle with excitement walking along the noisy, brightly lit Golden Mile, through Peter Pan's Playground and, of course, The Kursaal, a German word for amusement park. This late-Victorian pleasure ground, built like a royal palace, was the focal point of the entertainment. The Pier, the longest in the world, continued to be the town's most famous landmark. Several fires have failed to reduce its standing as a place to visit for anybody heading for the day tripper's paradise of Southend.

"A curtain of gloom dropped over the area I recall when a submarine, The Truculent, *plunged to the bottom of the Estuary after colliding with a Swedish tanker. in the winter of 1950. Sixty lives were lost. It was probably the saddest day in Southend's history. We had experienced the devastation caused by death during the Blitz, but this disaster was in peacetime. Southend's own lifeboat and its heroic crew were singled out for their efforts during the nightmare. The lifeboat was the first rescue vessel to the scene of the disaster and remained there from 8.30pm on the night of the sinking until the afternoon of the following day. Ever since I have made it one of my duties to raise as much money as possible for the Royal National Lifeboat Institute.*

"My education had been sketchy to say the least, and I did my best to catch up when attending first Southchurch Hall School and then Victoria Avenue School, which was situated in a grand manor house and after being demolished became the site for the Southend court room and police station. I preferred it as a beautiful school building that showed off Victorian architecture at its imaginative best.

"I remember one of my first protests was against plans to bulldoze Old Leigh to make way for a bypass but that plan was thankfully dropped. It remains a must-visit place, featuring wonderful restaurants, a nature reserve at Two Tree Island and a conveniently located beach close to the historic Bell Wharf. I've watched it grow and prosper since arriving as a wide-eyed schoolgirl in 1945.

"You have to remember in these mid to late 1940s there was no such thing as the NHS and Dad's poor health following his wartime service as a fire fighter meant we had medical bills that ate into our meagre savings. But we all pulled together and got ourselves through it.

"Our Uncle Bill Smith, a sailor throughout the war and eventually married to Dad's sister Aunt Grace, arrived home on leave just after we had moved to Southend and brought with him the rarest of things, bananas. Our then youngest sister Ann had never seen one before and was so confused

by it that she tried to eat the skin and threw the actual banana on the fire. We've never let her forget it.

"The thing we Palmer girls looked forward to once a year was our voyage on the Golden Daffodil from Southend Pier to Margate and back. Dad used to lead us on board like a Pied Piper and we'd explore the decks as if in a chapter from Enid Blyton's Famous Five. That was our annual holiday. No frills, no luxury but to we girls it was next to heaven.

"My memories of school are hazy, simply because I had so little experience of it, and at the then legal leaving age of 14 in 1948 I was released to the outside world with just a good head for maths and avid reading as my companions; oh yes, and I was addicted to my Singer Sewing Machine. I followed all my aunts and my grandmas as a sewing girl. That's the way it was in those days. You needed a dress, you made it.

"At least I was now a bread winner, and started work at the eye-watering wage of three pounds, ten shillings a week (that's £3.50 in today's money). Thanks to my ability to add and subtract, I joined Enever & Company in West Road, Westcliff-on-Sea as a clerk in the accounts office. They were wholesalers who specialised in mass buying of groceries and then distributing them to local shops. In those ration book days, there was tight government control of all goods and everything had to be rubber-stamped before it could be put in the vans for distribution"

"These were the days of the Clement Attlee Socialist government and I felt restricted and frustrated by their Age of Austerity approach. Even at that young age I sensed there was insufficient enterprise and imagination. I know they were having to pick up the pieces after the chilling years of war, but I felt they could have hurried our recovery by using bolder measures. The Tory in me was fighting to come out, and both Mum and Dad were keen followers of Churchill and used to vote Conservative.

"I felt I needed a greater challenge than the boring grind at Enever's and when one day Dad brought the London Evening News home with him, my eye fell on an advertisement. It was for somebody with clerical experience to work in the football pools department of the bookmakers William Hill.

"I applied, revealing my year's experience as a clerk with Enever's. To my surprise I was invited to take the job on a month's trial at a princely £5 a week.

"I felt as if I had won the pools.

"What an eye opener, working in London! To my young gaze, it was a huge and exciting place, and it's had a hold on me ever since. I was, of course, London born and bred but now it was such an exhilarating place to visit from my adopted home of Southend.

"I used to commute from Southend Central every day, getting the 7.30am train to Fenchurch Street and then catching the Number 15 bus to Blackfriars, where the William Hill headquarters were based. In the spring and summer I would walk from the station to the office to save the threepenny bus fare.

"This is when I grew up, because I had to be on my toes with my calculating and file-keeping. I was surrounded by girls from all over the country, and my ears became attuned to a multitude of dialects and accents. My workmates came from every corner of Britain and I particularly admired the Scouse girls who had come down from Liverpool to escape local humiliation. Several of them, along with the Dublin girls, had got themselves pregnant, and they used to live three-to-a-room in rented flats while their babies were being cared for by the local Catholic charity organisations. They were full of Merseyside wit and wisdom, and you could never knock them down.

"It was in those days at William Hill's that I fell in love with dancing, and at every opportunity went to the venues like The Lyceum in The Strand, Hammersmith Palais, The Marquee and the 100 Club in Oxford Street and jived away to the music of bands such as Oscar Rabin, Ken Mackintosh, Cyril Stapleton, Ted Heath and Johnny Dankworth.

"Our partners would usually be our office girlfriends until the boys, looking on shyly from the sidelines with their backs to the wall, would pluck up the courage to ask us to dance. They would often be Teddy Boy types, with greased hair, draped Edwardian-style suits, crepe-sole shoes and trying to hide their acne. Most would be waiting for their call ups to do their national service, which was when we used to lose touch with them because they were posted overseas.

"The dress code for we girls was calf-length sheath dresses, blouses or sweaters with pencil skirts and large leather belts to accentuate our waists. Trousers and jeans were a no-go for girls, and I can never recall anybody walking around like in these days with bottled water. We did not fear that we *were suddenly going to die of thirst!*

."Everything had to be bought using our ration book, all of this a decade before Mary Quant revolutionised fashion with her introduction of the mini skirt. To give myself height above my 5ft 2in, I used to wear smart stiletto heeled shoes and I ignored the sudden craze for ballerina pumps. We would be paid a £2.50 bonus for working on Sundays and I used to spend it on clothes, particularly basic underwear and make-up. Lipstick then cost 10 shillings (50p) a tube, and I could buy a dress with my clothing coupons for two pounds. Yes, it was another world.

"What became known as the 'Swinging Sixties' were still in the distance and we were, for the want of a better word, 'good' girls who were never tempted to bed hop, and the freedom provided in the 60s by 'The Pill' was strictly for dreamers. The most we 'good' girls allowed was a cuddle in the back row of the cinema when the likes of Clark Gable, Errol Flynn, Cary Grant and Humphrey Bogart were the pin-ups.

"During the football season, we used to go into the office on Sundays to pay out any punters who had selected the winning teams, which meant sending out hundreds of postal orders. Millions more did not get their forecasts right and it opened my eyes to what a mug's game betting was.

"In the summer months we would switch to the Piccadilly office of William Hill's to help out in the horse racing office. It was during this period that I discovered that many of the Crazy Gang – the Monty Python idols of their time – were addicted gamblers who were the best customers of the bookmakers. They used to lose scores of pounds and keep coming back for more punishment.

"We would regularly go from paying out the Sunday winners to the London Palladium to listen to the Ted Heath band or the Johnny Dankworth Seven. It was a huge blow to we jazz and swing lovers when the 'live' TV show 'Sunday Night at the London Palladium' took off and our concerts were cancelled.

"Rock 'n' Roll, Elvis and The Beatles had not yet made themselves heard and I was locked into singers like Ella Fitzgerald, Sarah Vaughan, Frank Sinatra, the Ted Heath trio of Dennis Lotis, Lita Roza and Dicky Valentine, and the big bands of Duke Ellington and Count Basie. I had taste.

"I honestly feel sorry for the kids today who have to listen to what to my

old ears is utter garbage. The musicians I listened to were masters of their instruments and could really swing.

"While working in Piccadilly I became a regular visitor to theatre land and started a love affair with musicals and plays that lasts to this day. Now days I sit in the best seats, but in those early visits I saw everything from the gods. I actually shiver with memories of shows like Oklahoma, Carousel *and – it had just opened and is still going –* Agatha Christie's The Mousetrap. All these years later my oath not to reveal the ending is still intact. Okay, it was the ... nope, not going to tell! My love of musicals has lasted right into my 90s, but I get so annoyed when the 'Woke' generation meddle with the shows I have loved since they were first performed. I have recently had to sit through My Fair Lady *with a black Eliza Dolittle and* Oklahoma *with four of the main cast black actors. As if George Bernard Shaw imagined Eliza as black and Rogers and Hammerstein saw their main characters in Oklahoma as black. What next, a white Sporting Life in George Gershwin's Porgy and Bess, and a white Carmen?*

"These are not racist comments, but just me getting angry at people messing with musical classics.

"My husband has told me off for going off track, but I just needed to get it off my chest.

"Back home in Southend, I continued my newfound hobby of dancing and was spoilt for choice of venues. There was The Kursall Ballroom, The Mecca, The Studio, Masonic Hall, The Odeon and, of course, The Pier. I could dance conventional ballroom or jive, and used to spend all my spare pocket money on decent shoes and of course, I made my own dresses to wear to the dances.

"I learned all the latest dance steps from the famous Victor Sylvester slow-slow-quick-quick-slow classes, and the newspapers in those days carried lots of diagrams showing the current dance crazes.

"All I needed was a regular partner. And I found him ... on his milk round.

Chapter Seven:
Pianos, Punches and Pie and Mash

WHILE Joyce was enjoying growing up in 'good old Southend on Sea,' I was tackling the immediate post-war years in the blitzed ruins of the East End. The sounds that for me ring across the years are of my Dad's piano playing and my Mum's singing … and, in stark contrast, my Dad's drunken swearing and Mum's terrified screaming as he used to pummel her with his fists in alcohol-fuelled rages.

Dad was a self-taught pianist who could pick up any tune by ear, and he had a wonderfully rhythmical left hand that he copied from the gifted 'Clap Hands Here Comes Charlie' Kunz. Find Charlie on YouTube and you will know how my Dad sounded.

Mum could sing like an angel and knew all the old songs that Dad played. Trouble is that when Mum stood and sang solos in the Crooked Billet pub in Cable Street, accompanied by her Jekyll and Hyde husband, he would later convince himself that other men had been ogling her and he imagined that she returned their stares. This would lead to irrational, jealous fury and once our flat door was shut he would often become violent with Mum, and as each of we boys grew up we took turns in punching him to protect our mother.

I would sob myself to sleep, dreaming of taking a machine gun into the Crooked Billet and shooting the beer barrels and whisky bottles. The next morning Dad would have no recollection of what had happened, and he would wonder why he had a black eye and bloodied nose. But the nightmare memories for we boys lived on and were the only blot on our childhood.

In mid-winter, Dad would fall into a drunken sleep with his leg up resting on the rail guard surrounding the fire. This would get red hot and he would eventually wake up with his trouser leg smouldering and painful burn marks on his calf. He called the scars his war wounds.

To do Mum a favour, I would often stay up and talk boxing to Dad and we would put on the gloves and spar, imitating the styles of our favourite champions. Then, when he had gone off into his inebriated slumber, I would take all the silver coins from his pocket and give them to Mum the next morning. Why should it all go over the bar?

A red-blooded Socialist, Dad used to have we Giller boys lined up outside the polling station at elections chanting: 'Who puts the boots on your feet and the food in your belly, Labour!' The fact that sitting Labour MP Wally Edwards always had a 30,000-plus majority meant we were preaching to the converted. Years later, when I told Dad I was switching allegiance to the Liberals, you would have thought from his reaction I had become Kim Philby confessing to being a traitor. 'You disappoint me, son,' he said. 'You're turning your back on the party of the working class who dragged this country out of the ruins of war.'

There was a lot of truth in that, but I still made the switch after watching the unions help bring the docks and Fleet Street to their knees. After making a study of the ideals and ideas of great Liberal thinkers like William Gladstone, Henry Asquith, David Lloyd George and William Beveridge, the real hero of the Welfare State and National Health Service, I decided to change sides to the middle ground of politics.

As I've often had to say to Joyce, 'get off your soapbox.

Sober, Dad was as good as gold and could not have been a more loving father and husband, and he was always looking to help others. He would throw his last pennies to the veteran, shell-shocked soldiers who used to walk through the grounds of our flats singing for coppers, and I remember him once, as a surprise, redecorating the Wapping flat of Nanny and Granddad Sims when they went away for a long weekend. Granddad, who could never show emotion on his paralysed face, just said: "I preferred the old wallpaper." He never did like Dad.

Drunk, he was not always a monster and could be hilarious. One Saturday he wallpapered half the living room and took a break to visit the pub. After a long drinking session and a late-night lock-in he came home and finished off the wallpapering. When we got up the next morning we were bemused and amused to find he had pasted the paper on the second half of the room with the pattern upside down. We called it his Picasso period. Yes, a true piss artist.

Out and about, everybody respected Dad, and few knew of his terrifying brutish side in drink. Poor, dominated Mum used to say that he was "an angel out, devil in." He literally had a nose for drink, and could sniff out booze like a hunting dog scenting the fox.

On summer Sundays Dad would take us on pleasure boat trips down the Thames from Tower Bridge. The one reason, the boats were allowed to serve alcoholic drinks after the pubs closed. He would often pay visits to Covent Garden and Smithfield Meat Market because he knew they had different licensing hours to the rest of the City, and he discovered how he could drink right around the clock when he had money in his pocket. There were a string of pubs where he knew the publicans would allow illegal after-hours lock-in drinking sessions, all done on a nod and a wink.

Another drinking excuse for Dad were the bi-annual beanos from the Crooked Billet. These were coach trips to the coast – Southend, Margate or Brighton – with the charabanc weighed down with crates of beer. Before leaving, it was a tradition to throw any loose change, "nobbins," out of the window, and we kids used to scramble for the coins. Dad, playing a borrowed piano accordion, and his mates would be legless by the time they got to their destination, sleep off the booze on the beaches or piers, and then drink the charabanc dry again on the drive home.

There were two occasions when Dad had the chance to get us out of the hellhole that was the bomb-blasted East End. First, Farmer Dart offered him work on the farm and a village cottage, but to East-London-born-and-bred Dad the country was like foreign land, they did things differently there. Much to Mum's lasting disappointment he declined the job offer.

Two years later he was given the chance to move us to a Council house in Chingford, then an Essex parish but now in Greater London. His excuse not to make the move was that he would lose his pub piano money. Dad moved just a few hundred yards in all his 66 years before losing a smoking-caused cancer battle in 1975.

Because most of Dad's money in those immediate post-war years was going into the pub cash tills, Mum slaved as an office char in the City of London each morning, and as a cleaner in the Queen Elizabeth Children's Hospital in Shadwell every evening, working herself into the ground to keep food on the table while my Dad was literally pissing his wages up the wall.

Bread pudding, bubble and squeak, scrag-end of meat, rabbit stew, Welsh rarebit, beans on toast, chicken as a treat on Christmas Day. This was our regular diet, and it was often just bread and jam for tea. Butter?

No chance, just margarine. Our Mum in a million performed wonders on a shoestring, and would see that we four boys were fed before feeding herself from any leftovers on our plates.

Our biggest treat was at Sunday teatimes, when we could occasionally afford winkles, whelks, shrimps and jellied eels from the popular Aldgate stall of Tubby Isaacs. The other favourite was pies, mash and liquor from nearby Watney Street market. Across all these years just typing the words has set my taste buds on fire.

To help make her life a little easier, Mum used to write down the day's chores on scraps of paper and then we brothers would draw from a school cap. I usually landed the washing and drying up, because older, stronger, bullying George would force that on me while he got away with the light polishing or sweeping jobs.

Four boys confined to a small apartment meant we inevitably got up to mischief and harassed Mum was always resorting to 'Wait until your father comes home' warnings. Dad used to take his belt off to us as a show of intent but rarely went through with using it. Deep down he loved each of us, and on the few occasions he did use the belt he would always finish up crying more than we did.

We three younger Giller boys wore hand-me-downs from big brother George, and Mum saw to it that we were always well polished and gleaming. Her favourite saying was: "Doesn't matter how poor you are, you can afford a bar of soap."

She made us have a spoonful of malt every single morning, and kept us regular with weekend doses of a vicious chocolate laxative called Exlax

Mum argued and scrapped with the education authorities to get us free meals at school, and took on a third cleaning job to help pay the bills and keep Dad in drink. What a woman, and for all the beatings she took from her husband she loved him intensely back in an era when wife-battering was, horribly, commonplace. There was lots of love and affection to go with the booze-driven rows bouncing off the walls of that tiny Ring House flat.

At my Chapman Street primary school in 1950 I was chosen to sing the Vaughan Williams classic *Linden Lee* during a visit from the Mayor of Stepney. My teacher, Mrs Kirwan, was so impressed she arranged an audition for me to join St Paul's Cathedral Choir, which would have meant me getting a scholarship to go to the exclusive St Paul's School.

I was ushered into the vast Cathedral, then the tallest building in London, and stood alongside redoubtable choirmaster Dr Dykes Bower, who sat at a small organ in a side chapel and invited me to sing a simple scale. I opened my mouth, reached for the notes and nothing came out. I had completely seized up with a sore throat that was on fire, and even at this distance I blush at the memory. I would have been better off singing Silent Night.

I often wonder how different my life might have been if I had not lost my voice and had made it into the prestigious Cathedral choir and school, but it was back to the smaller and less intimidating St Paul's at Shadwell.

Music, from swing to classics, has always played a huge part in my life, and the piano was magnetic for me. But it was George who very reluctantly got to take lessons. He used to break off from his scales and turn the clock forward half an hour, and tell Mum he had completed his practice. Finally caught out, the five-bob (25p) piano lessons were cancelled and, sadly, none of us got the chance to learn to play properly.

I have been struggling to play by ear for 75-plus years and can lay claim to being the world's worst pianist. I always maintain I was expelled from the Les Dawson pianoforte school because I was not good enough. You can find evidence of how bad I am on YouTube. Yes, a pillock.

When we were not praying, serving at the altar, cross bearing and singing at St Paul's, we were down in the crypt in the improvised boys' club playing table tennis, darts and snooker among the tombs and coffins. There were more than fifty sea captains buried in the churchyard, with another twenty entombed in the crypt. It was like partying on a Hammer House of Horrors film set.

Coming up for air from the crypt, it was coats on the ground as goals for street football or, in the summer, dustbins as stumps. We also used to play badminton in the church hall, where our closest family friend Norman Holland and his wife-to-be Lily were County-class and used to give us five-point starts and still whip us.

I once went up to my bedroom to put on plimsolls ready to go to the church to play badminton. An hour later my Mum found me undressed and fast asleep in bed. I was in such a dream that I forgot I was just supposed to be changing my shoes.

Football, for me, was the most compelling of all the sports, and from as young as seven I used to walk alone through Rotherhithe Tunnel to South London and the Millwall ground three miles away at Cold Blow Lane in New Cross. I discovered they opened the gates at half-time, and so I used to nip in for free to see the second-half of matches.

My eyes were at Millwall's Den but my heart at Tottenham on the north side of town. Dad's youngest sister, Emmy, and her husband, Eddie Baldwin – my Godparents – lived at Edmonton within goal-kicking distance of White Hart Lane, and they used to feed my young imagination with tales of Tottenham deeds when they were starting to dominate with their revolutionary push-and-run style of football.

After 40 years as a 'neutral' press box observer, I was able to come out of the closet as a Spurs supporter, all from the springboard of those schoolboy days of being a distant admirer.

Playing for the St Paul's Church team on Saturday mornings, I used to imagine myself as Wizard of Dribble Stanley Matthews. In truth, I played more like Jessie Matthews.

An enthusiastic young curate fresh down from Cambridge, Tommy Tucker, decided that we St Paul's choristers needed to learn the disciplines of boxing. He called my oldest brother George forward as a sparring partner because he was the biggest of the boys. Two minutes later, his nose bleeding profusely and with two swollen eyes, he decided that perhaps it would be better to teach us cricket. How was he to know that the Giller boys had been boxing almost from the cradle.

I had dreams of following my hero Bruce Woodcock as British heavyweight champion, and the fact that I was nine-stone lighter was not allowed to dent my ambitions. I packed my Dad's old Army kitbag with wastepaper and used it as a punchbag as I trained in a bombed-out house in The Highway. Brother Alan was already proving himself an outstanding boxer at our Chapman Street primary school, and he acted as my coach and sparring partner. He was far superior to me but never took liberties, and showed me how to throw fast, two-fisted combination punches.

My training schedule was interrupted when I fell off a wooden orange box fixed on to pram wheels as I steered it down the sloping Wapping Lane, fracturing my wrists. A few years later my boxing dreams died when in two minutes of fury in a schoolboy championship contest I stopped my opponent and managed to again break my wrists in the process. Both of my arms were encased in plaster for four months, and it was round about then I decided that it would be less painful to write about the sport.

One of my earliest sporting memories is of getting up in the middle of the night to listen to summary reports on the Wally Hammond-skippered Ashes tour back in 1946/47. Outside our freezing council flat, the ruins left behind by Hitler's bombers were covered in snow at the start of one of the coldest winters on record. But our concentration was on the second Test action 10,500 miles away in steaming-hot Sydney.

I can vividly recall Dad shushing us as he turned the dial on our highly polished, brown-wood Pye wireless, sliding through a dozen garbled foreign voices and smatterings of strange-to-the-ear music until he found the crackling BBC overseas service. I still remember the staggering news that Don Bradman and Sydney Barnes had each scored 234 runs, and Australia had declared at 659 for nine. One of my idols, Alec Bedser, went for one for 153. Years later, big Alec told me: "I had a sunburned tongue at the end of that Test."

For the second time that year I saw my sports-daft Dad close to tears in front of the wireless. He had actually cried seven months earlier in May when Bruce Woodcock was butted and battered to defeat in five rounds by Frank Sinatra-promoted Tami Mauriello in New York in an unofficial eliminator for the world heavyweight title held by the Brown Bomber, Joe Louis. I wonder from whom I caught my life-long sports bug?

I can even tell you the exact date off the top of my head. My youngest brother Kenneth was born that night in Whitechapel Hospital on 17 May 1946, and I recall going to the maternity ward to welcome the latest arrival to the Giller family in which there were oceans of love between the drunken squalls.

Most nights before going to bed, drunk or sober, Dad would come into our bedroom and tousle our hair, saying to each of us in turn: "Love you, son, night night, God bless." There was so much comfort in those words as we drifted off to sleep. I am painting an accurate, warts 'n' all portrait here of Dad the drunk, but he was at heart a good man, a loving father and husband, despite the violent rages.

He prided himself on being a master of the bon mot, and would often follow a quick punchline with, 'Get in there, Morton,' the catchphrase of a popular radio comedian.

Dad was just frustrated by the narrow world into which he had been born, and for all his quick wit, lightning mental arithmetic and natural intelligence he never really made it out of the starting blocks. I was determined to escape that existence where hope was stifled and ambition went no further than the next drink. Meantime, down the road, an older girl called Joyce had similar dreams.

Once every six weeks, Dad would herd we four boys into Albert's, the corner barber's shop in The Highway, where we would each have a sixpenny pudding basin haircut. There was an advertisement for Durex on the wall, and we would overhear Albert whispering to Dad, 'Anything for the weekend, George?' Then there would be a sleight of hand as Dad passed over a shilling and in return would get a small square, brown-paper sachet pushed into his hand. Back then I thought Durex was some kind of secret laxative for adults; after all we were always being force-fed Ex-lax.

Each Christmas would centre on the church services, with midnight mass the main event. A happily drunk Dad would come direct from the pub and sit outside in the porch on a seat specially left for him by our Ceylon-born vicar, Cambridge-educated Reverend Basil Jansz, who took a close interest in our welfare. Dad was unable to shake off the chains of his Roman Catholic upbringing, and never once stepped foot inside the Protestant St Paul's, but he was always stationed in the porch for our key solo performances.

Mum, who used to lend her sweet soprano voice from the front pew of the congregation, would usually buy on the never-never one main Christmas present to be shared between the brothers, and in a stocking we would each get an orange, walnuts, a bar of chocolate and one small personal present like a Dinky toy car or a tennis ball. One Christmas I remember crying with joy when I got a pair of rubber-wheeled roller skates as a present.

But it was the main family present that always became the focal point. I recall a game of Monopoly, the table football classic Subbuteo, new-to-the-market Cludeo, a 'Brain of Britain' family quiz board that lit up when you got the right answer, a Meccano construction set, and Lexicon cards that were the forerunner of Scrabble. I cannot remember a Christmas when we brothers didn't manage to hunt down the major present, and we would play it and then carefully place it back in the wrapping and act suitably surprised and delighted when it appeared in our shared stocking.

We used to make our own entertainment, and our most popular game was tuppenny-halfpenny football, provided we could dig out two old pennies (as the players) and a halfpenny (as the ball). Two matchboxes were put either end of the living-room table, and then using a comb (the shover) we would push the penny against the halfpenny and try to hit the opponent's matchbox. Then we needed fast feet to get away from Mum when she saw the mess we were making of her polished table top. All light years away from today's Gameboy, XBox and computer challenges.

Mum's roast dinner, always cheap chicken, never expensive turkey, was the highlight of every Christmas, and her unfussy cooking beat most of the chefs who have since fed me in some of the world's greatest restaurants.

Those 1940s Christmases were almost Dickensian in their atmosphere and innocence. Nobody had any money, but there was a spirit of goodwill around on which you could have warmed your hands, much more rewarding than modern Christmas celebrations that have become sickeningly commercial and far removed from the original meaning.

In this age of instant communications, mobile phones and the internet, it is timely to remember that few homes in the East End had a telephone, and it was almost an adventure to use the red boxes standing like guardsmen on many street corners. These were the days of 'Press Button A' to make a call, and 'Press Button B' to retrieve your money if you were not connected. Local dialled calls cost fourpence, and long-distance trunk calls made via the operator could be as much as a shilling. Queues used to form outside the phone boxes, and there were often arguments when people hogged the phone gossiping while others were waiting to use it for more pressing reasons. Many a romance was conducted on the phone, with a lover calling his/her mate from one red phone box to another.

There were also blue police boxes familiar to Dr Who fans for use by constables on the beat or, in an emergency, the public. Dad was once found standing fast asleep in a public phone box after one particularly heavy night of drinking. A friendly policeman on the beat brought him home rather than take him to the cells, because he considered him 'drunk but not disorderly.'

Our best friend was the wireless, and we spent hours listening to anything we could find on the BBC Light, Home or Third programmes. Children's Hour was must listening, presented by Derek McCulloch, who was known as Uncle Mac and always signed off by saying. 'Goodbye children ... everywhere.'

Comedy shows like ITMA (It's That Man Again, Tommy Handley), the Charlie Chester Show, At Much Binding in the Marsh, Ray's A Laugh, Life with the Lyons and Have A Go with Wilfred Pickles were huge hits with the Gillers between drunken squabbles.

Journey Into Space, Paul Temple, and Dick Barton Special Agent were never missed, while Man in Black Valentine Dyall used to put the wind up us with his chilling deep-voiced introductions to Appointment with Fear.

Sunday lunchtime meals always followed Family Favourites with Cliff Michelmore and Jean Metcalfe, and In Town Tonight presented by Franklin Engelmann and then Brian Johnston were highlights of each weekday evening.

It was all about feeding the imagination, and we used to provide the pictures in our minds. We were always laughing or crying, singing in close harmony around the piano, competing with each other in games and sporting quizzes, or arguing over which radio programme to tune into, or whether to have Bing Crosby or Beniamino Gigli on the wind-up gramophone. Life was never ever dull.

I used to escape between the covers of books borrowed from the Cable Street library, devouring Enid Blyton, Billy Bunter, Biggles, Just William tales and, later, Dickens and Hardy, before moving on to the great American authors like Hemingway, Steinbeck, Scott Fitzgerald, Irwin Shaw, Philip Roth, Allen Drury, Damon Runyan, Bernard Malamud and, my personal favourite, Budd Schulberg.

All helped lay the foundation to the writer I have become. So blame them, not me.

Comics were another source of eagerly consumed literature, and I always went for the ones with words rather than pictures, with *The Champion* top of my list because of the exploits of the unbeatable boxing master Rockfist Rogan, who flew wartime Spitfires and was forever beating "the Hun."

Between reading, writing, singing in the choir, stumbling around on the piano, playing street football and cricket, roller skating and cycling on my £2 wreck of a bike, I was already developing an inquisitive mind that was to lead me into a lifetime of probing into other people's lives and exploits. I was also garnering a reputation for being the classroom clown, and the first long word I learned was from my Mum, who used to say: "Norman, you are so aggravating." Nothing has changed.

The other long word I picked up was: offended, used in the message I learned by heart when regularly having to run to my Aunt Mary's flat at the far end of Ring House. She was Dad's eldest sister and in charge of paying the rent, because Mum would always be at work. "Mum says," I was programmed to ask, "please don't be offended but can she leave the rent until next week?"Thank goodness, nobody ever shot the messenger\

In those pre-betting shop days of the '40s it was illegal to gamble away from a racecourse or greyhound track, so Dad – just like Joyce's Norman – was among the law-breaking go-betweens who would collect hand-scrawled bets on street corners and then run with them to undercover bookmakers before the 'off' to the races; hence 'bookie's runner.'

Dad gathered pencilled bets from housewives, dockers, doctors, dustmen, schoolteachers, magistrates, even policemen, politicians and priests. Everybody but everybody liked a daily dabble on the gee-gees, and it was the height of hypocrisy that the Establishment refused to listen to campaigns to legalise betting until the revolutionary, barrier-breaking sixties.

Dad always had a mate riding shotgun as a look-out for the Old Bill, and if a policeman appeared Dad would drop into a shopping bag all the bets and money he had collected – mainly copper and silver coins – and his accomplice would run off with the evidence.

It was common for Dad to get arrested while collecting bets during regular clampdowns on street betting, and he would appear at the Thames magistrates court, always under an assumed name, have his thirty-bob (£1.50) fine paid by his bookie and then go back to his street pitches, often carrying bets passed to him by court officials. The police knew he was George Giller, the court clerk knew he was George Giller, but it was all turn-a-blind-eye time, because everybody liked a bet.

For Dad, the East End streets were his stock exchange, which had its own language and rules. He spoke fluent Cockney rhyming slang, a lingo that was first introduced to confuse the Bow Street runners back in the day when police enforcement was in its infancy. He mixed and shook this with smidgeons of Yiddish that he picked up in his youth when working in the schmutter trade as an assistant to a Polish-born tailor in the sweatshops of Whitechapel. He also earned extra pocket money as a "Shabbas Goy", lighting fires and candles for Orthodox Jews on Friday nights and the Saturday Sabbath.

It was as if Dad had stepped out of the pages of a Dickens novel. With his schnozzle, he could have passed as the W.C. Fields interpretation of Mr Micawber. He spoke the real rhyming slang, not today's Mockney. He just used the first word of the rhyme, examples: whistle (for whistle and flute, suit), would you Adam it (Adam and Eve, believe), take a butcher's (butcher's hook, look), here comes the trouble (trouble and strife, wife), he's losing his Barnet (Barnet Fair, hair), going up the apples (apples and pears, stairs), I'm crossing the frog (frog and toad, road), he's on the dog (dog and bone, phone), and his most common one, I'll be in the rub-a-dub-dub (pub).

He was the slave of superstition and illogically worked it out that he always seemed to be arrested on a Friday when Mum cooked sausages. "No more Friday sausages," he warned. "It has to be fish." This was Dad's conscience troubling him. He had been brought up on the fish-on-Fridays Catholic doctrine. Weeks went by and Mum forgot the instruction and was cooking sausages on a Friday evening when she realised Dad was late. His warning came back to her and she rushed to the rubbish chute, and was just in the process of tipping the sausages out of the frying pan when a very drunken and hungry Dad appeared. There had been no arrest, just a long session at the Crooked Billet.

A life of hustling on the streets and trying to keep one step ahead of the Old Bill ended for Dad in tragic circumstances. His bookmaker paymaster, a Jewish shopkeeper, committed the cardinal sin of not laying off with bigger bookmakers the scores of 1946 Epsom Derby bets he took on a horse called Airborne. It was a grey, which drew much of the housewives' support, and its name attracted many servicemen returning from the war. On paper it had no chance, but on the turf it raced to victory by a length at outsider odds of 50-1. The bookie was ruined, and that night he was found dead at home, with his head in the gas oven.

Dad was devastated, and it convinced him that he could no longer race around like he did pre-war as a twenty-something bookie's runner, working for among others Jack Solomons, who was to become the king of post-war boxing promoters.

He appointed Dad as a glovesman after the war, charged with looking after the top-of-the-bill gloves for title fights. No fee, just a free ticket to get in to watch the contests. Yes, a genuine boxing nut.

Convention and family commitments demanded that Dad get himself a proper job, and he became a packer and co-ordinator, first with the Gibbs toothpaste company and then with the toolmakers Buck and Hickman in Aldgate, a job he held for twenty years until his retirement.

Try packing a screwdriver, spanner and hammer in a brown-paper parcel for posting. Dad could wrap better than a Santa's helper.

For all his boozing, I never once knew him miss a day's work. He usually followed a heavy drinking session the next morning by swallowing two raw eggs in two inches of vinegar, and he never suffered hangovers. This was a pity, because it might have cured his unquenchable thirst for alcohol.

My love for sport grew in 1947 when my Chapman Street primary school teacher, Mr Frankel, took me to Lord's to see my all-time idol Denis Compton scoring one of his record 18 centuries that scorching summer.

There has never been a British sportsman to capture a bigger following of hero-worshipping schoolboy fans than the Brylcreem Boy, and we crowded the boundaries cheering every one of his record collection of runs in that glorious summer of '47. His only fault was that he played for the wrong North London football club, but here's a little trivia for you – Denis played more first-team games at White Hart Lane than at Highbury Stadium. That's because for the duration of the war and two seasons after, Arsenal played their home matches at the Lane while their ground was used as an Air Raids Precaution centre.

Many years later Denis would become a treasured Fleet Street colleague at *Express* newspapers, and I was able to get the inside facts on his astonishing career as a footballing cricketer. I wrote a book about it, as you do: *Denis Compton, The Untold Stories*.

In 1948 the Olympics came to London and this little, short-trousered sports fanatic was in heaven. We Gillers had an inside view on the Games because our near neighbour in Stepney, Frank Turner, was captain of the British gymnastics team. We were so close to him that we called him 'Uncle' Frank. He was one of the greatest gymnasts we had ever produced, an all-round master who specialised on the rings.

'Uncle' Frank gave we Giller boys Olympic badges and mementoes of the Games, and told us stories of what it was like to lead the British team. I helped my brother Alan decorate a wall at school with photographs of our local hero, and we followed every moment of the biggest sports festival in the world on the wireless and in the newspapers. We also wrote reports for our Chapman Street school on the highlights.

Forty years on, in harness with my close pal, the commentator and broadcasting master Brian Moore, I devised and scripted a *Games of 48* TV special involving all the legends of the London Games. It was like bringing my past alive and on to the small screen, with our John D. Taylor-produced programme featuring living legends like Emil Zatopek, Bob Mathias and Flying Dutchwoman Fanny Blankers-Koen. Emil told us how he used to scale over the wall of the ladies' team headquarters to steal a kiss from Czech javelin thrower Dana, who was to become Mrs Zatopek, and Fanny revealed that she was three months' pregnant while winning her four gold medals.

What we found out off camera from Zatopek was heartbreaking. He had refused to acknowledge the Russian-dominated Communist party ruling what was then Czechoslovakia in the 1960s. They stripped him of all privileges he had earned as one of the greatest athletes of any time, and he was reduced to sweeping the streets of Prague. But he had us applauding as he said in his broken English: "They never ever take away my pride and dignity ... and my heart."

We also interviewed the men's rowing pair who won a gold for Great Britain, one of whom was the father of multi-talented actor/pianist Hugh Laurie. With what could have been a line from a Fry and Laurie Jeeves' script, he said: "It was jolly good fun."

They should have been called the Miracle Games, because much of London was still rubble and ruins after the war-time bombing.

The Games of '48 were nothing like as huge and dazzling as the London Olympics of 2012, but for this sports-saturated eight-year-old schoolboy they were the greatest sports show on earth.

Our happy little world – blanking out memories of Dad's drinking – was devastated in 1949 when we lost our darling eleven-year-old brother Alan to a kidney disease. He was the best of the bunch, bright, gifted at all sports, already accepted for transfer to a grammar school and my best mate, mentor, boxing coach and playground protector as well as brother. There are tears splashing my keyboard all these years later. It was the blackest and bleakest time of my young life.

He was in St George's Hospital in Wapping for the last three months of his life, and we brothers used to stand in the car park waving up to him at his ward window. I knelt by my bed every single night and said a special prayer just for my beloved brother, who was also my dearest friend.

All these years later I can feel Alan with me, showing me how to box, and singing alongside me in the choir, and making our Mum and Dad cry when he, George and I used to harmonise every Christmas on *Away in A Manger.*

When he was diagnosed with Bright's Disease, none of us realised it was terminal. These days the nephritis would have been controlled and ultimately cured, but back in these 1940s it was rarely beaten.

While all my school friends went off hop-picking in Kent, I was sent packing to Devon for the summer holidays, little knowing that my parents didn't want me to be around for the final days. One morning I realised something was wrong when I came into the kitchen at the farm to find Mrs Dart crying. Joan, the schoolteacher wife of farmer's son John, took me into the garden that looked down into the beautiful valley, and gently told me my lovely Alan had 'gone to join the angels.' I cried for a week.

I wrote a short poem that I sent in a letter to Mum and Dad:

Alan was not only my brother but also my best friend
I loved him like no other and my heart will ne'er mend

Not exactly Masefield, but it was an early indication of my wanting to write down my thoughts and feelings. Already, I was a writer.

Alan's passing wrecked Mum and Dad. Our family doctor Hannah

Billig, famously 'The Angel of Cable Street' for her humanitarian work, advised Mum to take up smoking to help her nerves, which was, ironically, the root cause of her death at 67. Dad dived deeper into the bottle, and our little Giller gang was never quite so complete again.

We were so poor that Alan was buried in an unmarked pauper's grave, wearing one of 'Uncle' Frank Turner's Olympic vests.

I always vowed that one day I would give Alan the burial and gravestone that he deserved, but by the time I could afford it there was no registration of his last resting place.

Alan Thomas Giller, RIP. Gone, but never ever forgotten.

The new decade beckoned with me sitting my 11-plus exams, and in my last term at Chapman Street primary I was awarded a cherished, blue-marbled Conway Stewart fountain pen as a prize for my essay writing.

In my first week at grammar school it was stolen.

Welcome to the real world.

Chapter Eight:
Marrying the Milkman

JOYCE – six years older than me, remember – had entered the big outside world after an education that because of Hitler and the war was splintered and sporadic. But, taking after Granny Arundell, she had a good head for figures and quickly established herself in the football pools department of William Hill's in Blackfriars, just off Ludgate Circus and around the corner to my later hunting ground of Fleet Street. Joyce recalls:

"I loved the challenge and excitement of my work at William Hill's, and those early trips to London took in the imaginative 1951 Festival of Britain on the South Bank and the second term as Prime Minister of Winston Churchill. That was in the days when the Festival Hall became a regular haunt for jazz, and when the futuristic, cigar-shaped Skylon dominated the South London skyline.

"My new husband Norman has warned me against turning this into a political book, but I was delighted to see the grand old man of politics back in Number 10 after an overdose of Socialism. To my young eyes, it was disgraceful that the electorate had kicked Winston out in 1945 after all he had done to inspire us to beat Nazism.

"In those days I was not a political animal, but I was already a true Blue by instinct despite the poverty of the East End where I had been brought up in challenging circumstances. I felt back then and have always believed that the United Kingdom was was safer, more secure and better off under the rule of the Tories.

"As much as I was enjoying working life in London, Mum and Dad made it clear they were not so keen on my daily commuting to Fenchurch Street. They became concerned about the time I spent travelling back and forth on the train and it was my Mum who spotted that I was losing weight.

"I've always been Palmer small in my physique but there I was, nineteen and never more than a 10 in dress size. Mum said one morning, 'You've become so gaunt, Joyce. You're like a walking lollypop stick. This travelling back and forth to London is making you ill. It's got to stop.'

"Back then, even though a working girl bringing home a weekly wage, you still did what your parents told you, and the tragic floods of 1953 convinced my Mum and Dad that they wanted me at home.

"I remember going up on the train on a bleak, overcast winter Sunday and seeing all the fields under water. The sky was as black as a widow's dress and conditions became so bad that the Fenchurch Street line was closed and we had to switch to the Liverpool Street route.

"Suddenly the fields we always looked out on had disappeared under lakes of water, and the far-off houses of Canvey were submerged. It was only the next day we realised the full extent of the disaster, with more than 300 people drowned as the river and North Sea burst banks and spread death and destruction. We later learned that 38 of the victims lived in the Canvey Island area that we daily travelled past on the train

"The nation was plunged into mourning and my most vivid memory of the time is going to a hastily arranged jazz fund-raising concert at the Royal Albert Hall given by queen of singers Ella Fitzgerald, with piano legend Oscar Peterson sharing top of the bill. Out of the wreckage of a nightmare event I can vividly recall jazz at its finest. It's funny the way your memory blocks out the worst times and cherry picks only the best moments.

"The only good thing to come out of the tragedy was that the Government made plans for the construction of the Thames Barrier, a major flood defence structure to protect against the tidal surges and high water levels that had caused so many deaths in 1953. From this lowest point, we were suddenly pitched to the peak of national joy when our lovely Princess Elizabeth became Queen, following the cancer-caused death of her father, George the VI.

I was still working at William Hill's following their move to Clerkenwell, in North London and I thought I was going to burst with pride when it was revealed that Hillary and Tensing had conquered Mount Everest, an announcement held back until the day of the Coronation on June 2, 1953.

"My Uncle Dick Dixon, married to Dad's sister Beatrice, had rented a television specifically to watch the Coronation. The entire Palmer family traipsed to their house in Rayleigh Avenue in Westcliff to watch the crowning ceremony.

There were more than a dozen of us crowded round a TV set with a nine-inch screen, glued to a tiny, flickering picture in black and white. It's laughable now that this was State of the Art. Most of us were sitting on the floor squinting at the screen, while we were served with chips prepared by Aunties Beat and Min. This scene of unity was repeated across the country as the Coronation brought the nation together, with thousands of street parties and sing-alongs.

Owners of trestle tables did a roaring business. It was community spirit at its most heart warming, and I was a very proud nineteen-year-old singing 'God Save the Queen.'

This all came to mind when my new husband and I were queuing for 14 hours to pay our respects to the Queen as she lay in State in 2022. She did not put a foot wrong in all the years she reigned and never once did she not carry out her vow of 1953 to 'do my duty to God and country.'

And I watched it all on a 9-inch television screen in good old Southend..

"The Canvey Island flooding had added to the pressure on me to give up working in London and as 1954 dawned I reluctantly agreed to switch to the family tradition of machining in a local dress factory. I joined the rag trade in a small factory in the London Road, just a short bus ride or long walk from my Southend home, working the Singer sewing machine and stitching dresses and blouses with an ease that came naturally. No more getting up at the crack of dawn to catch the early-morning train to London.

"Every morning on my way to work I would pass the local milkman making his deliveries. We got to smiling at each other and then one day he stood directly in front of me and said, 'My name's Norman Lambert. Want to go to the pictures tonight?'

"I blushed and said, 'Uh, I'll have to ask my Dad.'

"That gives you an idea of the grip our parents had on us. My Dad was a disciplinarian with all five of we Palmer sisters and we dare not do anything bold without his say-so, and that definitely included going out with a boy. I'd had hints of romances but nothing serious. Then along came Norman the milkman.

"I recognised him as one of the best dancers at the Kursaal and I agreed that he could call for me at 7.00 pm. First, of course, I had to ask my Dad's permission and he reluctantly agreed on the understanding that I was back *home before 10.30pm. I almost chickened out but my best friends at work, sisters Barbara and Mavis Tribe, encouraged me, saying that I did not have to agree to see him more than once if I didn't like him.*

"*Norman arrived bang on seven, and was smartly dressed in a well tailored dark suit, crisp shirt and Windsor-knotted tie. I wore a white blouse and black, calf-length skirt, which was the safety-net fashion of the time. Dad gave him a once-over, approved of his appearance and also of the fact that he pulled up in a highly polished, black Austin Cambridge saloon.*

"*At 5ft 6in, Dad was two inches shorter than Norman, but he managed to sound authoritative as he warned, 'Back here by 10.30, or else ...'*

"*We went to the Rivoli in Alexandra Street where the feature film was 'Brigadoon' starring Gene Kelly and Cyd Charisse. Norman was the complete gentleman, and amused me on the way out of the cinema by singing the hit song from the film,* Almost Like Being in Love.'

"*I was later to discover that he was continually singing any song that appealed to him, and he could never resist a microphone.*

"*Two years older than me, I was instantly taken by him. He had a lovely smile, was easy to talk to and was a dreamer about the future, telling me his plans to conquer the world. Well, Essex at least.*

"*We chatted over a cup or three of tea (my tipple ahead of coffee) in the renowned Rossi's cafe in Southend High Street and he told me that he was not just any old milkman. He revealed that on the side he collected bets as a bookie's runner and many of the customers on his milk round were hush-hush gamblers in the days when betting was illegal. Norman would take their bets, usually written on a scrap of paper in pencil, and hand them over to a local bookmaker who would pay him 9d (4p) in every £1 commission on each bet he collected.*

"*From day one he could make me laugh like turning on a tap, and he had me in fits telling me about his 'military career.' He joined the Royal Air Force when called up for his National Service and had designs on learning to fly in somewhere exotic like Rhodesia or Malta. Instead he was posted to Hornchurch in Essex and went home every night without once seeing the inside of a fighter plane. The only good thing about that apart from the convenience is that he was excused wearing flying boots, and was able to keep on his everyday shoes that were made to ease the swelling where he had dropped a crate of milk on his foot. Doh!*

"*Norman could talk the hind legs off a donkey and I was infatuated with the stories of how his life started in Southend's Salisbury Avenue in 1932, and how he had plans to one day have his own business. He was a proper Del Boy of a character, always looking for the chance to make a few bob on the side. (as Del Boy had not been dreamed up then, perhaps I should say for older readers Arthur English, the Cockney spiv with the catchphrase, "Aye, aye. open the cage ...").*

"*There was an American Air Force base out at the beautiful Essex village of Wethersfield and he used to act as a go-between, selling on King Edward cigars and whisky supplied by American servicemen. He had ideas for other outlets from the focal point of his milk round but in those days the Agriculture and Fisheries department were in charge and came down like a ton of bricks on anybody caught selling anything other than milk and cream from a barrow that was like something out of the arc. The luxury of an electric float had not yet reached Southend.*

"*He talked and I listened and it set the tone for our next twenty five years together. Mind you, our relationship almost finished on that first date when we suddenly realised it was 11.30 and we were still chatting away without any idea of the time.*

"*Dad was a mix of worried and angry when Norman delivered me home in the Austin Cambridge saloon and he told me with real rage that we could never see each other again, but that following Saturday we went to a friend's wedding together and became inseparable. Unbeknown to me, he told the bride's mother that I was the girl he was going to marry, and we had only been out on one date!*

"*A secret Norman kept from me was that he had rented the Austin Cambridge for appearances sake and had to pay a fine for returning it late to the SMACS showroom in Elmer Avenue, Southend.*

"*That was Norman, a showman who had to be seen doing the right thing.*

"*The next morning he put our milk on the doorstep and raced off. No way was he going to face the wrath of my Dad.*

"*I instinctively knew Norman was my Mr. Right and we got engaged on September 21 1955 after he'd asked my Dad for permission to marry me, the way it was in those days. He was waiting nervously for me when I came home for a fish-and-chips lunch from the dress factory. I was overjoyed when he took me into our front room and gave me a ring that he'd bought for what was a small fortune of £90 at the Talza Arcade, a warren of little shops that later became swallowed up by the Victoria Circus development.*

"Everybody was delighted for us apart from Norman's sister Vera, who sulked because he went back on a promise to help buy her a pair of shoes. My diamond ring came first.

"We were determined not to sponge on our parents when married and Norman arranged with our friends Zelda and Arthur Waterfield to rent part of their house in Boston Avenue. It had a lean-to which we were going to convert into a kitchen and its own entrance door.

"Then, on the very day we got married on June 9 1956, Jimmy Morgan – Norman's milkman colleague at Eccles Dairies – discovered a flat on his round in St Helen's Road, Westcliff, was coming up for rent at £2.10s (£2.50) a week. Norman made enquiries while getting ready for our wedding at the historic St Mary's Church in Prittlewell that had stood there for a thousand years.

"We had a dream wedding, with my four sisters and two cousins as bridesmaids and my Aunt Flo's twin grandsons as angelic pageboys. Norman's close friend from his schooldays, Derek Johnson, was best man, and – because most of us were in the rag trade – we all made our own dresses, the bridesmaids in a blue brocade and me in a white, ballerina-length dress that a lady in the factory helped me finish. For my borrowed item I got a pair of white shoes from my dear friend Barbara Parker and I wore a lace veil. For something blue, I wore blue knickers.

"Norman was, as usual, very dapper in a new, tailored dark lounge suit and waistcoat. Everything had to be got on ration books, so we were limited with what we could do but the overall effect was grandly impressive. We felt like Royalty.

"It was during the reception in the local St John's Ambulance Hall that Norman told me we could get the flat in Westcliff. Only one problem. The flat owners required a £10 month's rent upfront. We had spent all our money on the wedding and the honeymoon we were about .to go on in Jersey. Norman's boss at the dairy, Mr Eccles, was a guest at our wedding and when he heard our predicament he generously gave us a tenner as a present. That was a huge gift back in the 1950s. The flat was ours.

"'This is the icing on the cake.' said Norman, who could be very witty.

"He was, of course, making a wisecrack about the main attraction at our wedding reception, a two-tier cake that had been made by my Dad's sister Aunt Flo with ingredients provided by my sisters and aunts in the days when food was rationed and hard to come by. It was very very tasty!

"We had ordered a photographer for our wedding from Richardson's studio in Southchurch, but because our finances were so stretched we could not afford to make a bulk order. I nagged Norman for years about collecting the photos and we had a running gag in which he would give a singing reply, 'One day our prints will come.'

"It must have been more than five years later when our good friends Alma and Nigel Wagstaff invited us round to their house, with the mysterious instruction, 'Bring a fiver with you.'

"That evening Nigel insisted that Norman hand him the fiver. Then he reached under the dining table and produced a plastic bag containing all our wedding photos. 'The fiver is for my brother, Tommy,' Nigel explained. 'He's a dustman for Southend Council and he found these photos as they tumbled out of the dustcart when it was being emptied. The photographic studio at Southchurch had obviously given up on you paying and had thrown them out.' Norman looked at me with a straight face and said, 'Told you that one day your prints would come.'

"For our honeymoon, we flew for the first time in our lives to Jersey from Southend Airport, accompanied by our close friends Zelda and Arthur, who were on their seven-day annual holiday. Each of us had to be weighed before we boarded the propeller-driven aircraft. I barely made seven stone and Norman was a skinny eight and a half stone, and we put on a few pounds with our Jersey cream teas during a relaxed week getting used to being Mr and Mrs Lambert.

"The hotel loved having Norman as a guest because after each evening meal he used to play the piano and sing. A highlight was when he found two straw hats and a couple of cane walking sticks in a basket under the stairs, and he persuaded Arthur to join him in a Flanagan and Allen take off of 'Underneath the Arches.' He always lit up a room.

"On our return from honeymoon, Norman's supportive boss Mr Eccles – I never did know his first name – was waiting on the doorstep of our new flat with the extra wedding present of a radio and an armchair, our only furniture at the time apart from a double bed. Eventually we invested in a dressing table and a wardrobe, and Norman's parents bought us a formica kitchen table and a couple of upright, wooden chairs.

"Both Norman and I refused to get hooked on that widespread curse – hire purchase. If we wanted something we were patient and waited until we could afford it. It's called discipline.

"Often it was kind people who bought us things we could not afford. Mr Eccles called again, this time with a beautiful Royal Albert bone china tea service that I kept for many years.

"We looked on him as our guardian angel, so it came as a bombshell in the 1960s when Mr Eccles drove to the shore in Shoeburyness, parked looking out to the estuary and shot himself in the head.

"The coroner's verdict was that he had taken his life 'while the balance of his mind was disturbed.' We had lost a good and generous friend.

"It threw a dark cloud over all who knew him, and my Norman – a new father – was suddenly out of a job."

Chapter Nine:
School for Scoundrels

WHEN Joyce was settling to her new life in Southend, I was starting out on my first day at grammar school wearing a funereal-black blazer two sizes too big that swamped me, and a peaked cap that came down over my ears, making me look geeky and gormless. Some would say it captured me perfectly. My grey-flannel, short trousers reached down below my knees, meeting grey, blue-topped woollen socks pulled up to full stretch on my stick-skinny legs. A brand-new, chestnut-brown leather satchel scraped the floor, and my blue and black striped tie hung diagonally from my too-large shirt collar.

The economic thinking was that I would grow into the clothes, and so worth a year of ridicule. Under the blazer's three-eagle badge was the motto: 'Do your duty to God and man'. I was ready to present my brain for indoctrination at the 'big boys' school.

This was my new uniform for entry to Raine's Foundation Grammar School in September 1951, and the first time I had not worn hand-me-downs since the end of the war. I looked a complete wally, and easy prey for the dead end East End kids who failed the 11-plus, and considered grammar school boys a suitable target for their frustration and contempt. The mile-long walk to school in Arbour Square – taking your life in your hands crossing Cable Street and then the hectic, traffic-jammed Commercial Road – was fraught with the danger of yobs trying to knock your cap off with a catapulted stone.

If caught by a patrolling prefect not wearing your cap you were punished with 100 lines for the first offence, and a slipper on the arse for a second. It was a lose-lose situation. The stone or the slipper?

I became a master of timing, knowing just when to stuff my folded cap into my jacket pocket until into prefect observation range two hundred yards from the school gates. There was a blue band on the back of my cap, signifying that I had been assigned to Dagger House. The school had four houses, all named after previous headmasters. Our present head was an imposing, 6ft 7in beanpole called Dr Shutt. The imagination would not stretch to having a house named after him.

My lasting memory of Dr Shutt is of seeing him break down in the assembly hall in February 1952, when telling us the news that George the Sixth had lost his battle with cancer. It was quite disturbing for an 11-year-old to witness this lofty, narrow-shouldered, stick insect of a man in his gown and mortarboard weeping like a baby as he said through sobs: "God rest the King, Long Live the Queen."

We sang the national anthem – for the first time, God Save the Queen – and then got sent home for the rest of the day, so that was all right then.

With Mum and Dad at work there was no problem getting into the empty flat. This was a time when you could leave your front door unlocked without risk of being burgled. We let ourselves in with a latchkey on a piece of string hanging from inside the letterbox. In truth, there was little worth stealing.

I had followed my older brother, George, to what was then arguably the most prestigious school in the East End, even though we had to put up with shouted taunts of, "Raine's get their brains from the drains." I have redacted the adjectives.

Alan had been all set to go, too, until tragically taken from us much too early. George was the brain box in the family, and got a shower of 'O' levels before taking an insurance clerk's job in the City with Lloyd's, where Mum worked as a char and opened the door for him. Back then, one in ten thousand boys went to university. They were needed as breadwinners.

Office life proved too claustrophobic for George, and after his two years' National Service in the Royal Fusiliers he became P.C. 508C in the City of London Police force, which then only recruited six-footers and above. George made it by half an inch. We used to jokingly describe him as the black sheep of the family.

As news got round that my brother had 'gone over to the other side', Dad found many of his regular drinking pals suddenly reluctant to keep his company. Among those who decided Dad was now persona non grata were a pair of boxing twins Dad had supported during their amateur and professional ring careers. They lived close to us in Vallance Road, and were making something of a reputation for themselves outside the ring, their names Ronnie and Reggie Kray

.Every East Ender from my generation seems to lay claim to knowing the notorious Krays, the gangland leaders who terrorised west London nightclubs and casinos with their protection rackets. Well, first of all through my Dad and then as a reporter on their manor, I really did know them. They interviewed me for the job of being their press agent in the 1960s, and I was also in the running to ghost their life stories, but the job eventually went to Fred Dineage, later of 'How!' television fame, who remained a popular ITV presenter on the south coast after more than fifty years in the media business.

Ronnie and Reggie really were good to their Mum, Violet, who used to pull pints for my Dad and me when she ran the Krays-owned Carpenters Arms pub in Spitalfields, just a short walk from where the twins grew up in Vallance Road. They were only violent against their own, rival villains trying to muscle in on their patch. Dad knew them when they boxed as amateurs at the Repton Club in Bethnal Green, where top-rated coach Tony Burns was loyal to their memory. He coached many leading amateur internationals, including a young Enfield tearaway called Ray Winstone.

In the 50 years I knew Tony – best man at Reggie's wedding – he never ever wavered in his belief that, at heart, they were "decent blokes who would always help anybody down on their luck."Another link of mine with the Krays is that the Blind Beggar pub in Whitechapel – where Ronnie murdered rival gangster George Cornell – was owned by Patsy Quill and younger brother Jimmy, who was at Raine's at the same time as me and an exceptional boxer we used to call 'Jimmy the Jab.' Boxing seems to be the common denominator in so much of my life.

In 1951 big brother George had been one of the King's Scout troop on parade at the Festival of Britain on the South side of the Thames, which was like foreign territory for we East Enders. I joined the scouts several times but always left when the knot-tying tests came around, which I am sure were designed to humiliate me. It's Giller family legend that I could never tie my shoelaces properly. Our troop leader, Scoutmaster 'Wick' Everett, whose flat I used to clean every weekend for half a crown, continually preached: 'It's better to know a knot and not need it, than need a knot and not know it.' I wanted to tell him to get knotted.

My brain is just not wired for such complicated tasks, as was proved at school where I was a dummy at anything practical. Woodwork, all the sciences and technical drawing went over my head like passing seagulls. History and geography held my attention, and I can come up with lots of fairly meaningless soundbites in French and German, but the only subject that really grabbed me was English, and I always got reasonable marks for my essays.

"Could do better" was a mantra that ran through all my school reports. The only grammar school prize I won was for Religious Instruction, and I was given a list of theology books as suggestions for my award. I chose *Cricket Is My Life*, by England captain Len Hutton. Yes, sport was my religion.

I excelled in most sports to such an extent that I was elected junior house captain and also captain of rugby, boxing, cricket, athletics and cross-country. One boy, impressed at the support I was getting across the board, put up his hand and proposed me for captain of the swimming team, not realising that I could just about doggy paddle a width of the pool. To this day, I feel queasy whenever I get a whiff of chlorine.

I was in a class of 30 lively East End boys and with a Victorian-strict form master called 'Donny' Lyons, who had himself been a pupil at Raine's and had become a linguist, specialising in German. At primary school we had been taught collectively, chanting the twelve times table together, and all of us reading aloud from the blackboard because there were not enough text books to go round. I cannot recall any of my classmates leaving primary school without being able to read and write

At grammar school it was down to the individual to concentrate and assimilate the river of facts flooding in from across a wide range of subjects. Most of the time I was out of my depth. One of my few talents, which I have retained, is being able to look interested when somebody is talking to me while my inner mind is elsewhere. Mr Lyons and all his well-meaning colleagues were convinced they were holding my concentration, while my imagination was taking me away to far more interesting thoughts and places. It is a gift that has carried me through many boring encounters with people who like the sound of their own voice.

Raine's, founded as a school for the East London poor by religious philanthropist Henry Raine early in the eighteenth century, had a long and proud tradition of educating the ragamuffins of the East End, getting in ahead of the Fagins to rescue the starving kids from the streets.

Let me give you the first verse of our school song:

Since upon the throne of England first was hailed the name of George
Raine's with unabated ardour set to work a chain to forge
Link by link a chain of honour, o'er two centuries the span
Ever Raineians learn their duty, duty both to God and man

At a Sports Journalists' Association awards dinner I sang this with another Raine's old boy, triple jumper Phillips Idowu. We went to the same school 40 years apart.

By today's namby-pamby standards, discipline at the school was strict to the point of brutal. We would stand to attention, hands down by our sides, the moment a teacher came into the classroom, and we had to show respect at all times and doff our caps to them if we saw them in the street.

One of our long-held traditions was if you wanted to go to the toilet you had to ask: "Please, sir, may I go forth?" New boys thinking they were being clever and original by saying 'fifth' would have to write 100 times: "I must recognise and respect school traditions at all times."

Grace was said in Latin, and at the start of every assembly we would sing a hymn as well as the rousing school song. All religions were accounted for, but the school was built on a Church of England foundation.

Donny Lyons, like all the gowned masters, carried a shiny-soled slipper with which he would administer six of the best at the least excuse. He used to call it Sammy, and was for my taste a little too fond of bending boys over his desk and giving them a whacking.

We would get thumped on the rump for dropping an aitch, saying 'fink' instead of think, 'ain't' instead of 'isn't', and 'done' instead of 'did'.

We had a kindly but very excitable English Literature teacher called Mr Norris, who once went ballistic when my good mate Ivor Bornstein, sitting in the next desk to me, said, "I done it, sir."

"No, no, no, boy," he said, jumping up and down. "I did it, I did it, I did it!"

I couldn't resist the open goal, and popped up with, "No sir, it was definitely Bornstein who did it."

It got me the slipper, but it was worth it for the laughter from my classmates. Yes, aggravating.

God help the boy foolish enough to back chat a teacher. He would be sent to the Head for caning, and the sight of the towering Dr Shutt wielding a cane was not for the squeamish. Worst of all was when he wanted to make an example of any boy who had brought the school into disrepute by fighting in the street, or been caught smoking behind the bike shed.

Dr Shutt decided such 'crimes' were worthy of public humiliation, and he would carry out the caning sentence – usually six vicious strokes – in front of the entire school at morning assembly. It certainly had the effect of making you think twice about stepping out of line, but it was brutal in the extreme and quite rightly banned by future administrations. No wonder we nicknamed the towering Dr Shutt 'Citizen Cane.'

.It is seared in my memory as if with a branding iron how I once dodged a PT period in the gymnasium with five other boys, and we were caught hiding out of the way in the woodwork room. Confirmed bachelor Donny Lyons was informed and kept us behind after school. He decided this was an 'in house' matter and not worthy of the headmaster's cane. The building was deserted as he shepherded us up the stairs to an empty classroom right at the top of the school. He then instructed all of us to strip bollock naked and bend over. As Donny, almost frothing at the mouth, whacked the first boy with the slipper on his bare arse, another lad started to have a screaming fit. Suddenly, like a man snapping out of a private fantasy, Donny ordered us all to get dressed and said: "That will teach you never to avoid PT again. Let it be a lesson to you."

We all got out of there as fast as we could, and the perverted incident was never mentioned again. We dared not tell our parents because they would have whacked us for misbehaving. Can you imagine the assault charges that would have been brought today? Yes, another planet.

I had as much intellectual depth as a thimble, and when I think back now I kick myself for not having made more of a wonderful school, where I could and should have drunk heavily from the sea of knowledge freely available.

But I was too much of a dreamer, lost in my own often surreal world, and I could only be fully motivated by writing essays and taking part in sport.

As well as the breaking of my wrists while winning a boxing contest in two minutes of painful action, I was prominent as the fastest runner in my year. I won the school sports 100 and 220 yards in back to back summers on the 1948 Olympic pink-cinder track that had been transferred from Wembley to Eton Manor in Leyton, and I was third in the London championships, beaten by two six-footers on the black-cinder Victoria Park track.

Between us, my brother George and I won a London Boy Scouts' track and field meeting for the 34th Stepney troop. It was mainly down to George, who finished first in the 220 and 440 yards races, also the high jump and long jump, and as the starter's gun sounded for the start of the 100 yards he, not unsurprisingly, collapsed with cramp.

My newfound love was rugby, and my best mate Ernie McDonald, a bus conductor's son from Bow, became one of the first East End kids to represent England schoolboys at international level. I played centre or wing in the school XV on Saturday mornings, and in the afternoon right winger for the church boys' football team. I was very good at all sports but outstanding at none. Yes, definitely a know-all sports critic in the making.

On leaving school I had one senior rugby union match, a trial with Wanstead Rugby Club. A giant second row forward hit me so hard with a tackle that I felt he was still with me two weeks later, and I realised I did not have the physique – I was nine-stone wet through – for senior rugby.

Ernie went on to play as a rugged hooker for Saracens and joined me in local newspaper journalism before starting an exciting new life with his gorgeous wife, Vera, in the United States, where he became a noted fabrics expert and ladies fashion designer.

He, sadly, died early in his fifties following a heart attack. I thought he was indestructible.

Another close schooldays pal was the 'I done it' boy Ivor 'Bingo' Bornstein, later a style-setting ladies hairdresser. He used to smuggle me into the exclusive Jewish Brady Boys' Club in Stepney, where I would compete more with enthusiasm than expertise at the table tennis table. I used my precious Johnny Leach bat – autographed by the world champion from Ilford and the envy of all, so much so that it was pinched while I was on what would now be known as a comfort break.

Ivor and I used to sit at the back of the class, making life exasperating for our teachers by clowning, chattering and specialising in humming and tuneless whistling. Yes, aggravating is again the word I'm reaching for..

At least 10 per cent of the pupils at Raine's were of the Jewish faith, and they included – five years ahead of me – a music-motivated boy called Ronnie Schatt. I caught up with him in the 1960s when he was running his world-famous jazz club in Soho, Ronnie Scott's. Goodness knows why he changed his name.

There was a lot of antisemitism poisoning the streets in those days of swaggering, hostile Teddy Boys, who used to clash in vicious East v. South razor-gang fights on the bombed sites of Aldgate and Whitechapel. Ivor sometimes got roughed up on his way to visit me, and scrawled on the walls around our flats were the menacing messages, 'HITLER WAS RIGHT' and 'KILL THE YIDS.' This explains why I do not feel comfortable with the 'Yids' nickname adopted by followers of Tottenham Hotspur. I wish they would drop it, but know I am preaching to the unconverted

The thugs with their Brylcreemed, high-quiffed hair, draped, velvet-collar jackets, brothel-creeper crepe-soled shoes, flick knives and knuckle dusters, had a new target for their xenophobia in 1956, when refugees fleeing the Soviet invasion in Hungary were housed down the road to me in a mission in Wapping. From Russian tanks to British bigotry, they must have wondered if their escape was worth it.

Included among those terrified by the Wapping street fights was a young Hungarian boy who would cross my path later in life; his name, Joe Bugner. I was his PR for a couple of years and to his face I would call him "the mad Hungarian." What a handful of ego, yet very likable for all that.

Next for the race hatred attacks was the new-from-West-Indies black community, terrorised at the friendly 1958 Notting Hill Carnival by gangs of rampaging Teddy Boys stirred up by the repulsive 'Keep Britain White' campaign. It was sickening to watch from the sidelines and dropped a curtain of caution on all our lives as we wondered and worried about where the next mindless riots would break out.

I have never seen people as Jews, Muslims, Catholics, black, white, brown, yellow, or any other creed or colour – just as fellow human beings, and I take them as I find them.

My first serious love in the late 1950s was a brown-eyed, auburn-haired Jewish beauty called Sandra, who also went to Raine's, where the girls were hidden from us like forbidden fruit behind huge wooden dividing doors. Sandy and I were introduced by her classmate Alice Carr, later my brother George's first wife, who was tragically taken from us by cancer at just 40. Sandy and I explored each other sexually like young men and women have been doing since Adam and Eve, and when her parents found out she was being romanced by a goy (non-Jew), they went berserk and broke us up. I thought of writing a musical about it called Goys and Dolls, but couldn't get any backers. Just as with Joyce and me nearly 70 years later, we were like an East End Romeo and Juliet, oy vey!

The wireless continued to be our main source of home entertainment, with a crazy comedy show taking humour off in a bizarre direction – *The Goon Show,* which ran throughout the 1950s, mainly on the usually stuffy BBC Home service. Several of the younger teachers at our school got swept along by the show's catchphrases and off-the-wall nonsense, and it got them into trouble with headmaster Dr Shutt, a smouldering-tempered Basil Fawlty type of character, who always looked as if he'd just been stung by a wasp.

In what was possibly an early form of hacking, I eavesdropped at the open door of the staffroom when the Head was reprimanding the teachers for what he called their 'juvenile behaviour, setting an appalling example for the boys by imitating the moronic conduct of some ridiculous wireless clowns.' I quietly passed on this intelligence to my classmates, and for the next few days all the boys were walking around the school corridors loudly mimicking the zany voices of Peter Sellers, Harry Secombe and Spike Milligan. Ying tong iddle I po (that's Enigma code stuff that will only ever mean anything to Goon Show lovers). The threat of the cane shut us up.

Rivalling the wireless for our attention was the cinema, and I used to spend most of the money I earned from a weekend round of delivering newspapers on 'going to the pictures'. It was a habit started in the immediate post-war years, when sixpenny Saturday morning pictures and episodes of cowboy adventures featuring Hopalong Cassidy and Roy Rogers sent my fantasies racing. I used to gallop home from the cinema with six-shooters blazing, and on a make-believe horse that could run like the wind. Yes, I could really ride my imagination.

There was also the Tuppeny Pictures run by missionaries at the Methodist Hall in Cable Street. Their budget would only run to old silent westerns starring Tom Mix and Buck Jones, and between each flickering black and white film we would sing such hymns as 'Yes Jesus Loves Me' and 'Onward Christian Soldiers.' 'Bingo' Bornstein singing lustily alongside me showed how far we would go to see a film in those pre-TV days.

Into my teens, most of the films that appealed to me were 'A' rated, which signified you had to be accompanied by an adult if under eighteen. This meant standing outside one of the four cinemas in our area – The Troxy, The Palaseum, The Poplar and The Mile End Odeon – and asking complete strangers, 'Can you take me in, please Mister.' I shudder now when I think of the chances I was taking, but it was worth it to see screen heroes like Humphrey Bogart, James Cagney, Jimmy Stewart and Cary Grant in black and white classics.

I can remember fighting back tears during the Jimmy Stewart classic *It's A Wonderful Life*, and sitting on the edge of my seat with tension when Public Enemy No 1 John Dillinger was being shot by the police.

The cinemas, with plush foyers and sweeping staircases giving them the feel and appearance of grand mansions, were the poshest places we used to visit to escape the reality of what were harsh lives, and the organist coming up out of the orchestra pit playing sing-along songs on a brightly lit Wurlitzer provided us with rare live entertainment. An evening at the cinema was an event, and these days I carry on the tradition by leading sing-a-long-a-Norm sessions of old Cockney songs while banging away on the old joanna in the style of my Dad playing the piano. Yes, I can still bore for Britain.

It used to be hilarious to watch us scrambling to get out of the cinema at the end of the programme to try to avoid having to stand to attention for the National Anthem, our shoes covered in discarded peanut shells and orange juice dripping from our plastic Kia-ora cartons. When the first notes of God Save the King (later, Queen) sounded you were duty bound to stop where you were, and it was common for people to be caught standing in the aisle trying to look suitably patriotic. We were a generation of robots.

Once, when sitting in the one-and-nines (8.5p) watching French seductress Brigitte Bardot in *The Girl in the Bikini*, the middle-aged man next to me unbuttoned his fly and started masturbating.

I froze for a few seconds. I could not report him to the usherette, because I had bunked in for nothing by nipping in a side door as picture-goers exited. I chose my moment to run out of the cinema, feeling sick and revolted. I never did find out whether Brigitte got her man.

One of the few times I went to the cinema with my Dad was to see Alec Guinness in *The Man in the White Suit* in September 1951, and we managed to get ourselves thrown out.

I can be specific about the date because the only reason Dad went was to see the newsreel report on Randolph Turpin's tenth round defeat by Sugar Ray Robinson in a world middleweight title defence in New York, just 64 days after taking the championship from the legendary American at Earls Court. My Dad had been in charge of the gloves.

There was controversy as to whether referee Ruby Goldstein was too hasty with his decision to stop the fight, with Turpin rocking and rolling on the ropes trying to avoid Robinson's two-fisted attacks.

Dad, who idolised Turpin, got so carried away he thought he was watching the fight live and shouted from the cinema stalls: 'It's a f***ing fix. You're a f***ng disgrace referee.'

Within moments we were invited to leave by the horrified cinema manager. Dad, still fuming, told him: 'Stick your pictures up your arse. The referee was bent.'

It would not be the last time that Dad and I were thrown out of a venue together.

A life-changing revolution started with the 1953 Coronation of Queen Elizabeth. H-shaped aerials started appearing on thousands of rooftops and chimney pots as everybody rushed to get in on the sudden boom in sales of television sets. We got our sideboard-top Pye TV with its 9-inch screen on a monthly 7s 6d (37.5p) Radio Rentals contract.

Televisions then used the cathode ray tube system, and the rental companies were responsible for the frequent repairs, so it made more sense to rent than to buy, not that Mum and Dad could have found the £45 plus £7 purchase tax for the prized TV set. That was more than six times the average weekly wage in 1952 of seven pounds, ten shillings (£7.50).

We used to take our lives in our hands hanging out of the top-floor window making adjustments to the aerial in a bid to get a better reception, and we continually had to manoeuvre the horizontal hold to try to stop the picture rolling. Mum had the best head for heights and performed most of the aerial positioning.

Once a month she would sit half outside the sky-high windows cleaning them, with one of we boys holding on to her knees. Dad couldn't even watch and would use it as an excuse to go out for a drink.

Our first TV set was delivered in May 1952 just in time for the FA Cup final between Newcastle United and Arsenal. Chilean international George Robledo, one of the few foreign-born players in the League, scored the only goal of the match for Newcastle, and my Dad, brothers – even Mum – and I watched it transfixed. To us, it was like a miracle that the match action could come live into our living room, all on the tiny screen that to us was like a window on the world.

There was just one channel, and virtually everything was 'live' because recording facilities were in their infancy. Between programmes, and often during them to cover breakdowns and shifts of scenery, there were short "interludes" while film of a potter's wheel, goldfish circling in a bowl or a field of corn being harvested were shown. We would sit there watching as if the filler films held some sort of fascination, listening to the pleasant accompanying music and feeling relaxed, and in no way getting irritated. Goodness knows how today's impatient, fast-food, must-have-it-now generation would have coped.

All of us were addicted to the small screen, and it was taken so seriously at the BBC that regular continuity announcers Sylvia Peters and Mary Malcolm often used to wear ball gowns, and co-presenter McDonald Hobley wore a dinner suit while introducing the programme we were about to watch. It made those of us sat at home watching feel scruffy and under-dressed. They were just glorified go-betweens, but quickly became among the most famous and feted people in the land.

To get the best television reception we always drew the curtains and viewed quietly and intently in darkness. Granny Giller was watching once, got up to go to the toilet in the dark, tripped over my youngest brother

Kenneth – spread-eagled on the floor watching the TV – and broke her hip. She died a few days later and from then on I always made the introduction, 'This is my brother Ken, who killed his gran.' Yes, I can be horrible.

That first Year of the Telly was immense for me. Spending the six weeks of my summer schoolboy holiday on the Dart farm in Devonshire, I hand-wrote my first book – a diary of the 1952 Olympic track and field finals in Helsinki. I remain a wearisome walking record book on those now obscure Games.

Just twelve days after the Olympics finished I was sitting alone in the conservatory at the farmhouse when the sloping glass roof started rattling and shaking as if being hit by machine-gun fire. A torrential rainstorm was sweeping across the fields and valleys, and farmer's wife Mrs Dart ordered me into the huge, stone-clad kitchen that was the hub of the house. The cascading rain continued non-stop throughout the day, causing havoc and tragedy across the glorious Devonshire countryside. A wall of water surged through villages and farmland, and it was so severe that the East and West Lyn rivers meeting a few miles away at the large Exmoor village of Lynmouth burst their banks. Homes were swept away, trees uprooted, motorcars submerged, animals drowned and, most heart-breaking of all, thirty-four people were killed and many more injured in what was then the worst post-war flooding disaster in Britain.

The next day I went with farmer's son John Dart in his Land Rover to see the aftermath of the storm. More than 40 buildings had collapsed, and the Army was drafted in to lead the clearing-up operation. Huge boulders had been driven down the surrounding hills, crushing anything in their path

Earlier in the week I had written home to describe how John had given me my first lesson in driving a tractor, and of how I was being trusted to bring the herd of cows home to the farm from a nearby grazing field. Now I wrote again, this time pretending I was a newspaper reporter giving a full description of The Day The Rains Came. Here I was, twelve years old, and already wanting to get on record everything I had observed.

I thought I was a healthy little boy, but in a routine school medical check it was discovered that I could not pull back the foreskin on my penis without it hurting. 'You will have to be circumcised,' said the nurse. My eyes are watering at the recollection .My comedian mate Ivor Bornstein told me it was nothing to worry about. 'I can't remember it hurting me at all,' he said, reaching back in memory to what happens to all orthodox Jewish boys when they are eight days old.

For the first time in my life, aged thirteen and a half, I went into dock at the Queen Elizabeth Children's Hospital in Stepney, where Mum was not only the cleaner but the best friend of the Matron, Miss Saunders, who was a regular visitor home for tea, biscuits and gossip.

The Matron assured me I had nothing to worry about and that it would all be over without me knowing a thing about it. Wrong! My nightmare started in the operating theatre when an anaesthetist placed a rubber, kidney-shaped gasmask over my face. This was not a Mickey Mouse lookalike as in the war, but a suffocating cup that had the nauseating smell of rubber and, worse, it was mixed with the whiff of real gas.

I instinctively turned my head away and it took two people to hold me still as they waited for the gas to take effect. Those of a nervous disposition should look away now. The gas only partly worked and I woke up in mid-operation to see the scalpel slicing into my defenceless, shrunken penis, and blood squirting over my thighs.

As my dear old mate Eric Morecambe used to say, 'Not a pretty sight.'

They then, thank goodness, put me out properly and I woke up the next morning wondering if I had dreamt it all, but my bandaged best friend proved that I had been through the operation.

I had to take two weeks off school because of complications, and – pardon the alleged pun – felt a complete dick head.

It would not be the last time I had a crisis in that department.

Most days on the walk to school I would take a detour to go past the house of my local hero Sammy McCarthy, the British featherweight boxing champion who lived half a mile away from me at the Limehouse end of Commercial Road, the main link from West Ham and Barking to Aldgate and the square mile of the City.

I was always hoping to bump into Sammy, who did not have a shred of arrogance and was happy to chat about his career and his plans. The huge, rambling, Victorian house where the McCarthys lived was always alive with life and laughter. He shared the home with his nine brothers and sisters and his mum and dad, Titch McCarthy, a barrow-pushing costermonger who was one of my father's drinking pals

.Sammy's nickname was 'Smiler' because he continually smiled in the ring, often applauding his opponent at the end of rounds, and he was the Gentle Executioner, almost apologising for landing his beautifully choreographed punching combinations.

I used to stand outside the Mile End Arena, a stroll away from where Sammy and I lived, to listen to the crowd when he was boxing. He never ever lost a contest at that famous old fight venue, and I recall crying the night he finally lost his unbeaten record to future world featherweight champion Hogan 'Kid' Bassey at the Royal Albert Hall to end his 28-fight undefeated record. I remember the Daily Herald back page headline: 'SAMMY SMILES EVEN IN DEFEAT.'

Back in those early fifties, Sammy was courting Sylvia Clancy, an attractive East End girl whose gran lived in Ring House, where Sylvia often stayed. Sammy would visit her along with his future best man at their wedding, Terry Lawless, later one of the world's top boxing managers and trainers. I used to follow them around like a puppy dog, fascinated by their conversations about boxing. They never once told me to push off, happy to put up with my schoolboy curiosity and, in Sammy's case, hero worship. It was the start of a life-long rapport with both of them.

Another boy who idolised Sammy used to play truant from his school in Canning Town, so that he could visit the McCarthy home. We often met on Sammy's doorstep and discussed his fights. The boy's name was Terry Spinks, who in 1956 won the Olympic flyweight title at the age of 18 and went on to capture the professional British featherweight title under the management of our mutual idol Sammy McCarthy.

When I delivered the eulogy at Terry's 2012 funeral Sammy was in the front pew. It was the only time I didn't see him smiling. They were like brothers, and along with Terry's cousin Rosemary Elmore he helped nurse Spinks through his last painful years when the punches he had taken in the ring caught up with him.

Sammy did not choose his friends well when he retired from the ring, and recklessly and rashly travelled the crime road as he tried to maintain the huge earnings he made in his fighting days. While running the Prince of Wales pub in Duckett Street, Stepney, he used to welcome some pretty dodgy company, and during after-hours lock-ins the talk was often about topics not for the ears of snoopers like me, or my policeman brother.

A brilliant defensive boxer, Sammy was rarely caught by punches but was always getting caught by the Old Bill. He served three prison sentences, first for three years, then six and, finally, after a crazy attempt at a completely out-of-character armed robbery, fifteen years.

Sammy and I kept our friendship going through all life's storms and calamities. "Whenever I talk to young boxers I tell them not to use me as a role model," Sammy told me, with his usual disarming charm. "I've been an idiot, but I guess I found it easier to cope with life in the nick than on the outside. Doing the crime, not looking to hurt anybody, was just my way of getting back the buzz I used to have climbing into the ring. Boxing was like a drug to me and I loved every second of my amateur and professional careers. I felt empty when it all finished and I had to find something to replace that feeling of danger. I never tried to harm anybody, and I'm ashamed of myself for letting down my family and friends."

He remained on the Christmas card list of his old prison governor right up to his passing at the age of 88 in 2020, and we mourners sensed him still smiling as we saw off this extraordinary East End idol.

A true one off, and I feel privileged to have called him a mate.

Chapter Ten:
Mother, mortgage and making do

W E rejoin Joyce at the start of her married life to the energetic and entertaining Norman Lambert in 1956 against the backdrop of the Suez Crisis that led to the humiliation of Britain, and Prime Minster Anthony Eden retiring soon after, claiming ill health but many thought it was in shame ,,,

"I was pregnant with Steven as Britain invaded Suez in union with the French and Israeli troops, and it revealed the shift in world power when the USA and Russia demanded we withdraw. My interest was much more concerned with bringing a new life into the world and fighting off milk fever that kept me confined to Rochford hospital maternity ward longer than I wanted.

"I was continually throwing up and unable to feed Michael the conventional way. I loved my new son dearly but had to pay a price for his birth.

"Norman and I had set our sights on getting a deposit together for our own house. This meant we spent many months making sacrifices and scrambling together a deposit of £300. It was easier said than done, and Norman worked his socks off to get the money. This included not only his milk round and bet-collecting cash but spending every spare second decorating people's homes and doing any odd job that came his way. He was never frightened of hard work, particularly with the motivation of getting our own home.

"Of course, it doesn't sound a great deal of money now but anybody who was around at the time will confirm it was a small fortune for we have-nots.

"I never smoked in my life, so could not make savings there but Norman cut down on his liking for Player's cigarettes. Penny by penny, we got our deposit together, me machining and Norman doing odd jobs on top of his milk round. We already had £100 in the bank, but Norman insisted this was untouchable. 'It's our roof money,' he explained. 'If we know we have a

waterproof roof over our heads we know all will be okay.'

"*We dipped just once into our savings – to buy a motorcar! This was not just any old car but a lefthand drive black Buick coupe, with a white-walled spare wheel on its side in traditional style of the 'mob' cars that featured in 1940s gangster films. Norman had been intrigued by a lock-up garage on his milk round in which the car had been kept on bricks since the fanatical motoring enthusiast imported it from America on the eve of the war. When the eccentric owner died in 1957, his widow asked Norman to take it off her hands for £100. He'd had a good Epsom Derby, taking in lots of bets and so was able to put his hand on the cash.*

"*The Buick Straight-8 was in amazingly good condition considering it had been off the road for so long and it started a love affair with American cars that lasted the rest of his life. In later years he had two Lincolns and another spectacular, gold-coloured Buick and he passed this fanaticism on to our youngest son Michael, inheriting a love for motor cars with style and elegance. Yes, my Norman was a man with impeccable if off-beat taste.*

"*We got some of our money back on the black Buick by selling its rare, six-cylinder radio to a wireless fanatic, and then eventually let the car go to a collector for more than it cost us. It set the pattern for a lot of car wheeling and dealing, a habit that Michael has continued. We had a string of cars including a Renault, Hillman Minx, Austin 30: Morris Minor, Fiat, beige Ford Consul, BMW, Ford Capri and, as our business picked up, a flash Jaguar. But it was our American cars that took the eye.*

"*I became a keen motorist after passing my test at the third attempt, and often took the left hand drive cars on head-turning journeys around Southend. The gold Buick was a real show stopper and its column gearstick and unique braking system was a mystery and a magnet to many curious people.*

"*The only car that rivalled it for claiming the attention of passersby and other motorists was our Lincoln Continental. That was the sleekest car I've ever ever driven. I would have called it Lincoln Presidential.*

"*It was 1959 when Michael arrived as a brother for Steven, and I again had to battle the fever caused by producing too much milk and I was grateful to my Mum and sisters for looking after me as I battled to keep any food down. Every day I felt drained and would have to lie down on my bed to combat the continual sickness.*

"*My dad was over the moon that he now had two grandsons after producing five girls in his marriage. I don't think I'd ever seen him so happy as when proudly pushing the boys around Southend in their prams, and he and mum would take the boys on holidays to Bournemouth and Torquay. Package holidays abroad had not yet arrived and we were far too busy getting our business off the ground to consider taking time out for a long break.*

"*Michael was a home birth in the early days at our first house in Beverley Gardens. Norman had spotted it was for sale and was taking a peep over the hedge when what seemed an old tramp asked him what he was looking at. Norman got into conversation with him and was astonished to discover that he was talking to the owner of the property who put him in touch with the estate agents. It cost us £2,300, and to clinch it we committed to a 30 year mortgage with Southend Council at £11 a month. Yes, 30 year! It was what our parents' generation called 'putting a millstone round our necks.'*

"*In the early days at Beverley Gardens, we had little furniture, no carpets and just basic china and cooking utensils, but this was our castle and if we had been millionaire landowners we could not have been prouder of our semi-detached, Tudor-style, three-bedroomed home.*

"*Because we knew the midwife was coming, we stretched to a carpet for our bedroom. When she arrived she took one look at it and said, 'You can get that up immediately! It's a dust trap and no good for your baby.'*

"*By then I was a devoted member of the Tory Party. I am often asked how a girl brought up near the poverty line in the East End could be a true Blue, and I reply that I have always followed the six Conservative commandments: Individual Freedom without government intrusion ... the Rule of Law ... Peace through strength ... Economic responsibility ...Free markets ... Human dignity.*

"*I joined the Tories in 1959 when a canvasser called Heather knocked on my door and found willing listeners in Norman and I. We thought Harold Macmillan was doing a great job and very happily signed up. I was reunited with Heather a few years ago and she recalled how enthusiastic I had been and said it seemed like yesterday. I pointed out that both my sons, babies back then, were now over 60.*

"*I have always found Labour too wishy washy and allowing themselves to be dictated to by the trade unions. This is why this East End girl will keep on demanding a fair and balanced society, and I'll continue to claim that Britain is only a small island and that it's common sense to limit the numbers who can live here. Racism? No, realism.*

"*I shall get off my soapbox and return to the story of my life.*

"*Dancing was always my major hobby, and I used to go with friends to lessons at Mimi Green's in Chalkwell and to Alan Mitchell's at the Talza Arcade. Then Norman became a perfect partner and with four willing sisters to call on as babysitters we were able to get along to Tory-sponsored events at Iveagh Hall and we also went regularly to The Elms in London Road, which is now a Wetherspoons.*

"*Our major venue was The Kursaal where Howard Baker's orchestra was the resident big band and there were guest appearances by the Cyril Stapleton and Ken Mackintosh bands. Norman was the life and soul of any event, a born entertainer who brought a buzz to all occasions. He could dance in conventional ballroom style or jive and he and I had a wonderful understanding on the dance floor.*

"*Norman would always look to steal the microphone and sing any of the current hits, and I recall that his favourite was Pennies from Heaven, and he would gently persuade his audiences to give their pennies for charity. Not just saying this because he was my husband but he was a great character who made parties go with a swing.*

If there was a dull moment he would get a pack of cards out and bewilder and entertain everybody with tricks he had spent hours perfecrting. The one unfulfilled ambition he had was to become a member of the Magic Circle, and one of the greatest nights of his life was when we were on holiday in Brighton during a magicians' convention. Guest of honour was the one and only Tommy Cooper, and we had an hilarious time with him. He, of course, was a born comedian and was even funny when he didn't mean to be. Norman and I were in hysterics when we visited a Chineese Takeaway with Tommy, and while we we waiting for our food he rang his wife to complain about a pain in his foot. He was being deadly serious explaining on the phone about his foot and Norman and I just creased up because it was like listening to a comedy sketch. You couldn't make it up.

"*In those days, we made do with listening to the wireless for our main home entertainment and programmes like The Goon Show, Lost in Space, PC49, At Much Binding in the Marsh, Paul Temple, Dick Barton Special Agent, Take It from Here, The Archers, Mrs Dale's Diary, The Charlie Chester Show, Ignorance Is Bliss, Family Favourites and Curtain Up were among our not-to-be-missed shows. Later on came Radio Luxembourg and the pirate radio ships and the wireless that Norman's boss, Mr Eccles, bought us, got a lot of use.*

"*When we finally bought a television it was second hand and reconditioned by a friend of ours, Harry Tidder, who built a flourishing business by buying old rented TVs, refurbishing them and selling them on from his shop in Leigh Broadway. He'd learned his trade at the famous EKCO factory set up by Southend-born engineer Eric Cole and which later merged with Pye and then Philips. My lovely older sister Eileen worked in the EKCO office where she was a noted sprinter, always winning the 100 and 220 yards on the firm's sports days. After retirement, she became quite a character in the Southend area as a Lollypop Lady, helping keep the schoolkids safe when crossing the road. I so loved my big sister and was heartbroken when she was taken from us by cancer in her early 90s.*

"*One of our favourite radio shows had been Educating Archie, which featured a ventriloquist called Peter Brough and on which Petula Clark and Max Bygraves first made their names. Archie was a dummy worked by Brough. It became so popular that BBC switched the show to television and it was a disaster because we could see that Brough's mouth moved more than the dummy's. Accidentally hilarious.*

"*So now we had Steven and Michael and both soon starting their education around the corner at the excellent Prince Avenue primary school. We were soldiering along quite happily when, out of the blue, a double whammy knocked us for six. The Tory Government, with Harold 'You've Never Had It So Good' Macmillan as Prime Minister, declared that gambling would be legalised and suddenly every high street had a betting shop. This meant the end of Norman getting a percentage of the bets he was collecting on the hush-hush.*

"*Soon after, everybody was stunned when Mr Eccles committed suicide.*

"There we were, Norman out of his milkman's job, and with two young boys and a 30-year mortgage that had to be paid. My Singer machining was all that was keeping us going.

"Norman did not have a lazy bone in his body and quickly got a job as a travelling salesman for a chemists' wholesale store owned by a couple we knew well. He travelled the length and breadth of Essex persuading village shops to take goods like shampoo, soap, toothpaste, cotton wool, Cow and Gate milk, and body lotions.

"My Norman was a born salesman and got huge orders and everything was going swimmingly until the wife of the owner of the chemists virtually accused him of stealing ten pound notes from his takings. He insisted on his innocence and demanded they make a thorough search of the store.

"The missing ten pound notes were discovered in an invoice book that the chemist's wife kept. His name cleared, Norman gave his accusing employers a mouthful and walked out of the chemists and his job without a backward glance.

"He had tremendous pride and strongly objected to being suspected of stealing. Yes, the Del-boy style occasional ducking and diving, but taking something that belonged to somebody else? Never.

"What to do next? Norman bought some thinking time by going to his barber in the London Road. This was a regular haunt because Norman liked his hair trimmed every ten days before it could go curly. He unburdened himself to the barber, a talkative, likeable Jewish character called Vic, who revealed he had a customer who was looking for a battery salesman.

"On his rounds for the chemist, he had discovered a lot of outlying farms, boatyards and houses and he was able to spotlight these as possible customers when he went for his job interview. This attention to detail impressed the battery business owner and in no time Norman had built up a network of contacts who bought special filters that were being imported from America.

"This was in the mid-1960s and went so well that Norman was not only earning good wages but also building up towards a huge Christmas bonus. He decided that what he was going to do with the extra money was carpet the entire house at Beverley Gardens.

We were as happy as a couple of kids in a toy shop.

"*Just before Christmas he went to see the owner about the bonus. 'I've taken an offer for the business,' his boss announced abruptly. 'I'm going to have to make you redundant.'*

"*'That's a helluva blow,' said Norman. 'But at least I've got my bonus to come.'*

"*'Sorry, I'll not be paying any commission' said the boss. 'The deal I've done with the new owners does not allow for any bonus money.'*

"*Norman told his now ex-boss what he thought of him and came home, seething and in a foul mood. He went straight to bed and thought things through.*

"*In he middle of the night he sat bolt upright and said to me, 'I've got him. I've got him'*

"*'What d'you mean?' I asked.*

"*'You'll find out in the morning,' he said. 'Nobody gets the better of a Lambert'*

"*The next day he went back to the owner of the business and told him he was going to report him to the local waterboard. He had been filing 'carboy containers' and turning the content into distilled water, so bypassing the meter. This cost the waterboard hundreds of gallos of water.*

"*'You're blackmailing me,' said his old boss.*

"*'Well it's no worse than what you're doing to me by not paying me the bonus that I've earned,' Norman said.*

"*The guv'nor reluctantly gave my husband the money to which he was entitled, buying his silence. Norman hated doing it but the experience hardened him and he became not only a skilled negotiator but a determined one. Nobody was ever going to get the better of him again.*

"*There was a twist in the tale when the franchise holder who had been selling the batteries heard that Norman was leaving. 'They must be mad to let you go,' he said. 'Since you've been with them their business has trebled. If you can get a premises I will deal with you.'*

"*We then contacted the filter people and they were happy to supply us ... if we got a premises.*

"*Over to me. I started searching for a shop that would be suitable to a battery business. One day I was on my way to see Jimmy Morgan, who had been instrumental in getting us our first flat, and as I drove down Westborough Road towards Jimmy's I saw a shop to let. I called in and a little old lady who owned it gave me the three degree treatment about what I intended to use the shop for. When I explained batteries and filters she envisaged oil being spilt on the floor and considered her property not right for that sort of business.*

"She had a friend with her who kept making negative noises. I was about to leave feeling disappointed when she asked what I was doing 'on the other side' of Southend and I said I was visiting Jimmy Morgan who lived nearby in St George's Road.

"Suddenly her mood changed. 'You know the Morgans?' she said. 'They are wonderful people and would only have good, reliable friends. Anybody trusted by the Morgans is fine with me.'

"And that's how Anglia Batteries started at a rent of £5 per week and in Westborough Road, Westcliff-on-Sea. Business jointly owned by Mr and Mrs Norman Lambert.

"We were as nervous as kittens but at the same time excited and elated at being our own bosses with our destiny in our own hands.

"The date: May 9 1967, and the first thing we did was come up with a name that would be high in the alphabet. One of our first major buys was an old second-hand post office van that was painted light blue, with the words Anglia Batteries on the sides in dark blue.'

"My silver-tongued husband then visited all our potential customers and convinced them they should have the Welsh-manufactured filters instead of the American version he had previously talked them into buying.

"Anglia Batteries was up and running."

Chapter Eleven:
Copy Boy to reporter

BACK to my story in our two-pronged tale. In the spring of 1955 a careers adviser visited Raine's to help the pupils map out their futures. When I told him I wanted to be a sportswriter, he failed to hide something of a sneer as he replied: "First of all you need to get an English Literature degree at university, and then take an extra course to study law and its correlation with sport."

There was as much chance of me going to university as swimming the Channel (remember, I struggled to do a width of the pool). We had a family conference, and I was given the choice of following my lighterman Grandfather on to the Thames barges, or to try to get into Fleet Street on the ground floor.

St Paul's priest Reverend Basil Jansz had a contact at the London *Evening News* – crime reporter Dickie Hird –and I secured a £5-10s a week job as a copyboy. The only question I was asked at my interview: "Do you have any objections to joining NATSOPA?"

I thought it might be the name of an old crooner, until it was explained that it was an acronym for the National Society of Operative Printers and Assistants. It was my introduction to the strength of the unions in Fleet Street. Nobody could get in without a union card. The whole of the Street was what was known as a closed shop.

I left Raine's when I was still fourteen just before the 1955 Easter weekend, during which I became legally allowed to work full-time for a living on my fifteenth birthday. And so it was that I landed in Fleet Street, the place of my dreams, and for the next two years – a card-carrying member of NATSOPA – it was like being at a university for would-be journalists.

If I had attended a thousand lectures, there was no way I could have gleaned half as much about the newspaper world as during that period on the bottom rung of the ladder in the long-gone hot metal days.

I worked as a dogsbody in every department, running editorial copy from reporters to sub-editors and then to the lino-machine operators, carrying metal photo bases to the printing stone as a block boy, rushing layout pages from the art desk, collecting photographs from the picture agencies and photo-telegraphy department, and – best and most important of all – working in the sports room as an unpaid statistician.

Facts and figures just stuck in my head, and I had an encyclopaedic memory on athletics, boxing and football. It quickly got to the point where major *Evening News* sports reporters like Jack Oaten and Terry O'Connor (athletics), Vic Railton (football) and Reg Gutteridge (boxing) were coming to me to check who-where-and-when statistics. For Google read Giller.

I learned to type and use carbon paper for copies on the huge, noiseless Remington typewriter in the sports room, and continually stayed after hours at the Carmelite House editorial office just off Fleet Street typing reams of major results from *L'Equipe*, the omniscient French daily sports paper.

As soon as I got enough money together I bought myself an Olivetti portable typewriter, and swanked around with it as if I was a reporter rather than a glorified teaboy. I also attended Pitman's shorthand evening classes, the only boy in a class of girls, twenty-six of them. This was in my painfully shy, blushing days, and I found it all an ordeal, but I stuck to it because I appreciated I needed shorthand for when I became a reporter. Nothing was going to stop me.

There was a team of fifteen copyboys, all of us working in relays on a 6am to 6pm rota in the era when the *Evening News* ran seven broadsheet editions a day, six days a week. They were all initialled A to G, and for late-breaking news stories they often went to an HH replate. I remember once an edition being rushed to press with a photograph of the winner of a big race being led into the winning enclosure by the Queen Mother. It was cropped so that all you could see was Her Majesty and the horse, and the hastily written caption read: "The Queen Mother (left) leads in the winner."

These were the exciting, heady days in Fleet Street when many of the buildings thundered with the roar of printing presses rolling out the latest news. Fleet Street had a smell, a sound, a feel and pace all of its own. Every time you stepped off the pavement you took your life in your hands as dozens of newspaper vans raced each other to be first to get the newspapers to their vendors.

This was life with the accelerator to the floor, and the rivalry between the three Evening newspapers – *the Star, News* and *Standard* – was cutthroat. There was a newspaper seller on every street corner, and their shouts of "Star, News, Standard" was part and parcel of the London background din, just as much as the engine noise of the red buses and black cabs, and the cries of the market stall traders. One Cockney newsvendor, with his armful of evening papers, was famous for always shouting: "La-di-da ... Evening Blues ... Stand-at-ease."

We copyboys at the *Evening News,* all fast-on-our-feet Cockney kids with sharp wits, quick tongues and wicked humour, could run rings round most of the mainly university-educated journalists, who were under huge pressure working against the clock as reporters and sub-editors.

We used to charge them threepence a time for a mug of tea from the canteen. It was a licence to make money. What they didn't know is that we had commandeered a small cubbyhole office on the same floor as the canteen, where we installed a boiler and made our own tea for about halfpenny a cup. We fleet-footed Fagins doubled our wages, because the journalists were a thirsty lot who each got through at least half a dozen mugs of tea every day.

There were many special sporting perks. I used to see the first twenty minutes of the major First Division match in London every Saturday when all games kicked off at 3pm. I would sit behind the goal alongside the *Evening News* photographer Dennis Hart, and at exactly 20 minutes past three would take his photographic plates and run with them to a motorcyclist waiting outside the ground, climb on the back of his bike – no crash helmet – and dash back to get the pictures developed in the dark room, before then sprinting with them to the picture desk for publication in the 5pm classified edition.

I saw all the top athletics meetings in the mid-50s from the White City Stadium press box, and every Test match at the Oval and Lord's for free, along with at least a dozen *Evening News* colleagues. Our sports department had two associate press passes, and once two of us were inside the ground we would take turns going outside with both passes in our pocket and coming back in through another gate with a mate in tow.

During the 1956 Jim Laker Ashes series – that included his world record 19 for 90 at Old Trafford – I worked as a copy telephonist in controversial circumstances. The newly knighted and newly retired Sir Len Hutton was signed to "write" exclusively on the Test series for the *Evening News*.

E.M. (Evelyn) Wellings, an Oxford Blue, former Surrey off-spinner and the *News'* cricket correspondent since the end of the war, went apoplectic when he heard of Hutton's appointment. I just happened to be in the sportswriters room at Carmelite House when he was told that Hutton would be commenting at the Lord's Test.

"The f*** he will," snapped Wellings. He was an awfully posh man with a cut-glass accent, and always wore either a cravat or an MCC tie. To hear the "F" word falling from his lips was as shocking to the ears as hearing your maiden aunt cussing.

Wellings was not revolting against Hutton becoming his unwelcome teammate, so much as the fact that his copy would be ghostwritten. This was a tinderbox issue throughout Fleet Street at the time, with the NUJ leading the fight against the employment of non-journalist sportswriters.

Using his influence as a distinguished founder member of the Cricket Writers' Club, Wellings managed to get Hutton barred from the press box at Lord's. The compromise was that three seats were made available alongside the covered, glass-fronted, pre-Gherkin press box: one for Sir Len, one for his ghost, Julian Holland (later the driving force of BBC's *News At One* programme), and one for the copy telephonist – little me

.I was not allowed to use a press box telephone, and had to gallop downstairs to a public phone box every 20 minutes or at the fall of a wicket with Hutton's priceless thoughts on a sheet of paper in my hand. We craftily kept a phone box occupied, with a *News* colleague making dummy calls

BBCtv was covering the match live, and when Brian Johnston referred to the "Hutton barred" story, the cameras panned the press box and then showed Sir Len on the outside, giving his views to the typewriter-tapping Holland.

Wellings was tipped off that the TV kept showing close ups of him and Hutton just yards apart. He waited his moment, and when the camera next started on a panning shot, he held up a foolscap pad on which he had written in large block capitals: BOLLOCKS.

The panning shots ended abruptly.

I got a rollocking from our NATSOPA FoC (Father of the Chapel) for being an innocent co-conspirator in the ghosting of Hutton, and was given

The Giller brothers during 1942 wartime evacuation to the Dart farm in Devon, left to right: George, Alan and Norman. 'Mum' Winifred Giller, called that period "the best years of my life." Below: Joyce with her friend, MP Sir David Amess, a fellow East Ender to whose memory this book is dedicated. Sir David was brutally and senselessly murdered by a terrorist while holding his regular surgery as a sitting Member of Parliament. He was due to become Father of the House after proud, long-term service to his country.

Norman the First with Joyce relaxing in 1964, three years before the launch of Anglia Batteries. They were married for 23 years before Joyce was widowed at the age of 45.

Right: Norman the Fourth's first wife Eileen, who died in 2006 after an idyllic 46-year marriage. Norman was widowed at the age of 66. He and Joyce were married a month before her 90th birthday. in 2024.

John Palmer proudly shows off the Palmer sisters, left to right, `Sheila, Ann, Eileen, Lorna and Joyce. This photograph was taken in 1972, when Joyce was 38. Below are the Giller brothers, left to right: George, a City of London policeman, Ken a sports and features photographer, and Norman, then chief football writer with the Daily Express. *The occasion, when George and Norman were jointly 'best man' at Ken's 1969 wedding to the wonderful Lynne.*

Joyce is installed as President of the South Essex Chamber of Commerce and (below) gets a honeymoon kiss from her new husband while appearing on television during ITV's Good Morning Britain 'We are just spreading the pollen of love,' Norman told viewers.

Norman kept good company during his writing and PR career ... evidence here with his friends Muhammad Ali, comedian Eric Morecambe (bottom left) and his close pal for 64 years Jimmy Greaves (bottom, right). They wrote 20 books together and 'scores' of newspaper columns.

Joyce and Norman were privileged to join in a Music Man Project rehearsal and (below) nine of the Ambassadors who are looking forward to performing on Broadway. Let's get them there!

Honeymooning on the Thames, with Big Ben in the background (above, left) and waking up together at the start of the rest of our lives (top right). Happy families below on our wedding day, left to right: John and Lisa East, son Michael and companion Julie, Roslin Hotel MD and good friend Jacqui Dallimore, Mick and Alison Lambert, Bryan Aston with wife Ann (far right), Steven and Lucy Lambert, Lorna Rayment with Richard Burrell in the background. It was the perfect day.

Happily hectic times: The proposal in front of the statue of Sir David Amess on September 9 2024 (below, right) ... the wedding at the majestic Roslin Beach Hotel in Thorpe Bay on October 15, 2024 (right) and then the presentation of Joyce's MBE award at iconic Buckingham Palace on March 28 2025. And now we have booked it all. Thank you for your support. All Profits going to the remarkable Music Man Project.

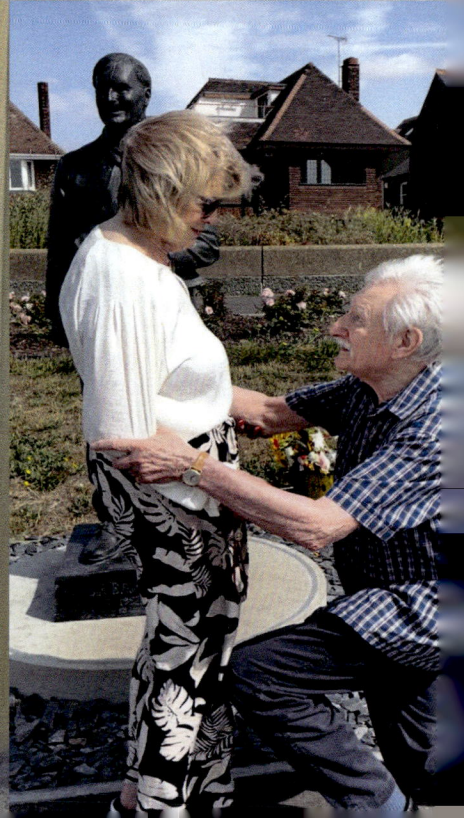

a lecture on the importance of solidarity.

Strange that much of my next fifty years was going to be spent ghosting the thoughts of non-journalist sportsmen.

After one dash downstairs with the copy, I returned breathlessly to my seat to find it occupied by an *Evening News* reporter on a day off. It was Leslie Thomas, who in his spare time was writing the *Virgin Soldiers* novel that was to earn him his fame and fortune. Every time I saw Leslie after that over the next forty years I used to jokingly offer him my seat.

There is an amusing punchline: E. M. Wellings (full name Evelyn Maitland Wellings) wrote for the *Evening News* for 36 years until it became unlovingly embraced by the *Evening Standard* in 1980. He received a letter about pension entitlements from the Associated Newspapers management that read: "Dear Mrs Wellings …"

The same company sent boxing guru Reg Gutteridge his gold watch for 40 years service in a brown paper envelope, a story I spotlighted when scripting Reg's *This Is Your Life* tribute in 1984. It was Reg – his promising boxing career finished when he lost a leg in the D-Day Landings – who battled with the amateur establishment to get Terry Spinks added to the British Olympic team at the last minute in 1956.

I was the copyboy who came racing from the telex machine with the newsflash that Terry had won the flyweight gold medal. As I shouted it across the sports room, Reg, dummy leg and all, jumped up on his desk yelling at the top of his voice: "He's done it. He's only gorn and f***ing done it."

It became our catchphrase for the next five decades of friendship..

Every Monday when there was a weekly boxing show at the National Sporting Club at the posh Café Royal Reg had to wear a dinner suit. He used to send me down to the Embankment, where his modified Standard 10 car was parked, to collect from the boot his spare leg that was fitted with a polished black shoe. I used to do Jake the Peg with the artificial leg long before Rolf Harris recorded it. Forever after, Reg used to introduce me as 'Norman, my leg man.'

From making Reggie's tea, running his copy and collecting his spare leg, we became good mates. He used the telephone like a garden fence and called me for a regular gossip for more than 50 years.

Running in tandem with my work as a copyboy-cum-sports-statistician, I had started a love affair that still burns passionately today – with jazz. It began with regular visits to London's New Orleans traditional jazz headquarters at the Humphrey Lyttelton Club at 100 Oxford Street, and the Cy Laurie Club, situated in a dank basement room in Great Windmill Street. It was two floors below the Jack Solomons boxing gymnasium, so I could visit both my favourite worlds in one go.

I also used to creep into the theatre opposite, the notorious Windmill, with its statuesque naked girl models who were not allowed to move on stage.

My curiosity about the opposite sex was, as in the jazz standard, *Running Wild*, and I took every opportunity to peep and touch in what were sexually constrained times. The Wolfenden Report – containing the historic phrase "homosexual behaviour between consenting adults in private should no longer be a criminal offence" – was about to be published.

There were several in my circle of friends I suspected of being what we used to then call 'queer'. For them, it must have been like being trapped in a prison, and it is impossible for a straight person like me to imagine the torture they went through in those blind, bigoted days that were heaving with hypocrisy and intolerance.

I got in to the Windmill Theatre pretending to be eighteen when I looked more like fourteen, and sat among the salivating, mostly rain-coated men ogling the girls in nude tableaux – pornography masquerading as art. The establishment ruling of the time was: "It's all right to be nude, but if it moves it's rude."

I did not only go for the fleeting glimpses of female flesh but to hear the best comedians of their generation, and among those who learned their art at The Windmill were mirth masters like Tony Hancock, Benny Hill, Tommy Cooper, Peter Sellers, Bruce Forsyth, Max Bygraves and a young Des O'Connor, a fellow Stepneyite of mine. He told me years later: "It was the hardest audience of all because all they wanted is you off stage and the girls on. You would perform every couple of hours, often infront of the same blokes who were there throughout the day with not just their binoculars out. I once dried up doing my act and somebody in the front row shouted, 'You do the parrot joke next.'"

My magnets at Humph's club were the Chris Barber Band (with Tony Donegan on banjo before starting out on his skiffle adventure as Lonnie) and the more mainstream jazz of Scottish clarinetist Sandy Brown, who doubled up as the chief BBC acoustics engineer. He had a wonderful collaboration with fellow Scot and former schoolmate Al Fairweather, who later played with Acker Bilk and piano master Stan Greig.

From that platform I moved on to the swing of Count Basie, the seventh heaven of Duke Ellington, Johnny Dankworth's orchestra with a jesting Dudley Moore on piano, and more cutting-edge modern jazz sounds at the Flamingo Club and the newly opened Ronnie Scott's in Soho.

A lone wolf with what many considered peculiar tastes, I always went on my own – often to all-night concerts – standing as close to the bands as possible completely wrapped up in the music and unaware that around me many were there to smoke pot and stronger stuff. Naïve Norman never ever had anything to do with that world. I was just obsessed with jazz, and as with my sport I knew the line-up of every band exactly as I did the major football teams of the time. What a sad young man.

With old friends from Raine's, we started our own New Orleans group called the Redmans Jazz Band, named after the primary school in which we rehearsed in a hired room (which I later learned was the same Redmans Road where Joyce's Granny Arundell lived!). Our leader was Michael 'Wag' Williams, a clarinetist who later became a successful banker in Hong Kong. I began on piano until they found Friz Stevens, who could actually play properly. Then I switched to drums, dragging them up and down the eight flights of stairs at Ring House, and driving our neighbours mad with my single and double paradiddles (Eric Morecambe: 'You can get arrested for that.'). I occasionally played with my Dad in the Crooked Billet, but his left hand provided its own tempo and did not really marry with my attempts at jazz cross rhythms. Drumming to Danny Boy and Galway Bay was not, it's fair to say, within my jazz compass.

I lost my drum seat in the band to a less competent drummer, who just happened to have an old London taxi that became the band bus. Then, total insanity, I switched to the double bass, which needed not only lugging up and down the Ring House stairs but also the 70 steps at the local Shadwell tube station long before they installed a lift.

The bass, bought on the never-never at seven-and-six (37.5p) a week, was taller than me, and during a gig in a South London pub my fingers – blistered from all the practising – started to bleed. In a foul mood, I idiotically drank down a bottle of sickly VP wine in virtually one swig. On the way home I was so drunk that I was swinging the bass around my head as if in a hammer-throw competition, and I snapped the neck as it hit a wall. Stupid boy.

That weekend my Dad, much better at DIY than me, glued it together using a clamp and stood it up against the wall in the passage to dry. During the night, the bass fell to the floor, and the neck snapped again, this time with a crack like a rifle shot … so much like a gun shot that within twenty minutes police, called by frightened neighbours, were banging on our door with truncheons drawn.

I sold the bass to a music hall comedian for ten pounds, and I later saw it on stage at the Queen's Theatre in Poplar with a telephone fitted inside its body.

It was while at Humphrey Lyttelton's club that I stumbled on the story that gave me my first published headline: OFF THE TRACK. I was at the White City Stadium one Saturday afternoon in May 1957 watching Yorkshireman Ken Wood win an international mile race, and could not believe my eyes in the evening when I literally bumped into him at Humph's, where the Chris Barber band was in full swing.

I plucked up the courage to speak to Ken, and congratulated him on his victory and asked if he was a jazz fan. We spoke for all of thirty seconds. When I got home I sat at my trusty Olivetti as if I was my sportswriter hero Peter Wilson of the *Daily Mirror*, and wrote ten paragraphs on what top miler Ken Wood did when he was off the track.

On the Monday morning I presented my exclusive to *Evening News* features editor Don Boddie, who I am sure wanted to put it straight on the spike. But he saw the enthusiasm shining from my face like a searchlight and did not have the heart to disappoint me. Five paragraphs of my story found their way into the *News* diary and I was paid 21 shillings, an old-fashioned guinea. I was a professional journalist. Don, later Editor of the paper, was kind enough to tell me the same thing that rugby/athletics reporter Terry O'Connor had been saying for months: "Don't stay a copyboy too long. Get out and learn the business in local papers."

I sent job applications to six local editors, and the *Stratford Express* replied with a job offer at the union minimum of £6 a week. I transferred from NATSOPA to the NUJ, and my career as a journalist was up and running. I was replacing Ivor Davis, a prominent local amateur footballer whose newspaper reporting career was being interrupted by National Service in the Army.

Ivor later became a distinguished correspondent on the West Coast of America in partnership with his beautiful Irish wife, Sally, all from the launching pad of the *Stratford Express*, which could not have provided a better grounding for a young, ambitious sportswriter. It covered much of East London and the edges of Essex, sold 100,000 copies, and had at its heart West Ham United and Leyton Orient Football Clubs.

There were also boxers by the busload, including my schooldays mate Terry Spinks, who had just turned professional with Sammy McCarthy as his manager after winning the Olympic flyweight gold medal. My news beat was Bow and Stepney, embracing the Krays' empire

I had an extraordinary first week in the reporting life I had been dreaming of for so long. On the Monday I was sent to East London Juvenile Court to cover the day's hearings. The usher saw me wandering into the courtroom and pointed me to a seat. I took a pad out of my jacket pocket and started taking a shorthand note, when a young, twentyish man approached me from a bench seat on the far side of the court.

"What you doing, son?" he asked

."I'm reporting the case for my paper, the Stratford Express," I said proudly.

"Then why are you sitting with the defendants?" he asked. "Come over with me to the press bench."

I looked so young that the court usher thought I was a juvenile on trial and had put me in the dock.

"I'm Norman Giller," I said, introducing myself to my saviour.

"Colin Hart," he said, shaking my hand. "I'm with the East London News Agency."

Yes, the same Colin Hart who would become the doyen of boxing writers. He was a worldly man of 22.

My brief at the *Stratford Express* was to cover East London as a news reporter, doubling up as assistant sports editor to Harry Miller, four years my senior and a gifted all-round journalist. Both Harry and Colin were in the foothills of careers that would take them to impressively successful futures in Fleet Street. I was in good company.

Harry's first assignment for me was to cover the Tuesday boxing show at Shoreditch Town Hall, where promoter Harry Grossmith and his young matchmaker Mickey Duff were launching their inaugural promotion at a venue that over the following twenty years would become a famous cockpit of a fighting arena. In the top of the bill contest for my first fight as a ringside reporter unbeaten prospect Terry Downes came a cropper against an unknown Liverpool-based Nigerian middleweight called Dick Tiger.

The spectators could not believe their eyes when the squat, wide-shouldered Tiger flattened Downes in the first minute of the fight. It was suddenly the lion versus the Tiger, as Terry picked himself up and battled back in a swinging, two-fisted style that was to become his trademark. Manager Sam Burns finally pulled Terry out of a fight that had become a war at the end of the fifth, with his eyes swollen, nose busted and ego bruised.

Years later, matchmaker Mickey Duff told me that it cost the little matter of £195 to stage – £135 to Downes, £60 to Tiger, plus his petrol money. During the 1960s, Tiger became world middleweight and light-heavyweight champion, and Downes world middleweight king. By then, it would have cost a fortune to bring them together in the same ring.

There was the usual hush of a losing dressing room when I joined the big-time boxing reporters looking for after-fight quotes.

Defeated Downes, his face a bloody mask of pain, did not disappoint: "When the first bell rang I thought, 'F***ing hell, they've put me in with a giant.' Then I realised I was flat on my back looking up at him. I don't remember much after that. I look forward to reading your reports to see what happened next."

It was Bill Bateson of the *Islington Gazette* and later *News of the World* sports editor, who came up with a fairly straightforward question that drew one of the all-time great responses.

"Who d'you want to fight next?" Bill asked.

Back came Downsie: "The bastard who made this match."

Mickey Duff, wise man, was nowhere to be seen. It was all priceless copy for this young, new-to-the-road sports hack, but I was brought down to earth the next day when I switched to my news-reporting role. I was given the dreaded "Dead Door" assignment. This meant knocking on the door of a bereaved family to ask for a photograph of the deceased. The Stratford door I had to knock at belonged to a middle-aged couple, whose only son had died a few days earlier working as, wait for it, an apprentice lighterman.

He had fallen into the Thames while jumping from one barge to another, struck his head and drowned.

His parents were only too pleased to invite me in and talk about their 17-year-old boy, and when I told them about my Granddad Sims and his life on the River they almost tried to adopt me. I left with the prized photograph.

So it was that in my first three days as a bona fide journalist I had been put in the dock of a juvenile court, reported one of the greatest small-hall fights of any time, and written about a young man – who could so easily have been me – being claimed by the dark, swirling, unforgiving waters of the Thames. Welcome, Norm, to the world of reporting.

I quickly settled to the unpredictable life of a reporter, never ever worrying about the hours I worked, even though it was often way over what the union had negotiated. I was living my dream, and it reached paradise pitch when Harry Miller agreed to a feature I suggested called, The Apprentice. This was long before Alan Sugar's TV programme

The idea was that I would interview a West Ham apprentice footballer and get him talking about his life and aspirations as he started out on his playing career.

Harry put the plan to the then West Ham manager Ted Fenton, who agreed to let me talk to a young unknown hopeful called Bobby Moore. It was the autumn of 1957 and it set me back threepence to entertain Bobby, whose shyness matched mine. That was how much it cost for a mug of tea at Casettari's, a café opposite the Upton Park ground, where he had been employed as a Hammers apprentice for a year.

Bobby turned down a bacon butty. "Watching my weight," he said, which was something he often repeated throughout a career in which he kept to a strict diet, because he was worried about putting on surplus pounds. The round-faced Bobby I first met was known behind his back as Chubby Boy.

We were meeting in the basement of our careers, neither of us realising that within ten years Bobby would be king of the football castle and I would be at the peak of my newspaper profession as chief football reporter for the *Daily Express*.

It was the first interview given by Bobby, and my plan was to write a similar interview with a young, 17-year-old East Ham-born boy who was just making a name for himself at Chelsea. I arranged to meet him at Stamford Bridge, and when I got there he told me: "Sorry mate, the Boss (Ted Drake) has ordered me not to talk to the press. He thinks the publicity is affecting my game." This, of course, was one Jimmy Greaves.

Mooro, Greavsie and me. We would move up life's escalator together

I learned a valuable lesson at the end of my first month at the *Stratford Express* – don't gamble at cards unless you can afford it, and if you can afford it don't gamble at cards. (Card-fanatic Joyce tells me her first Norman used to play for money in a hard card school but she has only ever played for buttons, sensible girl).

One Thursday afternoon on publication day and after the paper had been put to bed, I got drawn into a marathon session of blind brag with our brilliant chief news reporter Keith Cade. I lost my week's wages and gave over IOUs for two further weeks, fifteen pounds in all.

That night I cried to my Mum when I told her I could not give her any housekeeping. She hugged me and said, "Just put it down to experience. You won't do it again."

I did and I haven't. Keith came with me when I sold my treasured Olivetti portable typewriter to pay my debt to him. "I am going to take your money," he said, wisely, "because the more it hurts the less likely you will be to do it again. If I let you off, you'll think losing at the card table doesn't matter."

A year or so later I was best man at Keith's wedding to features writer Pat Heaton. It was a private joke when I said in my best man's speech: "Keith is quite a card." He was also an exceptional journalist who, along with chief sub Bill Coller, had a huge influence on this young, raw reporter.

Another lesson I learned was not to take my Dad with me to football matches. I was reporting a Second Division game at Leyton Orient, and before the kick-off I introduced Dad to a couple of the club officials in their small boardroom that doubled as a private bar.

I freelanced for several papers as 'Giller of Stratford' and I had to write 200 words on the final whistle for the *Sunday Express* and for the *Sunday Pictorial*, before it morphed into the *Sunday Mirror*. As I was dictating my report in a now virtually deserted ground I saw out of the corner of my eye somebody lurching down the terraces from the direction of the boardroom. It was my Dad, drunk out of his head and waving to me with a dopey grin on his face. He had not seen a single ball kicked.

I poured Dad on to a bus home and vowed never to take him with me again.

On the afternoon of 6 February 1958, I was sitting on the top deck of a bus coming back to Stratford from a news reporting assignment when I saw a newspaper placard screaming: 'MAN UNITED PLANE CRASH'. I jumped off the bus at traffic lights and dashed to buy a paper.

The story was just breaking, and the early facts were that the United plane had crashed on take-off heading home from a European Cup tie in Belgrade, and after refuelling at Munich. All we knew then was that there were casualties.

Over the next hours and days it transpired that twenty-three of the passengers had been killed, including eight United players and eight travelling sportswriters.

Of the eight United players who died, Duncan Edwards was the last to submit to his injuries fifteen days after the crash. We had lost our greatest young footballer of that era.

Chillingly, it was a disaster that would change the career paths of several journalists, including mine. What a way to get promotion.

Chapter Twelve:
The Committee Years

W HILE I was launching my career in journalism, Joyce and Norman
the First were establishing Anglia Batteries as a major power outlet
in Southend, building a business that was to bring them happiness and
heartache in equal measure…

*"Norman and I threw ourselves into the business, working flat out six
days a week and often opening on Sundays, too. This was in the days of rust-
bucket cars and customers would come to us for batteries and accessories
while washing their motors at the weekend. The worse the winters the better
we did, and in those late 1960s the weather was bitterly cold leading up to
each Christmas and car batteries had to be regularly replaced. Bingo!*

*"I'm giving away trade secrets when I tell you that people who bought
Fiat models were among our best clients, because back then they rusted
very quickly and batteries continually went flat. We had drivers coming to
us from all over Essex, because they knew they would get a good deal and
we sold repair kits with which people patched up their cars.*

*"They were hard times and very few could afford new cars, so they went
for second and often third and fourth hand vehicles that needed constant
repair. Their first stop after putting in their early mileage was invariably
Anglia Batteries, and Norman often went out in the refurbished GPO van to
help motorists who had broken down. We became known for being reliable
and helpful, all good PR. Word of mouth was our best advertisement and
drivers continually returned on a regular basis.*

*"In the early days I worked behind the counter while Norman would
go out touting for business, and with his easy-going personality and gift
of the gab he was brilliant at talking people into buying our batteries and
accessories such as wheel trims, seat belts, wiper blades, floor mats, brake
pads and light bulbs. He got us business with the boatyards and talked
the owners of the machines that loaded the moored ships into using Anglia
Batteries. He could talk for Britain..*

"Norman could always think one step ahead, and he quickly caught on to the growing demand for seat belts before the Harold Wilson government made them compulsory, with that Jimmy Savile 'clunk-click-every-trip' campaign. He convinced many local secondhand car dealers that it was a good selling point to include safety belts in their vehicles, and he set up a profitable chain with a manufacturer in Dagenham.

"Our foot fall started to increase to the point where Norman brought in an enthusiastic and efficient full-time accountant named Stan Crabb to do the bookkeeping, and then he talked his younger brother Geoffrey into switching from being a food salesman to selling batteries. Geoff became a key member of our staff and Anglia was quickly an established business in the Southend area and people started to come from far and wide to buy our batteries and car extras.

"We started to do so well that we felt we could invest in a new Ford Transit walk-in van with all our accessories on show in the back. We had only recently got it when Norman's brother Geoff drove the van to a local garage to do some business. While it was parked with the keys in the ignition, somebody drove off in it, leaving Geoff angry. bewildered and without transport.

"We were, of course, insured but anyone who has done business with insurance companies will know they become slow coaches when they have to pay out, but are slick and professional in collecting your premiums. I had the brainwave of taking out a small-ad in the London Evening News offering a reward of £100 for anybody giving us information leading to the return of our van. We put in the registration number and van details. There had not been time to have the Anglia Batteries logo painted on the side of the blue van, so there were hundreds like it on the road.

"Four days had passed since the publication of the advertisement and not a single response. Norman and Geoff were beginning to nag me about what they had always considered a daft idea when the telephone rang with somebody claiming the £100 reward. They had found the van abandoned on the marshes near Chelmsford and it had obviously been stolen by joyriders.

"It pays to advertise!

"We had been up and running a couple of years when our landlady Mrs

Smith, the owner of the house who had been letting us the downstairs part, asked out of the blue whether we would like to buy the whole house. Norman and I both gulped when she said her asking price was £5,000. That may sound peanuts now, but back in the late 1960s it was a fortune and remember we had a mortgage to find each month for our home at Beverley Gardens.

"This meant a visit to our bank manager at Barclays in Rochford, Alan Smith. We had followed his early advice to put any takings into our business account every day, which gave us a high credit rating. He said that he had just received clearance for big loans to the local farming community and he was happy to release some of that in the shape of a commercial mortgage to Anglia Batteries on the premise that we had been helping farmers with tractor problems.

"It was going to cost us £150 a month over five years, a big whack but the shop was doing so well that we were confident we could afford it. Just one snag, the house came with a sitting tenant!

"She was an eccentric and very independent elderly lady with health problems, and occupied the upstairs back room in a reclusive fashion. We used the rest of the space upstairs for overflow shop storage but rarely had any contact with our extremely private tenant.

"I started to have sleepless nights because I could smell that she was using a paraffin-fired stove to heat her room. We could easily have all gone up in flames. I went first to her and then her Southend-based brother to ask if either could help with the problem but both claimed they were unable to afford a proper electric fire. I then went to social services and they financed a replacement for the death-trap paraffin stove.

"We had employed a school leaver called Kevin to do odd jobs. One day after our tenant had not appeared for a while I asked him to climb a stepladder and look through the fanlight into her locked room. He almost fell off the steps as he reported, 'She's lying on the floor ...'

"I made an instant 999 call and the police and fire brigade were quickly with us and they broke down her door. She was unconscious and an ambulance whisked her off to hospital. While I was making tea for the fire and police teams I was urgently summoned upstairs by the chief fire brigade inspector.

"'I want you to be a witness to this,' he said, pointing to a row of jars and biscuit tins he had found under the bed. They were all stuffed with pound notes and fivers, hundreds of pounds.

"I thanked the fire brigade officer for his honesty and telephoned the brother. He came round at a rate of knots, while refusing to visit when I was asking for help to replace the stove. This despicable man disappeared into the night with all the money jars and tins, Later that week his sister died a lonely death in Southend General hospital. Comedian Norman described it as a very jarring experience.

"Our next drama involved me. One afternoon I collapsed with terrible stomach pains. A doctor was summoned and he put it down to a severe period, but my Mum insisted I be taken to hospital for a check up.

"'I've got five daughters,' she told the doctor, 'and I know when there's something serious going on. I insist she gets a proper check over.'

"Within 24 hours I had my uterus removed in an emergency operation and after the hysterectomy I found out just what wonderful sisters and neighbours I had. They could not do enough for me and insisted on bringing in meals, helping with the two boys and doing my housework. I felt blessed.

"Come late 1971, Norman said that rather than drive every day from Prittlewell we should move nearer the shop. We found a large bungalow at Westbourne Grove that was just a few minutes away from the business. It was for sale at £27,000 and such was the sudden rise in house prices that we got around about that amount for Beverley Gardens, so no mortgage!

"Norman and I were just congratulating ourselves on a shrewd bit of business when on the very day we were due to move the lady selling to us said she had changed her mind and wanted to stay put!

"Both Norman and I were struggling with 'flu at the time and feeling like death warmed up. This is not what we wanted to hear and we had to get our solicitor to explain that as we had exchanged contracts there was no way she could not go through with our deal.

"We eventually moved in and over the next couple of years turned our new home into an impressive chalet bungalow, with several extensions and a double garage at the rear. Our next door neighbour asked if we would be willing to buy part of his overflow garden and we were able to spread even wider. It was a wonderful family home, and our sons Steven and Michael commandeered the back of the garden and had their mates round helping them restore old cars. It was a messy hobby but it kept them out of trouble and they were perfect teenagers. When we added a large swimming pool they were in their element.

"Norman used to keep our spirits up with his engaging sense of humour. I remember him once getting one of those realistic model's heads from a closing-down hairdresser's sale and playing lots of pranks on people, with the head suddenly appearing in most unexpected places and frightening the life out of staff and customers. Norman could be a scream.

"I was now getting ambitious as our bank account grew and I talked a very reluctant Norman into expanding our business to take in the shop next door. This was a women's underwear outlet that had failed to keep step with the modern trend in clothes. With the support of our friendly bank manager Alan Smith, I offered the landlady a reasanble sum for a premises that came with sitting tenants upstairs. She held out or an extra £500. Alan gave the go-ahead and suddenly we had a massive, double-fronted property on the junction of Westborough Road and Southbourne Grove. Anglia Batteries now had a substantial presence to go with Norman's atomic energy. The Lamberts were really swinging.

"Our youngest son, Michael – or Mick, as most call him – joined our shop staff straight from school and gradually became a crucial member of the Anglia team. He took after his Dad and was full of ideas and enterprise and we turned the shop into quite an empire.

"Meantime, our eldest boy Steven had joined the Essex Police and after graduation at Hendon college was stationed at Chelmsford. Nobody was prouder than my Dad and Mum, who were renting a home in Southend.

It seemed like only the day before yesterday they had been pushing their grandsons around in prams. We were one big happy family.

While the rest of the country was struggling, we had a bonanza during the three day week crisis of 1974 when Ted Heath's Government took on the miners, and it seemed the whole town of Southend was relying on Anglia Batteries to help out with their lighting. Out of adversity somebody always earns and it just happened to be us! An ill wind had blown us a lot of good.

"Like everybody else, we struggled through the 'winter of discontent' of the late 1970s when a series of national strikes meant we could not bury our dead or get our dustbins emptied as strikers protested against the then

Labour government's wage limits. Another nudge, as if I needed it, towards the Tories. Mrs Thatcher was waiting on her white charger.

Norman was determined to make my life easier by always doing the shopping in Southend High Street and he was a master at finding bargains and making our hard-earned money go a long way.

"He was socially active, drinking increasing amounts between playing lots of snooker at the local Services Club in Hamlet Court Road, where his two years with the Royal Air Force meant he could become a member.

"It was mainly for men but we ladies were allowed there once a month for an evening out when we would sit chatting while our husbands played snooker. The favourite drink of we wives was the mildly alcoholic Babycham, while Norman would knock back pints of Guinness followed by port.

"We mixed with colonels, captains and sergeants, while Private Norman was the man who made them all laugh and enjoy themselves.

Everything in the garden was lovely.

"Nobody, certainly not me, could have seen the cruel blow that was waiting just around the corner. Never ever take life for granted.

Chapter Thirteen:
The Swinging Sixties

THOSE of us born like Joyce in the 1930s or me right at the start of the 1940s saddled the 1960s as if they were a bucking bronco and rode them for all we were worth. Many of us were thrown off, but got back on and continued the ride through the most exciting, exhausting and exhilarating decade of the 20th Century.

The era has been accurately defined as the Swinging Sixties, captured by the emergence of The Beatles and the Stones, a new freedom for fashion, drugs and debate, establishment-bashing satire, and a sexual revolution triggered by the birth control pill, and – thanks to the Wolfenden Report – homosexuals dared show themselves in public and became what we called 'consenting' adults.

We finally shook off the shackles of Victorian discipline, ration-book austerity, and a depressingly grey world, and changed our attitude from 'you can't do that' to 'we can'. With two fingers to the lawmakers, we even refused to stand to attention for the National Anthem at the cinema, and they were forced to drop the ridiculous ritual.

After the Age of Austerity, things in Britain were brighter, better and electrifying, and I had a privileged spectator's seat at the banquet. Just before the decade started I was learning my trade as a local newspaper journalist; by the time the curtain dropped on the 'sixties I was chief football reporter on a national newspaper selling 4.2 million copies a day, married with two children, and far away from the poverty trap of my Cable Street roots.

When England won the World Cup in 1966 I got to hug our captain and my good friend Bobby Moore on the day he held the Jules Rimet trophy aloft and watched Geoff Hurst checking the Wembley scoreboard to make sure he'd actually scored a hat-trick. I was the only journalist to get into the dressing-room until turfed out by manager Alf Ramsey on the reasonable grounds that if he let me in there were 500 other reporters from around the world who would have expected to join me! Yes, I was right at the heart of it all and, like England's footballers, felt on top of the world.

The Munich air disaster that robbed us of so many outstanding footballers and journalists meant an unplanned shuffling of Fleet Street staffs. This led to an unexpected vacancy for a reporter/layout man at *Boxing News*, the fight game's trade paper. One of my first *Boxing News* assignments was an early-morning meeting with a boxer who was to become the most popular of all British sportsmen. It was 5.15 a.m. on a freezing December morning and Henry Cooper was standing alongside me stark naked, apart from a pair of heavy-duty size eleven army boots.

No, I am not uncovering a sordid, kinky secret from Henry's past. I had asked for an interview for a feature I was writing as Ross Martin, and Cooper's manager Jim Wicks told me in raw, unadulterated Cockney: 'The only time Our Enery's got to rabbit to you, my son, is when he goes on his early morning gallop. So get a pair of strong daisies and join him on the old frog if you want any nannies.'

It was like listening to my Dad. So I got my daisy roots (boots) on and joined Henry on the frog and toad (road) to get some nanny goats (quotes). Meet The Bishop – Jim Wicks, the most influential and important man in Henry's life and boxing career. Jim was not just his manager. He was his minder, mentor and best mate, and an unknowing master of malapropisms. Very misleadingly, he was called 'The Bishop' because of his distinguished, benign looks and bald dome that would have fitted perfectly into a mitre. But ex-bookmaker Jim's church was the betting ring and his altar rails were at the racecourse. Dad had run street bets for him and Jack Solomons when they were operating as bookmakers before the war.

My meeting place with Henry for the early morning road run was the Thomas à Becket gymnasium, deep in Del Boy territory down the Old Kent Road, where Henry was training for an upcoming British and Empire heavyweight title fight against his old foe Brian London.

I had just stripped off and was about to pull on a tracksuit when The Bishop arrived, looking immaculate as if he were on his way to morning prayers. A smart, grey trilby protected his bald head from the cold morning air and he was sheathed in a fine-check Crombie overcoat. He had probably just come from a Mayfair casino or an all-night card school.

'Bleedin' 'ell,' he said, catching sight of my skinny-as-a-pipecleaner, nine stone featherweight frame. 'I've got greyhounds fatter than you. You need a good meal rather than a good run. For gawd's sake, Enery, don't let him fall down any drains.'

Henry came to my defence. 'Don't listen to him, Norm,' he said. 'You can't fatten thoroughbreds.' From that day on it was a catchphrase between the two of us, as what started out as a working relationship blossomed over the next fifty-plus years into strong friendship and encompassed four books together.

The 'can't fatten thoroughbreds' line came back to me when I got the exclusive story that when he first fought Clay/Ali in 1963, crafty Jim Wicks slipped racing handicap weights into the soles of Henry's boots for the weigh-in. He didn't want Cassius to have the psychological advantage of knowing that Cooper weighed just 12st. 12lb.

The official weight announced was 13st. 4lb. "It was just a case of self reservation," said Jim, whose delightful, unintended Malapropisms deserve to be preserved for all time.

The Bishop took it upon himself to offer me advice about my new Ross Martin column. "You've got to be bold and write what you think, son," he said. "No good being a shrinking violation in the old pen and ink business."

Enery and Jim, a priceless pair of characters..

When Henry was adjudged to have lost his last fight on points against Joe Bugner, we became united in our loathing of referee Harry Gibbs. Most good judges had Henry winning by two rounds. What a way to treat a hero.

My dislike of Harry was on a much more personal level. He had been a close family friend, not only through boxing but because he worked in the docks with my favourite Uncle Ted Clark, my Mum's brother-in-law who was an affable, larger than life character loved by all.

Harry was foreman of the gang in which Ted worked, loading and unloading docked ships. It was one of the unwritten perks of dock life that sometimes imported things fell off and found their way into the homes of the dockers. I am not condoning the practice, but it was a way of life.

Ted and half a dozen of his mates got caught doing a bit of pilfering by the Old Bill, and it just happened to be a day when Gibbs was off on one of his boxing trips.

My Uncle Ted was 62, and his worst punishment should have been a help-the-community sentence, but the judge decided to make an example of him. He was sent down, despite – in East End jargon – having no previous.

Gibbs, lucky to have missed the police raid, found an excuse not to come forward as a character witness for Uncle Ted. For that, he was never forgiven, and to all his old docker mates he was out for the count.

I became Godfather to Ted's son, Ian, who later in life emerged as chairman of the insurance company Aviva. He has done Ted proud.

Working for *Boxing News* meant I was able to polish the page-designing skills I had started to learn while employed as a copyboy in the art department at the *Evening News*, and I studied the balance of typefaces and body text as preached by master typographer and dedicated Marxist Allen Hutt, who while showing me the way to display type properly also tried (and failed) to convert me to Communism. He just wasn't my type.

I was free on Saturdays to follow my favourite Tottenham team, that in 1960-61 became the first side of the century to win both the League championship and FA Cup, the elusive Double. They set a record by winning the first eleven matches of that First Division season, and played with a rhythm, style and coordination I have not seen equalled by any British club team. Like a hero-worshipping son, I had a rapport with manager Bill Nicholson, who throughout my journalistic career continually told me: "Football is not about fairytales. Always write the truth."

The truth is that Bill was one of the finest managers of any time, and it was disgraceful that the Establishment did not reward him with a knighthood for his services to Spurs in particular and football in general.Spurs legend Steve Perryman and I got the Nicholson story into a book called 'Sir Bill'. The Master.

There was an off-beat front-page story during Tottenham's Double season when Spurs skipper Danny Blanchflower became the first person to say 'no' to Eamonn Andrews and his famous *This Is Your Life* book. Many years later I did some detective work and found out just why Danny Boy, hardly a shy, retiring type, ran off when Eamonn appeared with The Book.

I briefly jump forward here to when I joined the *Life* team as a scriptwriter in the 1980s. Their editorial office was based in Tottenham Court Road in the heart of London's West End, and I was fascinated to know exactly what happened the night that Danny politely told his fellow-Irishman Eamonn where to stick his book.

The programme was scheduled for the evening of 6 February1961, and here I was some twenty years later with the actual script in my hand.

The date that the BBCtv producers had chosen to go 'live' to the nation was the third anniversary of the Munich Air crash that decimated the Manchester United team, and from which Danny's younger brother, Jackie, had escaped with his life but injured so badly he could never play football again.

I read through the script and saw that they had planned to end the show by reuniting Danny and Jackie. It had tearjerker written all over it. They had played together a dozen times for Northern Ireland before Jackie's career was so cruelly cut short after he had established himself as a key defender for the Busby Babes. Eamonn was scripted to tell how Jackie had been given the Last Rites at the scene of the crash, so his story was even more dramatic and moving than Danny's. There were family guests who had been brought over from the United States and South Africa, and Spurs manager Bill Nicholson and the entire first team squad were lined up at the Shepherd's Bush studio to welcome their captain, with whom they had trained at Cheshunt earlier that day.

Relatives and old friends flew in from Ireland and several of his international team-mates were ready to tell their Danny stories.

So many myths have been perpetrated about the show that never was. Even to this day I meet people who say they saw Danny saying "no" to Eamonn on television. Oh no they didn't. Only one man apart from Danny knew exactly what happened. This is what the sole eyewitness, Eamonn Andrews, told me: "We got Danny along to Broadcasting House for what he thought was going to be a radio interview about the season so far. He didn't know, but we had hidden cameras filming his every move from the moment he came into the studio. We were recording it to show as the introduction to a live broadcast from Shepherd's Bush. He was sitting at the microphone ready to start his interview when I came in carrying the Red Book.

"He took one look at me and was like a startled rabbit caught in the headlights. As he stood up, he just said: 'Oh no ... oh no ... no way.'

I didn't have a chance to say a word to him before he dashed out of the studio as if shot from a cannon. If I could have got to Danny I might have been able to talk some sense into him, but he was away and out of range of our television cameras.

"One of our production team caught up with him and tried to reason with him, and explained that we had friends and relatives from all over the world waiting to greet him.

"He replied, 'That's your problem, not mine. You should have asked me and I'd have told you my private life is my private life.' We were stunned. It had never happened before, but thank goodness we had a show from the previous month in the can – a Somerset doctor – and we ran that, with the viewers watching at home having no idea that it was supposed to have been a live show featuring Danny. I've been asked more about this programme that never was than most we've screened!"

Many years later, when Danny and I were colleagues on *Express* newspapers, he confessed to me that it was a mixture of embarrassment and his belief that private lives should stay private that made him instinctively run away. He did not want to be dishonest or hypocritical about his family life in front of the cameras. His three marriages and various dalliances give a clue to the fact that he had an eye for the ladies. He had yet to tell his unsuspecting wife that a divorce was on the horizon.

I wrote a book about it: *Danny Blanchflower, This WAS Your Life.*

Around about the time that Danny was running away from the *This Is Your Life* book I was playing the lottery love card. In May 1960 Ernie McDonald and his wife-to-be Vera set me up on a blind date with the *Stratford Express* switchboard operator, a beautiful divorcée called Eileen Seeger. I married her in a side room at Limehouse Town Hall just eleven months later, when I was still twenty, four years younger than my bride.

We were refused a request to have a church wedding because Eileen was a divorcée, escaping from her first marriage after just a few months. We later had a quiet, private service at a side altar in St Paul's, Shadwell, conducted by my faithful mentor Reverend Jansz,

Our closest friends, Terry and Sylvia Lawless – in their nine-year-old Austin A30 – drove us from our small wedding reception at the improbably named The Cock pub in The Highway to our humble home in Stratford, next door to Eileen's parents. We were renting the downstairs half of an Edwardian terraced house that had an outside toilet, and a pre-war Butler sink for washing and bathing. To outsiders it looked as if I had returned to the back of the queue.

I call it the lottery of love, because what else can it be, when I now know that at twenty you have little grasp of the real world. Eileen gave shape and meaning to my life, but it was more luck than judgment that led me into her arms.

Throughout the next four decades she was the sensible one, leading this incurable romantic through the minefield of marriage. I was so blessed to find her, and we had wonderful times together, despite my occasional, uh, adventures. When she was taken from me by a kidney disease after 46 years of a blissful marriage that produced daughter Lisa and son Michael little did I guess that I would remarry down the line to a 90 year old granny! And again I had won the lottery of love.

Chapter Fourteen:
Facing the world alone

W E now enter the period of Joyce's life when fate smacked her in the face. She has found it tough talking about it even at this distance, but – deep breath – here goes …

"Nothing prepared me for the shock of Norman's death. We were living if not the high life, certainly a very comfortable one. Both of us were workaholics and we took great pride in the success of Anglia Batteries.

Norman continued to be the life and soul of any party, but I could detect that all was not right.

"I used to lie alongside him in bed at night and could actually feel his heart racing, and he was wheezing, coughing and struggling for his breath. He was never one of those men who willingly faced a doctor and was convinced he could shake off any illness. He started to hide behind the bottle, drinking lots of port which dulled whatever he was feeling but it affected his happy-go-lucky personality. The slimline Hamlet cigars he used to smoke started to become a crutch and his health visibly began to go downhill.

"On top of all this, I was knocked over by the same terrible dose of quinsy that affected my Dad just after the war. This was in the winter of 1979 just as we were all preparing for Steven to get married to Lucy Pickering, his policewoman girlfriend from Southchurch.

"The two of us were also planning a rare break, a holiday in America. We had been talking about it for weeks and were hyper excited. Then everything started to go wrong.

"I was ordered into hospital to have the painful abscess in my throat pierced, and I had a constant stream of concerned visitors – everybody but Norman. He suffered from a fear of hospitals and just could not bring himself to visit me.

"By the time I got home his health had really deteriorated to the point where he was skin and bone, and I decided that I would have to trick him

into seeing a doctor. I kidded him that we were going to see his brother Geoff, who just happened to be living in the same road as our family doctor. This was his private house. I dare not try taking him to the surgery because he would have bolted.

"Suddenly, as we approached Geoff's home, I stopped outside the doctor's door. Poor Norman was like a trapped animal and agreed to seeing the doctor under protest.

"As I feared, he was told he was seriously ill. and needed to take things easy. A few days later I was worried and called a heart specialist, who instructed that he should go to Oldchurch Hopsital in a blue-light dash.

"He was allowed home after emergency treatment but within a matter of days it was obvious that he needed to be back in hospital, and he was taken to Southend General. It had still not entered my head that he was never going to come home again, so it came as an earthquaking shock when he died in his hospital bed without me or the boys with him. The date: November 9 1979. Black Friday.

"I was still in a state of severe shock when we cremated Norman at Southend cemetery just five days after his passing. The details of the day are a blur to me because I was completely in pieces. All I can recall is that it was an appalling wet, rainy day that suited the mood of all the mourners, me in particular. We had lost a good man to what was diagnosed as lung congestion.

"Norman had been a wonderful husband, generous but never flash with his money, always supportive of me and our two boys and a born entertainer. To say I was in shock is an understatement. I had never envisaged being a widow, and suddenly I found myself having to climb life's mountain alone. I had lost my best mate, a man who had always laughed at life. If only he had not been born with a fear of doctors and hospitals, we might have caught his condition before it took hold. Ironically, he had always been quietly cautious to the point where he had to have £100 in the bank in case the roof needed mending, but he didn't have the same safety-net care and attention to his health.

"We had poured ourselves into making a success of the Anglia Batteries business to the detriment of our health. I had been knocked over by pesky, painful throat problems that I had inherited from my Dad, and it was while I

was run down to the point where I had to go into hospital that Norman went downhill and quickly lost his fight for life.

"This is when being a Palmer came to my rescue. My large family – Mum, Dad and each of my wonderful four sisters – gathered round me and nursed me through the worst of times. They were all there for me and I started to battle back, because I had to. It was their love that carried me through, along with my sons Steven and Michael stepping up to the plate and giving me the motivation to carry on.

"Just three months after his Dad died, Steven went through with his marriage to Lucy, as Norman would have wished.

"I wore a grey costume rather than depress everybody with black. It was a union that produced my wonderful grandchildren Ryan and Rachel. How sad that Norman was not around to see them become model citizens and presenting me with smashing great grandchildren.

"So there I was, a widow in my mid-40s after 23 years of a good, solid marriage and with a business to run and two mortgages to pay. To be honest, I was numb with shock but my Mum and Dad and sisters propped me up with their love and I eventually pulled myself together and decided to get on with the rest of my life.

"It's fair to say I became a changed woman, facing up to my responsibilities and taking a determined, independent view of life. The experience had toughened me. I decided I had to stand on my own two feet. I was a Palmer girl and we had been taught to be self sufficient and not rely on the State to clothe and feed us. Sounds dramatic, I know, but Norman's death made me adopt the attitude of 'It's me against the world.'

"First thing to do was see what Norman had left in his will, so that I could get our business shipshape. He had put it away in a box deposited at Barclays Bank after we had moved our account to Chalkwell branch, where John Wakering was a caring and conscientious manager.

"John came to see me with the box under his arm back in the days when bank officials were humans, not robots locked into credit ratings. He took out the will and started to read it to himself, smiling at each codicil and then when he reached the last page his face suddenly altered and he blew out his cheeks.

"'I hate to have to tell you this,' he announced solemnly, 'but your *husband has not signed it. The will has been witnessed but there is no Norman Lambert signature. I'm afraid this will is not worth the paper it's written on."*

"I looked at the name of the witnesses and quickly deduced that it had been signed on a boozy night at the Services Club and that dear, daft Norman had forgotten to sign it himself.

"Oh what a palaver. It meant everything had to go into probate and as anybody who has experienced it will testify this can take months. Meantime I had mortgages and pressing bills to pay. Talk about going in at the deep end.

"Barclays and my creditors – mainly the firms who supplied our batteries and accessories – were very understanding and allowed me extra time to clear the debts, but I did it and gradually put Anglia Batteries back on firm footing. What an introduction to widowhood!

"Around about this time, our first-born son Steven was making steady progress in the Essex police force. One day he was called out to Canvey Island for what the police describe as 'a domestic', a husband and wife quarrel,

"He had just, so he thought, sorted it out amicably when the wife involved in the altercation spat full in his face.

"This unsettling incident sent him into a depression, and he told me, 'Mum, I joined the police to try to put something into society. I didn't expect anything as horrible as this.'

"I talked him into quitting the police force and joining our Anglia Batteries team along with brother-in-law Geoff and youngest son Michael. It was now truly a family affair – sadly without Norman – and we went from strength to strength. My two boys did the memory of their Dad proud with the diligent way they went about their duties. Each one of us became an expert on fitting, repairing and switching car batteries, and we spent so much time under the hoods and bonnets of cars that we were in danger of getting round shoulders. You try doing it for more than fifty years and see how it affects your posture, and ridiculously the more modern the car the more difficult it was to find and change the battery.

"We managed to get the business on such a firm footing that it got to the stage where I took Mum and Dad to see a terraced house at Ambleside Drive

in Southend. They looked around approvingly and were gob-smacked when I handed them the keys. 'This is now yours,' I said, feeling fit to burst with pride. 'It's in return for all you've done for me and my sisters throughout our lives.

"Mum and Dad just couldn't believe it. I just wish I could have bottled the moment. It gave me so much satisfaction, and I truly learned the full meaning of what Jesus is quoted as saying in the Bible, 'It's more blessed to give than receive.

"When Mum passed on at the age of 82 in 1982.my sister Ann and her jovial husband Bryan took Dad under their wing and I was so grateful to them for caring for him and making his last years wrapped in care and love. He left us at the age of 83 in 1989. The Palmer Sisters had lost their hero. What a man. He courageously fought fires during the London Blitz, and always set standards of decency and devotion for we girls. The fact that I was able to buy he and Mum a house in which to spend their final years was the best thing I ever did..

"My younger sister, Lorna, bought the Ambleside house from me and so it stayed in the family. All we Palmer sisters were ever thankful for what Mum and Dad did for us. We had come a long, long way from the old East End.

"Now over to my latest Norman, who was still in the East End and starting to make his way in life ..."

Chapter Fifteen:
Expressing opinions

THE day before my 1961 wedding I took a call from John Jenkins, a gifted journalist I had left behind on the *Stratford Express*. He had been appointed Editor and offered me the job as Sports Editor in place of Harry Miller, lured to the *Daily Mirror* in Manchester in the continuing fall-out from the Munich air crash.

I enjoyed every second of my time at *Boxing News*, where I had a ringside seat for every major promotion in London. But they could not match the weekly £10.10s (£10.50) wage that John Jenkins was offering me, plus the convenience of living around the corner to the *Stratford Express*. Yes, an offer I could not refuse ... and this a dozen years before the making of the first *Godfather* film..

One of the great perks of being Sports Editor at the *Stratford Express* was sitting at the feet of West Ham manager Ron Greenwood. He and his assistant John Lyall used to almost purr with their love of pure football, and they talked the same language as Spurs boss Bill Nicholson, that the game should be about style and invention. Ron and Bill Nick shared the same principles and I was privileged to learn about football tactics from both of these professors of the Beautiful Game.

Because of the foundation of friendship I had forged with Greenwood while I was on the *Stratford Express* I was one of the few pressmen he fully trusted. He knew I would never break a confidence, and shared with me the news that Bobby Moore had gone into hospital during the 1964-65 season to have a cancerous testicle removed. This was shortly after he had skippered the Hammers to their FA Cup final victory over Preston.

Those were the days when you whispered the 'C' word. The cover story Ron released was that he was being treated for a groin injury. How much bigger a hero would Bobby have been had England supporters known he had battled with testicular cancer before collecting the European Cup Winners' Cup and then the World Cup to complete a remarkable hat-trick of climbing the Wembley steps for three successive years?

It had all started with West Ham's victory over Preston in the 1964 FA Cup final. On the following Monday Ron and I had been driving to Pathé Pictorial's Wardour Street studio for a colour film premier of the match when we got snarled up in a traffic jam. We abandoned the car at Mile End and continued our journey on the Central Line by tube train.

Legendary photographer Monte Fresco snapped Ron and I on the tube train, the FA Cup in a bag on the manager's lap. The unique picture featured on the back pages the next day, with the hilarious caption:: 'Ron Greenwood and a West Ham official go underground with the FA Cup.'

The punchline is that Ron got his knuckles rapped by the Football Association for giving their treasured trophy such a public airing. This was two years before the Jules Rimet World Cup trophy was stolen while being exhibited in London. From then on they made replicas of all the major trophies and the originals were tucked away in safe places once the presentation had been made. Nobody will ever again travel with the FA Cup on a London tube train. And to think I have photographic proof of it on the opposite page. You couldn't make it up..

I was a headstrong, know-it-all (nothing's changed), and benefitting from having been among the first of my generation not to be caught up in the net of national service conscription.

Disillusioned by *a Stratford Express* decision to redesign with smaller type faces, I put out feelers for a Fleet Street job and landed a three-month holiday relief position as a sub-editor on the *Evening Standard* sports desk. I did not want to worry my six months pregnant wife and told her I had a staff post. Knee-knocking time.

On the Friday evening before starting my new job I went to the Crooked Billet pub in the East End to have a celebratory drink with my Dad, who was still picking up a few extra bob knocking out the old songs on the piano. We sank a couple of pints, and then Dad took a break from playing the joanna to go to the loo. I can never resist a keyboard, and on an impulse I decided to sit down at the battered old upright and play my banana-fingered jazz numbers. Not the best selection for a spit-and-sawdust pub in notorious Cable Street.

I was into the second stanza of *Careless Love Blues* when a rather drunk Irish docker, as wide as he was tall, staggered over and demanded: "Play *I'll*

West Ham manager Ron Greenwood holds the FA Cup like a baby, alongside reporter Norman Giller in 1964. It was the only time the treasured trophy travelled by tube.

*Take You Home Again, Kathlee*n."

"Sorry, pal, but it's not in my repertoire," I said, a little too cockily. It was another bad selection, this time of vocabulary and the sarcastic delivery.

"Don't give me that f***ing repertoire bollocks," he slurred . "Everybody knows that song."

Now a third bad selection, I elected to stand up and say: "If you're so clever, *you* play it."

That was the breaking point, and the end of negotiations. No more song requests, just swinging punches, but first the overture of him calling me "a f***ing long-nosed young c**t." Long-nosed, I thought, was out of order

All my lessons in defensive boxing came in handy as I ducked inside the furious lefts and rights that were suddenly coming my way, but I could not avoid his following head butt. I hung close to him while clearing my senses.

At this moment Dad came out of the gents, giving a classic double take as he found his son in a wrestling match. He had only been gone a couple of minutes.

Dad instantly started firing street-fighter punches at the ox holding me, and then the docker's mates decided to join in. Now there were half a dozen of us throwing punches as if in a Wild West brawl.

Les, the landlord who paid Dad's wages, 6ft 6in tall and with a nose spread across his face, sprang over the bar, took a panoramic view of the four hefty dockers, his pianist and skinny son and after all of a second's deliberation made the wise choice of throwing my Dad and me out into Cable Street.

I went home to my pregnant wife with a closed right eye, which was still black with bruising when I started my Fleet Street career with the *Standard* the following Monday.

The sports editor on the *Standard* was a cold, ex-Army officer type, who was a cross between David Niven (looks) and Attila the Hun (temperament). My main task was to edit the constantly changing cricket scoreboard through six editions, in the days when the county game had huge support. It was the most aggravating job of my life, with people continually standing at my back looking for their county scores.

One afternoon I took my eye off the ball and let through a literal, or rather a joke by the boys in the composing room. These were the days when The Nawab of Pataudi was gracing the Oxford University team. To get his title to fit in the scoreboard we would abbreviate it to N'w'b of Pataudi. This particular day it got into the paper as Nob of Pataudi.

The grumpy sports editor took the laughter it generated as aimed at him personally, and soon after I was going cap-in-hand to the *Daily Herald* to beg for a staff job on their sports desk. I felt a complete knob.

The *Herald* was a quirky, quality broadsheet with which I broke into the national newspaper world back in that summer of 1962. Our editor was the cerebral Sydney Jacobson – later Baron Jacobson of St Albans – with Tony Boram and Ted Castle alongside him on the backbench.

Ted was the husband of MP Barbara Castle, and I spent many an hour listening to them planning the dawn of a bright new world in the Cross Keys pub opposite the old *Herald* editorial building in Long Acre, within a tenor's Top-C range of the Royal Opera House.

Opposition leader Harold Wilson and his often inebriated No 2 George Brown were regular visitors, and the political conversations blew powerfully in from the left like a Siberian gale.

I once wormed my way into the barroom chat by mentioning Huddersfield Town and the feats of their manager Herbert Chapman before he moved to Arsenal. Harold – not yet knighted – knew the history of Huddersfield Town inside out and regaled us with tales of when he watched them on their way to three successive League championships in the 1920s. Our Editor Sydney Jacobson, a warm and approachable man, called me on one side and said quietly: "Norman, the football talk is fascinating, but we've got Harold here to talk about the next Election. Can we have our conversation back?"

In the summer of 1962 I had one of my most expensive rounds of drinks within five weeks of joining the *Herald*. My wife Eileen had gone two weeks over the predicted date for the birth of our first baby when the barman held up the phone and shouted: 'A good news call for Norman Giller.'

"Drinks all round," shouted the excited new Dad.

When I got to the phone it was heavily pregnant Eileen on the other end. "*Weekend Magazine* has bought your short story,' she announced. 'They're going to pay fifteen pounds. We can put it towards a cot for the baby."

The round came to a fiver.

I was on the National Union of Journalists' minimum of £21.10s a week, Doh!

My gorgeous daughter Lisa – still my Precious Precocious Princess – arrived during that night, arriving backwards as a breech birth. The date: August 5th 1962. The headlines the next morning were about Marilyn Monroe committing suicide. But for me it was one of the best days of my life. And Lisa remains my Precious Precocious Princess.

I was in the *Herald* office on the 22 November 1963, the day that Kennedy was shot, and I watched the master James Cameron at work writing an extraordinarily moving account of the effects of the assassination..It made me strive for new standards.

My closest friend on the *Herald* was talented and witty Welsh writer Peter Corrigan, with whom I enjoyed memorable experiences and escapades. He had a classic half exclusive in the summer of 1965 when he got a tip-off that Wolves were appointing Les Allen as their new manager in the wake of the sensational sacking of Stan Cullis.

The first edition was due to go to press, and so Peter dashed into print before he could make the proper checks. It was no secret that veteran QPR striker Les Allen wanted to get into management.

Next day came confirmation that Allen was indeed being appointed the new master of Molineux … West Brom's Ronnie Allen. "Oh well," said Peter through his chagrin, "I was half right."

We move forward two years to the Arab-Israeli war of 1967 for the facts of my second cracking Corrigan anecdote, which I have since seen borrowed to dress up invented stories. This is the true, original version.

The England Under-23 summer tour that year coincided with the Six-Day War, and at the height of hostilities the squad was briefly stranded in Bulgaria.

There were sixteen players, six doddery members of the FA blazered brigade, Manchester United trainer Wilf McGuinness, Tottenham manager Bill Nicholson and seven of Fleet Street's finest football writers. I would say that; I was one of them.

Peter is the central character in the story, a few years ahead of becoming the highly regarded sports editor of the *Observer* and certainly one of the matchless sporting journalists of my generation. At that time he was reporting for the broadsheet *Sun* two years before it became the tabloid toy of Rupert Murdoch.

As the war reached its peak, it suddenly became impossible to make telephone or telex contact with our London offices. I was earning my daily bread with the *Daily Express,* and along with my colleagues I sat fretting and frustrated in the team's hotel headquarters in Sofia as the edition deadlines for our copy approached and disappeared into the distance.

Ike Robinson, the octogenarian chief representative of the Football Association, had called an emergency meeting of the media and told us he was going to ask the British government to send an RAF plane to "rescue" the England team if the war escalated. It was a great story but we felt as frustrated as pianists trying to play with the piano lid locked.

In those non-STD days you had to order your telephone calls through the hotel switchboard, and we were informed that all lines were down. You have to remember the mood at the time. There was wild rumour of Russia getting involved and nuclear weapons being used as Israeli tanks and jet fighters destroyed the combined forces of Egypt, Jordan and Syria.

We agreed among us that if anybody should be lucky enough to get through we would put over a shared story that could be distributed at the London end. After two days of total silence, it was Peter who suddenly got the desperately awaited call and found himself being put through to the Sun sports desk from the lobby of the hotel.

It was an appalling line and he was reduced to screaming "Peter Corrigan" into the mouthpiece in a bid to make himself heard at the other end. The rest of us were gathered around, willing him to keep the precious line open. We couldn't believe it when he suddenly threw down the receiver without having dictated a word.

On the other end of the line was a veteran sub-editor who had a pronounced stutter.

Peter, tearing out what little hair he had left, looked at us wild-eyed and said: "I've just been told that P-P-Peter C-C-Corrigan is in B-B-Bulgaria, and then he put down the phone and cut me off."

I seem to remember saying something like f-f-f-fancy that. Or words to that effect..

The *Herald* was ripe for a change of direction in 1964, and after an initial spurt the revamped paper made even less of an impact in its new guise as the broadsheet *Sun*. It was then given the kick of life when a young Aussie called Rupert Murdoch bought it on the never-never for £800,000, beating off a rival bid from the oily and openly ambitious Robert Maxwell, and changing the format to tabloid.

It was a few months later that the *Daily Mail*'s exceptional chief football writer Brian James was overheard making the dismissive remark: "The No 2 football reporters these days are such an insignificant lot."

Instead of getting angry and precious we No 2s were highly amused, and at an impromptu meeting agreed to form a club called The Insignificant Seven. We took it very seriously and had a special tie manufactured by the manufacturing company run by Spurs maestro Dave Mackay.

Brian James was installed as President, and we had plans for golf days and liquid-propelled jaunts. The Insignificant Seven founder members were Peter Corrigan (*Sun,* later *Mail* and *Observer*), Steve Richards (*Sun*, later Pelé's PR), Harry Miller (*Mirror*, later *Mail*), Brian Scovell (*Sketch*, later *Mail*), Bryon Butler (*Telegraph*, later *BBC*), Peter Blackman (*Evening Standard*, later a distinguished artist) and – most insignificantly – me.

Sadly, our little club fell apart because too many insignificants proved themselves somewhat magnificent in the pursuit of the written word, and they all went on to distinguish themselves in the sports reporting and broadcasting world.

One more Peter Corrigan tale. We both harboured ambitions to become comedy scriptwriters, and we got ourselves a top agent in former impressionist Ted (Voice of Them All) Kavanagh. This was in 1966, when one or two things were happening on the football front as something of a distraction.

There was a comedy series on ITV at the time called *Mr Aitch*, starring Harry H. Corbett in the lead role, not as a rag and bone man as in *Steptoe and Son*, but as a Cockney spiv (it always amused me how a Mancunian could be passed off as a Cockney). It was the first sit-com ever produced by an independent company, and was scripted by the Hancock and Steptoe creators Ray Galton and Alan Simpson (both football daft, incidentally).

The independent company, run by a Mr Aitch-type character called

Johnny Arrow, hit funding trouble and could no longer afford the great G&S team. Arrow was pointed in our direction, and he said he wanted one full script and seven synopses for the rest of the series by the end of the week.

He told us this as we sat swanking in the back of his Rolls Royce, feeling like the next Galton and Simpson but more like Bart and Homer Simpson. We were suitably seduced. Johnny offered us "magic pills" to help our output, but both of us declined. We wanted clear not stoned minds.

Peter and I were each paid 50 quid up front in readies, and spent the next morning in Harry H. Corbett's bedroom. He was unselfconsciously in his vest and boxer shorts, and his latest lady, in off-the-shoulder negligee, sat in bed alongside him while we ran through a shaft of ideas. Harry kept lapsing into Shakespeare-speak, booming out lines as if on stage, and sharing out-of-school stories as to why he despised his Steptoe co-star Wilfrid Brambell. He continually referred to him as 'The Poofter'. It occurred to me that perhaps this would have made a better sit-com scenario than Mr Aitch: In Bed With Harry H.

By the end of an exhausting week we had a full 30-minute script written about Mr Aitch running London's buskers as if he was Lew Grade; there were also seven outlines for the rest of the episodes. Another deadline met

We eagerly took the scripts to Johnny Arrow's Richmond office only to find it locked. The production company had gone bust and the smooth-talking Mr Arrow disappeared from our lives along with Mr Aitch. What you might call an initial blow.

As with all good comedy, there was a punchline. A month later Clive Toye resigned as chief football reporter on the *Express* to become a soccer pioneer in the United States, where he was the man who brought Pelé into US Soccer with New York Cosmos. I was proudly promoted to the No 1 football reporting role, and my pal Peter Corrigan was interviewed for the job that I vacated and which was later filled by the inestimable Steve Curry.

Years later I asked sports editor John Morgan why he had not given Peter the job. He drew heavily on his Mr Aitch-style cigar, and said: "Clive Toye tipped me off that if I appointed Corrigan to work with you, all you'd be interested in was writing comedy scripts.

'It's a funny old game (a catchphrase, incidentally, that Greavsie always insisted I ghosted into his mouth. Wish I'd put a copyright on it! It's a funny old game).

Frank Nicklin, the most electric of all the sports editors I worked with and more responsible than anybody for The *Sun's* soaraway success when switching to tabloid, arrived at the *Herald* in 1964 like a tornado. He held the secret that the paper was about to morph into the broadsheet *Sun*, and wanted to gather the best possible team ready for the launch.

He sat at his desk in our open plan office, quietly getting an assessment on all the subs at the table from assistant sports editor John Kendrick, a larger than life character from the Black Country. John crouched alongside Frank giving a whispered rundown into his ear about each one of us.

When John pointed to a Scottish sub-editor called Ron Trevorrow, he said: "Ron is a brilliant sub but so slow we call him Tomorrow."

Frank followed John's pointing finger, but somehow managed to look at me rather than Ron Trevorrow, who was sitting next to me. So it was burned into his mind that I was very slow. A few days later I applied for the boxing writer's job for the new paper, but Frank told me: "You need to be quick to do ringside reports. Sorry, but you're not right for the job, Ron."

I scratched my head and wandered off disappointed, and annoyed that Nicklin could not even get my name right. I have never been the best, but prided myself on being one of the quickest writers in the business, and to this day – 122 books later – I've never ever missed a deadline. Ends bragging

The boxing reporter's role went to John Kendrick, who on his first assignment at a European title fight in Austria got so legless that he failed to file a single coherent sentence. He was given back his old desk job, and the boxing correspondent post went to the sports news editor, one Colin Hart, who went on to become arguably the most respected and revered ringside reporter in the world. A long way from out first meeting at juvenile court!

Meantime, I was head hunted for the football writer's job on the *Express* as successor to the hugely talented Mike Langley, and I left the *Herald* just before it became the broadsheet *Sun*.

I had no idea about the Trevorrow pantomime until 10 years later when Frank Nicklin told me: "I owe you an apology. I didn't give you the boxing job because I thought you were so slow your nickname was Tomorrow." Suddenly, I felt a yesterday's man.

I reported football from 35 countries for the broadsheet *Express* while travelling the world in five-star splendour, the highlight coming with a five week stay in Mexico for the 1970 World Cup finals, the greatest celebration of the Beautiful Game ever. Even now – more than 55 years since Bobby Moore was arrested in Bogota, accused of stealing a diamond bracelet from a hotel jewellery shop in the Colombian capital – I am often asked with a whisper and a wink, "Come on, tell us ... did Bobby nick that bracelet?"

Of course he didn't, and it was long ago proved he was the victim of an attempted sting, but it is human nature that people like to think the worst. I found out within 48 hours of Bobby's arrest that he'd been framed, but it was long after his tragic death from cancer at the age of 52 before he was officially cleared. I was in Mexico City at the time and at the insistence of my London editor, Derek Marks, went to every embassy, where I was repeatedly told that Bogota was notorious for this sort of con. There were a string of complaints from tourists on record at each embassy, and an aide to the American ambassador told me: "We call it the Bogota boobytrap."

That inspired the headline they put on my front page lead story filed to the *Daily Express*: "BOBBY CAUGHT IN THE BOGOTA BOOBYTRAP."

It was a nonsense to even suspect Bobby of the theft. As his closest pal Jimmy Greaves said on hearing the news when he arrived in Mexico City at the end of his London-to-Mexico World Cup rally drive: "Bobby's nicked a bracelet? Why? He could afford to buy the bloody shop."

Jimmy gave me this quote while sitting on a floating armchair in the middle of a pool in the luxury Camino Real hotel, drinking gallons of Mexican beer after going dry through the rally in which he and co-driver Tony Fall finished sixth out of 96 starters

I discovered where Bobby was hidden in a British embassy house, and got a cab and took Jimmy there. Nobody was being allowed in, but that did not stop Greavsie. I gave him a leg-up as he shinned over the garden wall. He was found wandering around the grounds by the ambassador's wife, who showed him out and told him to try the conventional way. Jimmy rang the doorbell and was invited in by the ambassador's wife, who almost fainted at his first words to Bobby: "Come on, Mooro, show me the bracelet."

Bobby never dared take the shop owners on in a legal battle because he feared false evidence being produced. Yes, a funny old game.

Chapter Sixteen:
Have Passport, Will Travel

WHILE I was travelling the world reporting football, Joyce was expanding Anglia Batteries, and matching me for exploring foreign lands. We two East Enders were piling on the air miles between us ... me on five-star expenses while visiting the greatest sporting venues, while my wife to be was paying her way out of her own purse, simply because she loved seeing how others lived....

"I always wanted to travel from the earliest days when my teachers showed me world maps, largely coloured pink to reveal they belonged to the British Empire. My generation were taught that British was best and that we should take great satisfaction from what our ancestors had achieved. We were not going to allow Hitler to trample on our pride.

"Norman and I were too busy trying to put Anglia Batteries on the map to bother with holidays, but even so we managed breaks in Canada, France, Holland and Spain before he was taken from us so cruelly. My best friends Barbara Beech and her husband John insisted I accompany them on their holiday to Barbados a couple of months after Norman's passing. They were concerned at the way I was run down by my painful battle with quinsy followed by the death of my husband. These were, to say the least, difficult times.

"I had such good experiences in Barbados that I vowed to take every opportunity to travel and I have since visited scores of countries, but am always happy to come home to England, still the greatest place on earth to live. I continually bless having been born British and will always wave the Union Jack. Some people, including my current husband, seem to think I am on the edge of Fascism but I am simply preaching pride in our untouchable country.

"On one of my earliest trips abroad as a widow in the company of my sister Ann and her lovely husband Bryan, I had the wonderful experience of meeting my gifted distant relation Bill Bond. He had been born in the East End in the 1920s, served in the Royal Navy and then emigrated to Canada.

"He had the natural eye and skill of a born artist and when he sent examples of his sketches to the prestigious National Geographic Magazine in the 1950s they paid for him and his family to fly to Washington DC where he took up the role of one of their main illustrators.

I admit to having tears in my eyes when he showed me his office and revealed hundreds of his majestic drawings. Here was a Stepney boy who had climbed to the very top of his profession, and we kept in touch with each other right until he died in his 80s. You can find his brilliant illustrations on line by tracing the work of William H. Bond. I proudly claim him as ;one of ours. Bond, William Bond.

"I was so lucky to have friends and family helping me adapt to being a widow, and one regular customer – the improbably named Cuthbert Thresh – came into the shop one day and demanded that I start accompanying him to his sailing yacht berthed at Wallasea near Burnham-on-Crouch, This introduced me to a wonderful community, many of them motor dealers like Cuthbert who used Anglia for their battery needs. I knew them all.

"Cuthbert, happily married but keen to share his knowledge with me, was one of the most interesting and energetic men I ever met. He was a very short man and his interviewing officers sneered at him when he volunteered to join the RAF as a pilot at the outbreak of war. But they changed their tune when he showed how he could strip down and replace a Spitfire or Hurricane engine in minutes. He was a born mechanic.

"Even though he was a qualified pilot, he was posted to Newfoundland where he taught hundreds of young pilots vital mechanical skills.

"He had the patience of Job and showed me how to sail his 50-foot yacht round the waters of Wallasea and down to Hullbridge and back along the River Crouch. Cuthbert was an expert on the fantastic wildlife that we saw on our travels and he passed this interest on to me.

"I looked up notes I kept in his log book of sightings I made of Marsh Harrier, Kestrel, Owls, Waders, Avocet, Curlew, Black-tailed Godwit, Grey and Golden Plover, Lapwing Redshank, Greenshank, Knot Dunlin and Oyster catchers.

"Wildfowl I spotted included Teal, Wigeon, Shovelet, Mallard and Shelduck, and we used to watch Atlantic grey seals and the occasional

Harbour Porpoise swimming and relaxing at the beautiful nature reserve that was being extended with earth transferred from the erection of the Queen Elizabeth tube train line. This was a million miles from the blitzed East End where I had grown up.

"Cuthbert, ceaselessly amazing with what he could do, used to fly us down to Le Touquet from Southend Airport for lunch in Northern France. It was so exciting and eccentric.

"Among his many hobbies was hair-raising speedway riding at Rayleigh, and he also drove a stock car with the name emblazoned on the side, Careful Cuthbert. He was continually the butt of jokes by entertaining MC Maurice Jardine, whose lovely wife worked for us at Anglia Batteries as a van driver. She once asked me for some time off without explaining exactly why. Imagine my utter shock and devastation when during her voluntary break she died of cancer, that brutal disease that was to cause me so much heartbreak.

It was around about this time that I got actively involved in politics after being invited to join the Southend Chamber of Commerce by Ron Price, a friendly man of many parts who later became a dynamic Mayor of Southend.

A brilliant engineer called Bernard Vincent-Pryke talked me into standing for the Conservatives in the local Council elections. Our Southend West MP Paul Channon further encouraged me to have a go, and although I was beaten the first time around I got the appetite for serving the community.

I think it was my way of handling the despair at losing Norman, but just as I felt I was feeling back on top of things another family blow took, so to speak, the wind out of my sails. And again it was cancer that caused the nightmare and, eventually, the grief.

"My lovely younger sister Sheila, fourth of the Palmer girls, lost her darling husband David to a sudden heart attack, and I am convinced the shock of it brought on what proved to be her terminal cancer.

"I gave up my sailing weekends to join my sisters Eileen, Ann and Lorna in taking turns to look after our beautiful Sheila, who was fading away in front of our eyes. When the hospital informed us it was time to call in the Macmillan Nurses to care for Sheila, Lorna and her supportive husband Colin elected to have her spend her final days at their home.

"It was terrible to watch and took me back physically and mentally to *where I had been when I lost Norman. Life could be so unkind*

"I was hardly what could be called a Merry Widow, more a cautious one, but I did have my share of romances that helped me cope with the demanding responsibility of transforming Anglia Batteries into a solid and successful business.

. "The family joke was that I chose Normans so that I got their names right. As well as my lovely Norman Lambert, I became very close to life-long friend Norman Ball and also Norman Hammond before finally agreeing on the eve of my 90th birthday to marry what my new husband laughingly refers to as Norman the Fourth.

"The third Norman – Hammond – also mentioned marriage but by then was on his sick bed and things were just not right for such a commitment. This Norman and I had known each other for 15 years when we were both married, and we got together after my Norman had died and Norman Hammond's wife had left him in distressing circumstances.

"It was our mutual friend Francoise – his sister in law, married to his brother, Don – who brought us together, inviting us both round for a beautifully prepared Sunday lunch at her place.

"Norman Hammond was owner of the small Strathmore hotel in Westcliff and we had a shared love of going to the pictures and visiting London, and a romance slowly developed. The relationship gathered strength when he joined me with my sister Ann and brother-in-law Bryan on a 1987 holiday trip to the United States.

"We had a wonderful time and were on our way from Disneyland to Las Vegas when we became concerned that none of us were getting replies to our messages home. It was a worrying 24 hours later before we discovered that all communication lines were down because of the infamous hurricane ripping through Kent and Essex.

"I went through with the holiday even though at the time Anglia Batteries were being taken to court by Southend Council in what became a farce known as the 'Red White and Blue' revolution. We had a franchise for Excide Batteries and innocently decided to paint the eaves of our shop front with red, white and blue stripes, marrying in with the Excide logo.

"Oh dear, you would have thought we had desecrated a holy place.

Neighbours complained about our choice of colours, and somebody suggested we were promoting the National Front, which was total nonsense.

"The Council poked their nose in and demanded that we repaint it white, green or cream, and they took us to court for breaking Council uniformity rules. It was a classic example of Big Brother politics and strengthened my resolve to get involved in a bid to introduce what I considered my brand of common sense.. We eventually lost the court case and had to pay a fine of £600. But the publicity we got was worth far more than that, and most people contacting us thought we had been hard done by.

"We settled on green paint at the court's bidding, which was the colour of the faces of the small minority of busybody people who hated seeing our business thriving.

"While in America, Norman Hammond and I became very close. How painful and ironic that we later had a repeat of a health scare that had forced me to trick my husband into seeing a doctor.

"I had noticed Norman H. having problems with his breathing and again had to be cunning to make an appointment with a hospital consultant. What is it with these men that they are frightened of doctors?

"As I had guessed, Norman H. was seriously ill and his condition was not helped when his brother, Don, died suddenly of a heart attack, leaving the lovely, French-born Francoise a widow, just like me.

"I discussed the situation with my son Michael, and he agreed that Norman H. could move in with us while he recovered. One snag – and I am not making this up – he said he would only come if he could bring his best mate, Bob – a parrot.

"This led to some hilarious incidents, the most unbelievable being when the next door neighbour complained that Norman was wolf whistling her when she was sunbathing topless in her garden. I had to explain that the whistler was in fact Bob the parrot.

"Bob was very talkative and could imitate any of our voices. He continually confused us by repeating things we had said and leaving Norman and I looking at each other in a mixture of amusement and amazement..

"When he felt better, Norman returned to his hotel (thank goodness, taking Bob with him), but quickly realised he could no longer cope, and *he sold the Strathmore and returned to live with Michael and me. He was telling people that we were going to get married, and I was wondering what to do when he died from a brain aneurysm while putting the rubbish bags out in our garden.*

"Norman was 62. How tragic – and I was back to being alone and devastated at the age of 55.

"All this was against the background of Anglia Batteries finding a new home. It was the summer of 1988 when my son Michael asked me to join him on a secretive car journey. It was like a magical mystery tour.

"He drove me round to the busy London Road, bottom of Woodfield Park Drive, and parked opposite a fenced-off site with some advertising hoardings.

I looked blankly at him. 'What's this?' I asked "You've brought me here to show me advertising hoardings?"

"Michael pointed to a 'For Sale' board above the hoardings.

"'I think we should make this site the new home for Anglia Batteries,' he said.

"Michael, who had inherited his Dad's nose for an opportunity, explained that companies like Halfords had decided to move to Westcliff and that we were too much off the beaten track to compete with our rivals.

"The site included a semi-detached house at 109 Woodfield Park Drive. I thought Michael's brainwave was a winner and we entered into a sealed-bid auction.

"We first of all put in our bid, then had second thoughts and raised it by a couple of thousand. We felt like we had won the World Cup when we were named as the winners. I just wish my Norman Lambert was around to see what we had achieved.

"The timing was not good because the bottom had dropped out of the commercial buildings market, but by converting our old shop into three flats we managed to climb above a financial crisis that was sending many businesses to the wall.

"As the new site included the Woodfield Park Drive house, we had got ourselves a real snip. Barclays came on board with a loan to help us clinch

the bid. This aggravated Norman Hammond who was still alive, and he insisted on giving me an interest-free loan to help with the building of our new premises. My Normans always came up trumps.

"Michael decided in 1989 that he was going to move in with his girlfriend Alison, who was to become one of my best friends and close confidants. She is a hairdresser of the highest calibre, and we have shared many jokes, much gossip and secrets over the 35+ years that we have known each other. Few have ever had a better daughter-in-law, and I love her dearly. Michael and Alison have given me fantastic grandchildren in Hannah and Lucas, both of whom are making their way in the world. Hannah is an intelligent and successful air-hostess with Emirates and is based in Dubai with her boyfriend Nick, while her brother Lucas is showing Lambert-style entrepreneurial skills down in Brighton, where he lives with his marvellous nursing girlfriend, Meghan.

"This flying-the-nest move by Michael meant I was suddenly rattling around in the vast chalet that we had continually expanded in Westbourne Grove, and I took the plunge and down sized to a bungalow adjoining the huge Tower Court complex in Westcliff-on-sea, looking out on to the Thames Estuary.

"Meantime, I had started a 'non-Norman' relationship with an interesting character called Ron Saunders. I used to tend his large garden for him because it satisfied the horticulturalist inside me. If ever I come back, it will be as a gardener or a London tour guide. It's fair to say that I know my way around a garden and also London, for me the greatest capital city in the world. I know its history and its geography inside out, and even in my 90s get excited at the thought of making what are regular visits to the museums, art galleries, opera houses, jazz clubs and theatre land. My current Norman shares my tastes, otherwise I doubt I would have agreed to marry him!

"But back to Ron Saunders. Like me, he was an East Ender by birth, served in the Royal Navy during the war and later took a German bride, which made him less than popular with some people of our generation. There are many who will not forgive or forget the inhuman Holocaust crimes. They should certainly not be forgotten.

Alf Ramsey. This was a priceless moment in his extraordinary career...

He has had (and is still having) a five-star, exciting and exotic life sryle – a long, long way from his near-poverty East End roots. His family were poor but he was a bright, enterprising lad and managed to get into an East London grammar school, which he left when he was just 14 to start his climb into the sportswriting world. He stresses in a fascinating book that there was no hope of him going to university, so he decided taking the bottom-up route to his dream of becoming a leading Fleet Street sportswriter before becoming an author, top boxing PR and television all-rounder.

His first job was at the London *Evening News* as a copyboy. Two years later, the sports-mad Norman was a junior reporter on the *Stratford Express*, a weekly paper in West Ham that was something of a staging post for Fleet Street. He ws learning his alliteration at the same time as West Ham's famous trio of Bobby, Geoff and Martin were serving their football apprenticeships.

He didn't stay long in local papers - he has never stayed long at one task - and managed to land a job as a sub-editor on the *Boxing News* for a couple of years before returning to Stratford as its sports editor.

That didn't last because he soon moved on to the London *Evening Standard* and just as quickly to the *Daily Herald* before he joined the *Daily Express* in 1964, being promoted to chief football reporter. two years later.

Over the following nine years, Norman met every famous footballer and club manager of the era. No, he didn't just meet them or report on them. He befriended them. He was mates with Bobby Moore, Geoff Hurst and particularly Jimmy Greaves, with whom he has penned 20 books! Also among his close confidants have been Spurs manager Bill Nicholson, West Ham's Ron Greenwood, Liverpool's Bill Shankly, England legends Billy Wright and Kevin Keegan and he was George Graham biographer after his fall from grace at Arsenal. He liked them and they liked him. It was not just football. He has had books published in harness with Hanry Cooper, Frank Buno, Tom Graveney, Sir Roger Bannister, Eri Morecambe, Ricky Tomlinson ... the list just goes on and on.

They all trusted him and shared secrets with him in a way that modern sports writers and football stars would find inconceivable.

Once he became a freelance, aged 33, and then started to write books, aged 38, he became the voice of his footballing and sporting friends, winning a reputation as the maestro of ghostwriting and biography..

For nine years he also ghosted sports columns for the comedian Eric Morecambe who took to introducing him to friends as "Norma, who I have known since long before the operation."

He turned his hand, and his nimble mind, to a host of projects. He wrote scripts for several television series; devised and produced TV programmes; was an early blogger and Tottenham Hotspur advocate, acted as PR to several boxing promoters and boxers (remember Jim Watt and a certain Muhammad Ali?); and was even interviewed for the job of PR to the Kray twins (a gig he is glad he failed to get).

Norman also created dozens of newspaper puzzle games, and was the ideas man who came up with such TV shows as *Who's the Greatest*, *The Games of 48*, *Stand and Deliver* for Sky and *Petrolheads* for BBC2. He was *The Sun's Sports Judge* for 10 years, settling hundreds of sporting arguments, and he confesses to being the man who first coined the phrase 'It's a funny old game' while writing a script for his best mate Jimmy Greaves.

Along the way he churned out books by the score. He claims to have had "more words published than Shakespeare and Dickens combined." And it's true. His autobiography is his 100th publication. He also works out that he has travelled more miles than Captain Cook and Christopher Columbus combined! I have also checked that our, and it's fact. Mind you, he did have the advantage of making his journeys by air.

He also specialises in leading sing-along sessions of Cockney songs while accompanying himself on the piano. 'Dad was a pub pianist who played by ear in the old East End,' he reveals in his fascinating autobiography, 'and I have followed in his finger steps.'

After the TV success of the *Royle Family*, he teamed up with one of its stars, Ricky Tomlinson, to write four books based on his character's catchphrase, "My arse." The first, *Football My Arse*, sold a staggering 100,000 copies. It is Tomlinson who has written the foreword to *Headlines, Deadlines*, which begins:

> *"I have known and avoided Norman Giller for many years, and have agreed to write this introduction to his life story just to get him off my back."*

Amid the light-hearted banter and the namedropping there are odd tender moments in this book, with warm memories of a 46-year marriage, and none more so than his recounting of how he and Jimmy Greaves overcame their drinking habit.

In February 1978, the two boozers, having returned from the funeral of a Fleet Street friend who had died at just 57, were in maudlin humour while sharing a coffee. Norman takes up the tale:

"I raised my cup and said to Jim: 'Let's go and get sober out of our minds.'

'What a great toast,' Greavsie said.

'Neither of us has had an alcoholic drink since."

All in all, this is a remarkable book by a remarkable man. And I wouldn't be surprised if he isn't already writing his 101st book.*

Roy was on the ball with his prediction that I was already writing book No 101. In fact I have had 22 books published since the one he reviewed that took me to the century. This is my 122nd book, with Joyce as my latest writing partner, following in such illustrious footsteps as Jimmy Greaves, Eric Morecambe, Ricky Tomlinson, Frank Bruno, Brian Moore, Steve Perryman, Tommy Docherty, Tom Graveney, John Newcombe, Jim Watt, Sir Gareth Edwards, John Newcombe, Sir Geoff Hurst, Kevin Keegan, George Graham, Billy Wright, Roy Ullyett, Sir Henry Cooper, Sir Roger Bannister, Bob Wilson, Gordon Banks and Pelé.

I also found time to have an enjoyable 13-year relationship with the very independent Jackie Wright and her wonderfully gifted family, co-produced more than 50 sports and showbusiness videos with multi-talented author, TV director Brian Klein, have written 500+ blogs for the Spurs Odyssey website and was a member of the *This Is Your Life* scriptwriting team for 14 years; plus I was resident columnist for the Sports Journalists' Association website, and regular correspondent for the nostalgia football magazine *BackPass*. I'm tired even thinking of it all (conceited, moi?).

We launched my *Who's the Greatest? series* on ITV with George Best against Kevin Keegan, and when the jury voted 9-3 in favour of Kevin, Best's advocate Michael Parkinson threw a hand to his head and said on television: "If this is British justice, then I hope the day never comes when I have to face a jury."

It was only weeks later that we discovered that the man we had trusted to put together the jury was a former member of a Kevin Keegan fan club at Southampton! Uh, a funny old game.

There is no question that if I'd been on the jury my vote would have gone to Best. He was without any argument the greatest British footballer of my lifetime.

In a later *Who's the Greatest?* programme, David Frost showed just what a great professional he was by throwing himself into the task of presenting the argument for Ian Botham against the untouchable Garfield Sobers.

It would have been easy for David to have taken the money and run. But he poured himself into the assignment as conscientiously as if preparing to argue with Richard Nixon.

He invited Producer John D Taylor and myself to his sumptuous London apartment to go through the script inch by inch, fact by fact, stat by stat.

"To paraphrase Nye Bevan," he said, "I don't want to be sent naked into the studio courtroom."

At the last minute the BBC inexplicably refused permission for us to use their footage of Ian Botham's innings of a lifetime against the Aussies at Leeds in the famous 1981 Test. Botham snatched victory from the jaws of defeat with an extraordinary knock of 149 not out that turned the game on its head.

I gave David the news of BBC's refusal to let us have the footage just before he was called from the green room to shoot the show that was being recorded "as live" in front of a studio audience.

His eyes suddenly glinted with a hint of steel.

When it came to the Headingley Test segment, now covered with a gallery of still photographs, David stepped out of camera shot and addressed judge Brian Moore and the jury: "I am relying on the director to cut this," he said. "but I just wanted to tell you that because of a ridiculous political war between BBC and ITV we cannot show the footage of Botham's fantastic innings in the 1981 Ashes Test at Headingley."

He then proceeded to describe the innings in graphic detail, bowed to the jury and then returned to his place in front of the camera and carried on as if there had been no break. David lost the vote 8-4 to Willie Rushton's case for Sobers. Before disappearing into the night, Frostie told me: "I'm pleased with that, because even Botham would vote for Sobers. The Jury got it wrong. It should have been 12-0."

Who's The Greatest broadcaster? No contest. That title belonged to Sir David.

Michael Parkinson, despite his defeat in the courtroom, was so taken by the *Who's the Greatest?* format that he helped sell it to a New Zealand broadcaster. We were a few weeks away from going to Christchurch to shoot the Down Under series when the stock market collapsed and the TV production company went bankrupt.

I was going to get paid £5,000 a show, and we were due to fly to and from New Zealand first class. Easy come, easy go.

The saddest memory of my *Who's the Greatest?* series is that it was during the shooting of the Muhammad Ali v. Rocky Marciano episode that I first realised that one of my most respected mentors, Eamonn Andrews, was seriously ill.

Eamonn had taken me under his wing, and used to invite me to his riverside Chiswick apartment to give me tips on scriptwriting, while his lovely wife Gráinne cooked for us. We used to talk boxing for hours, because it remained his first love. He was all-Irish amateur middleweight champion when he was eighteen, and would have boxed professionally had he not stumbled into broadcasting from the mundane world of insurance.

A skilled writer, Eamonn was one of the first to recognise that I was proving fairly prolific with the amount of books I was having published, and he featured me in his *Catholic Herald* column. I don't know which of us was more embarrassed that the typesetters managed to have me down throughout the flattering article as Norma.

He reluctantly took on the role of *Who's the Greatest?* advocate for Rocky Marciano against Muhammad Ali, a boxer he considered the finest heavyweight of all time. He wanted to represent Ali, but that role went to 'Minder' star Dennis Waterman, whose brother Peter had been British and European welterweight champion.

As we were preparing to shoot the show I found Eamonn sitting slumped on the sofa in his dressing-room. "Are you okay?" I asked.

"Nothing a glass of brandy won't cure," he said.

I went and got him a large brandy, while presenter Brian Moore and producer John D. Taylor monitored him, both expecting him to have to pull out of the show. But once the cameras were on, Eamonn suddenly became his old self and gave a magnificent (though losing) performance as Marciano's courtroom representative.

As soon as the show was over, he was again feeling unwell and had to be examined by the studio doctor. I was writing a script at the time for a *This Is Your Life* tribute to rugby legend Cliff Morgan.

I telephoned producer Malcolm Morris to warn him that Eamonn was unwell, and that weekend he was rushed off to hospital with heart problems. There had been concerns when preparing the Cliff Morgan show over the cost of having a reunion of the 1955 British Lions, with which Cliff starred. They were now spread all over the world.

Eamonn took my script to hospital with him, and was editing it with his distinctive green-ink pen. When he died, lying on his chest was the script with the instruction written in capital letters and in his distinctive green ink: "Cancel the British Lions."

One *This Is Your Life* show I regret putting my name to featured Sir Jimmy Savile. It was just after Eamonn had been succeeded as presenter by Michael Aspel, and the man we all now loathe was at the peak of his popularity, and continually in the headlines for his astonishing charity work

We had a production team meeting to discuss whether to make a second show starring the wildly eccentric disc jockey. Eamonn had featured him in 1970, and it was being suggested we should surprise Savile again with the famous Big Red Book.

Chief scriptwriter Roy Bottomley, who had been a sharp news reporter on the *Daily Sketch*, said: "Well I'm not going to write it. The man's a notorious paedo." Roy then told us how former Fleet Street colleagues had been trying to find evidence to support allegations that Savile molested under-age girls and boys but he frightened them off with legal threats.

To my lasting shame, I accepted the assignment after Roy had refused to have anything to do with the show. We ignored research that revealed Savile had often been under suspicion of abusing children. I will never forgive myself for putting my name to the programme as scriptwriter. I should have followed the lead of Roy Bottomley and declined the job. The

£2,400 fee bought my blind eye. Nice one, Norm.

Professor Roy Greenslade briefly mentioned in his *Guardian* article that I was the only newspaper reporter to get into the England dressing-room after England's extra-time win in the 1966 World Cup final.

Shrewdly, I tied myself to Wembley public relations officer Len Went, who talked and walked me past all the jobsworth stewards. On the way round Wembley's back doubles I came face to face with Her Majesty the Queen, about to climb into her Roller after she had presented the Jules Rimet trophy to Bobby Moore.

Dressed in a beautiful neutral canary yellow coat and matching hat, she gave me a dazzling smile (okay, it might have been to the people behind me) as she was chauffered away.

Minutes after the players had performed a victory lap of honour and returned like frolicking schoolboys to the dressing-room, I managed to hug my mate Bobby Moore and to touch the Jules Rimet trophy before being x-rayed out by Alf Ramsey's famous baleful stare.

Even in that moment of Everest-high euphoria, he insisted on the dressing-room being hallowed ground for players only. He later explained: "If I'd let you in there were 500 pressmen from around the world who would have demanded the same privilege."

That night – way after midnight – I tracked Bobby Moore down to the Playboy Club in London's posh Park Lane. He was happily inebriated and leaning against the grand piano while drunkenly singing *Magic Moments*.

Accompanying him at the piano was the song's talented composer, Burt Bacharach.

Yes, that was another magic moment.

Chapter Eighteen:

In the world of politics

JOYCE was settling into her new existence in her Tower Court bungalow overlooking the Thames Estuary as she entered a phase in which she became politically and community minded and motivated. Three local Conservative MPs – Paul Channon, Sir Teddy Taylor and Sir David Amess – figured large in her insanely busy life and took turns persuading her to become heavily involved in the world of politics ...

"I got particularly close to Teddy Taylor and then David Amess. Both were charming gentlemen as well as being sharp-as-a-tack politicians. What I liked about both of them is that they were happy to help anybody despite their political persuasion, colour or creed. Anybody who knows me well will, I hope, think I am cut from the same cloth.

"Happily, I carried out a lot of door to door canvassing, putting the Tory side of things to Southend residents and showering them with booklets and pamphlets. My enthusiasm and energy caught the eye of Lady Sheila Taylor, Sir Teddy's wife, and she encouraged me to stand as a Councillor for Southend's Milton Ward. I managed to get elected and became engrossed in local matters and emerged as a busy body on many committees.

"I was privileged to become a Trustee of the Darby and Joan retirement homes and also active on the committee to improve our wonderful Pier, famously the longest in the world and a huge day-tripper attraction.

"Sheila Taylor was a fascinating person, who used to give interesting after-dinner talks, and she would tell us how she and Teddy first got together He was at death's door in hospital and she was the ward nurse who helped him through his crisis. It was a wonderful, true love story, which I didn't know that one day I would eclipse!

"Teddy and Sheila had three children, and it was so cruel that she finished up nursing him again when he became a victim of the horrible Alzheimer's disease (that, incidentally, also claimed two of his early colleagues in the House, Margaret Thatcher and Harold Wilson).

"My interest in local history inevitably led to me joining the inspiring

151

Southend Society, and I have been quite fanatical about preserving historic parts of our town (now, of course, a City, thanks to Sir David).

"There was one headline-hitting affair when uncaring people were trying to demolish the 18th Century Royal Hotel at the bottom of the High Street, overlooking Pier Hill and Royal Terrace. Sir John Betjeman, Poet Laureate and lover of Southend, got to hear of our campaign to save it and put his weight behind the protest and it still defiantly stands as a Grade 11 listed building. Hands off!

"One thing that fills me with pride is when I see old Leigh packed with masses of people at the many excellent waterside restaurants. I fought against Council opponents who wanted the area retained as a boat-building yard. That was pie in the sky, while the restaurants were in demand by people coming from far and wide. It is also a vicinity where a lot of local youngsters can get useful work experience and many go on to greater things. As President of the South Essex Chamber of Commerce I was more interested in boosting local employment than reviving a dead profession.

"I smile with satisfaction when I now eat at what is, ironically, called The Boatyard Restaurant, where we staged the annual, hugely popular Whitebait Festival. It came agonisingly close to not being allowed to expand into one of the outstanding restaurants in Essex. Old Leigh is on the map for the right reasons and brings colossal footfall to the district. If you want a good meal in a buzzing atmosphere and with a waterside setting then head for Old Leigh!

"It was my privilege to be treasurer of the Southend Society and we joined forces with the Clifton Conservation committee – ably run by Laura Khan and Jo Clark – to give the area a refined look. On Churchill's orders, all the railings had been cleared for the War effort and we organised a sprucing up of the bowling green area and surrounding vicinity with smart railings paid for by residents who shared our pride in good old Southend-on-Sea. What a way to celebrate the centenary of the bowling green that is overlooked by the quaint La Petite Petanqu restaurant and all in the heart of the beautiful preservation area.

"When I finally stood down as the Southend Society treasurer, I was so proud that it was my niece Sarah Fulcher, a solicitor, who volunteered to take my place.

"People tend to take for granted all the work that is done free of charge by concerned citizens who want Southend to be represented in the best possible light. I would, for example, come down heavily on fly-tippers who spoil the environment with their lazy and careless disposal of their rubbish.

"Norman has told me to come down off my high horse, but I know a lot of people, the silent majority, agree with me. I shall shut up.

"Sir Teddy Taylor was a dynamic character, who was often in the headlines as outspoken MP for Rochford and then Southend East. I always found him a friendly yet fiery Scot, eager to get his teeth into local matters. I recall him getting behind our campaign to save the Rivoli cinema in Alexandra Street and restore it to its original grandeur as the New Empire Theatre. It had been originally built in Victorian times by the grandfather of Roger Marlow and it was Roger who invited me on to the committee fighting to revert it to a theatre for affordable entertainment by local dance troupes, amateur theatre players, pop groups and mass choirs.

"Teddy Taylor helped me arrange coachloads of Southend folk to have supper at the House of Commons, all to raise funds for the campaign. I had lots of feedback from people who found the trip and the tour of the House fascinating, and Teddy always put himself out to meet as many as possible.

"Ron Martin, former Southend United owner and quite a controversial figure, showed his human side when he allowed us to take £8,000-worth of seats, lighting equipment and carpet from his Odeon Cinema and transfer it to the Rivoli, soon to be re-established as the New Empire Theatre.

"It was invigorating being a member of such an energetic committee, and Tessa Davies – from the wonderful Stagecoach School – was a driving force who helped get the theatre up and running and we kicked off with a highly successful production of Little Shop of Horrors.

"I was astonished by the input from a dedicated family, the Robertsons, who poured themselves into the project. Mum Winnie and Dad Dougie acted as cleaners and odd-job workers, son Danny was the lighting man and daughter Julie worked the box office. They were supported behind the scenes by husband and wife Anne and Ron Coulidge. It's these volunteer workers who are the backbone of amateur theatre and we were so lucky to have them working on our ambitious project.

"All seemed to be going well and we were planning a Christmas pantomime to raise extra funds when, aggravatingly, the roof was declared unsafe and everything was put on hold.

"Southend Council were invisible in giving us any breathing space, and the miserable Landlord ran out of patience and closed down the theatre. It was the end of our dream – particularly that of Roger Marlow and the industrious Robertson family – and everything was turned to dust when the grand old building was demolished. That broke a lot of hearts.

"There was more heartache for me when I lost my seat on the Council by a single vote. The election came on the very day I was taken to hospital with painful appendicitis. I am confident I would have held on to my seat if I could have had those vital final hours to get supporters out.

"But my interest in politics and loyalty to the Conservative cause had been sharpened, and I joined the Iveagh Club in Leigh where I eventually became chairman (I detest all that nonsense about chair person!).

"The Iveagh was to play an important part in my life over the next quarter of a century. Fittingly for a social club, the name has a direct association with a world-famous drink. Paul Channon, who was Southend West's Conservative MP at the time of its launch in 1963, was the only son of Sir Henry 'Chips' Channon and Lady Honor Channon, who in turn was the eldest daughter of Rupert Guinness, the 2nd Earl of Iveagh. Yes, the famous Guinness family. That explains the long-standing 'Iveagh' name of the club, with its roots in County Down and the charitable side of the Guinness dynasty..

"I have spent hours at the club, playing cards, taking part in all the social events and, just occasionally, talking politics. Oh yes, and cooking sausage rolls! I was as famous in the kitchen as at the card table.

"The kitchen got me into an unfortunate war with some of the club's members. When I took over as chairman the facilities were, frankly, unhealthy and I refused to allow food to be served for fear of spreading something as dangerous as Legionnaire's Disease.

"A small section of the members decided to quit rather than see the sense of what I was trying to do. It was almost literally a storm in a teacup, and several of those who walked out in protest have since apologised and accepted that I was looking out for their health. If I had continued using the *kitchen in the state it was in we could have lost our licence to operate.*

"If I upset some people with my stubborn attitude at the time, I beg their understanding and hope they will now accept that I was acting in their interest.

"The large majority of members, I'm glad to report, understood and agreed with my stance on the kitchen. To this day I remain close friends with the two Judiths, Suttling and Canham, who has succeeded me as an excellent chairwoman of the Iveagh club. I also had the full backing of the loyal staff workers led by conscientious and industrious bar manager Scott Brown. He is a driving force behind the scenes and when my new husband led a sing-along at the club showed he was also a whiz at computers by helping Norman transfer lyrics from his laptop. The sing song was an enormous success and so reminded me of my original Norman and his 'Some day my prints will come' running joke.

"David Amess and I hit it off from the moment he arrived from his Basildon constituency to win a popular election at Southend West on May Day 1997, taking over from Paul Channon. We shared an East London background, so had a lot in common, and I was only too happy to help him with his Friday surgeries, superbly organised by his office manager Gill Lee.

"He and his wife, Julia, were a charming couple who threw themselves into local affairs, and their arrival coincided with Margaret Thatcher taking over at 10 Downing Street. Somehow Sir David – knighted in 2015 – managed to juggle his Westminster affairs with helping Julia bring up their five children and pouring energy into his Southend duties and demands.

"David had been a committed Southend admirer from his youth in East London, and his campaign to have it recognised as a city was something to marvel at. We all know that he eventually got his wish, but in such tragic circumstances

"As befits a man on the brink of becoming Father of the House, he had a superbly appointed office overlooking Parliament and I was privileged to often be invited there where the ever-efficient Gill was in charge. Sir David was always keen to reward those people who supported him, and there was a memorable day when he invited me and my grandchildren to be among the first to take a ride on the imposing London Eye, the world's largest

cantilevered observation wheel. Fittingly, I had a sweeping view over my beloved London and I delighted in pointing out landmarks to my grand children. It was a capital day out!.

"My dear friend Sir David – by then quite rightly knighted for his political and public service – was the main instigator for me to be awarded Freeman of the City of London because of my work with the Farringdon Ward, where I had started work all those years ago in the office of William Hill.

"This meant I had the right to drive my sheep through the City, but more realistically it meant I could participate in London's ceremonial functions, various civic events and ceremonies within the City, including parades and dinners hosted by the Lord Mayor. Plus, of course, the Lord Mayor's Show. It was as if I had a season ticket to the grand Mansion House and Guldhall.

"Unbeknown to me, my local newsagent's husband Alex Dumon was a distinguished Sergeant-Major in the Coldstream Guards. He helped organise all those magnificent public displays like Trooping the Colour and Beating the Retreat at Horseguards Parade.

"Imagine my surprise and delight when one year he invited me to the Trooping of the Colour in the days when Her Majesty the Queen was still taking part on horseback. It was an absolute privilege to have a front-row seat on one of those spectacular occasions that make the hair on the back of your neck stand on end. Nobody does it like the British.

"All this time I was enjoying life at Tower Court, where I made lots of lasting friendships with many lovely neighbours, most of whom lived in the enormous block of apartments that dwarfed my bungalow. In later years we had good gossips on our WatsUp group, and we made human contact in regular tea and coffee mornings in the nearby Cliffs Pavilion café.

"WatsUp! Yes, I had come a long, long way from the East End and our days of 'push button A' telephone box calls.

Chapter Nineteen:
Farewell My Lovely

THE dawn of the new Millennium darkened for me when my beloved Eileen was diagnosed with renal failure. She had first started suffering undiagnosed pain a couple of months after we had got back from a tour of Australia. I took her off to Barbados for three weeks, hoping the sun would cure the problem. But she had no energy or appetite to walk the beautiful beaches, and when we got home she was immediately put on to three times a week dialysis treatment.

I had always been a BUPA client, but the first time we needed them they pointed us to the small print that revealed we were not covered for kidney problems. The NHS took Eileen under their wing, and for the next six years were continually attentive and caring.

In a panic, I cashed in two pension policies so that I could cut down on my workload and give my attention to Eileen. Stupid boy. I frittered the money and am paying for that rash decision now, and if you know anybody facing a similar dilemma talk them into hanging on to the policies, if possible.

My son Michael and I became experts at loading the home dialysis machine. We were offered care workers, but preferred to do it ourselves for a wonderful woman who had always willingly devoted her time to others. I gave Eileen her EPO injections, and we'd joke about her winning the Tour de France.

We celebrated our Ruby Wedding by retaking our vows, and became closer and more loving than ever in what were last precious years together. Eileen, who had a laugh that lit up any room and company, never once complained throughout the long battle, and was surrounded by the love of her family. Daughter Lisa and son-in-law John, son Michael and daughter-in-law Sarah and grandchildren Alexander, Katharine and James were the driving forces that kept her going long past the three years that the doctors privately gave as her likely survival span. Daniel arrived after her departure. How she would have adored him, a real bright spark with his grand mum's intelligence and tolerance.

Eileen suffered six bouts of the dreaded MRSA infections, and was finally reduced to wanting to pack it in after an operation had failed to clear a complication. It was at her firm request that the hospital quietly agreed to switch off her life-support machine. It was 15 August 2006.

As I prepared to spend the last hours with her in a private side room, I made a point of making sure my last words to her were what I had been saying for 45 years: "Night night, darling. I love you."

She, as usual, replied: "And I love you."

Wonderful last words, I thought.

A sister came into the room with a camp bed that needed (simple) erecting. I was telling the sister that I was the type who got trapped inside deck chairs when a voice came from the bed: "He's an idiot.."

Yes, famous last words.

We gave Eileen a smashing farewell, a celebration of her life at a humanist funeral with no black and everybody encouraged to wear bright clothes. Jimmy and Irene Greaves and Henry and Albina Cooper were among those who came all the way down to Bournemouth to share in the send-off.

I set up a Wall of Love online, with people pledging to buy a brick in Eileen's memory. We raised more than £15,000 for a dialysis machine for Dorchester Hospital, with the indefatigable Ricky Tomlinson kindly handing over the cheque.

Throughout her long illness, Eileen used to nag me not to be on my own after she had passed on. She, understandably, considered me useless at looking after myself. I think even she would have been dumbstruck when I took Joyce as my bride a month short of her 90th birthday.

It was not long after I had discovered that Eileen was seriously ill that I was rocked by the sudden death of Brian Moore. I was sitting at home in September 2001 watching England destroying Germany 5-1 in Munich when I got a telephone call during the match from Simon Moore, telling me his Dad had died following a heart problem. For the last 15 minutes of that England triumph, I watched the screen with tears rolling down my cheeks, and dwelling on the poignancy of the timing of Brian's passing.

I was privileged to be trusted with the eulogy to one of the nicest people I'd ever met, paying respects to Moore the Man, while Bob Wilson beautifully and emotionally talked about Moore the Broadcaster.

My family started calling me The Undertaker after I had been privileged to deliver the eulogies in a short, chilling time span for a dozen friends including Mooro, Jimmy Greaves, Terry Spinks, Terry Lawless, journalist pals Peter Batt, Dennis Signy and cartoonist genius Roy Ullyett.

And I'm still here. Just. But I've got my love to keep me warm. Thanks, Joyce.

In the new Millennium I teamed up with that Scouse rascal Ricky Tomlinson for a series of four books inspired by his *Royle Family* catchphrase, '*My Arse*'. To be in the company of Ricky is like being caught up in a whirlwind of mischief and banter. In all the years we've known each other I don't think we've had a conversation that makes sense. His laugh sets me laughing, and I'm gone. Thank goodness, he has a gorgeous and wise wife, Rita, who keeps him tethered to a semblance of sanity.

It was Rita who did all our negotiating with the book publishers, and got us a joint writing deal that helped me through the barren times when Eileen was desperately ill.

I have rarely met a couple like the Tomlinsons, full of Liverpool love and good humour. They are also people who put action where their mouths are. Without fuss or fanfare, they gave more than £1million to an Alder Hey hospital charity that houses the families of sick children.

He will tell me off for writing about it here, but I am determined to broadcast it because it's a gesture that restores faith in human beings. It would have been easy for Ricky and Rita to go and spend the money on flashy cars and huge villas, but that is not their style ... and I love them for it.

Our four books together, written and published over a span of eighteen months, were *Football My Arse* (a collection of true, funny soccer stories), *Celebrities My Arse* (anecdotes about famous people), *Cheers My Arse* (tales revolving around bar-room tales), and the one of which we are most proud, *Reading My Arse*, the search for the Rock Island Line.

It is a short novel about a young Scouser going to America in the 1960s to trace the route of the Rock Island Line railway that features in Ricky's favourite 1950s skiffle song hit by Lonnie Donegan.

The book was written for the Government-sponsored *Quick Reads* project along with more than a dozen other celebrity-driven books aimed at first-time readers, and ours was officially voted the best of the crop.

We tried to get another project off the ground, *Ricky's Joke Shop*, which we made with director/producer Brian Klein as a pilot for BBCtv. Ricky was the proprietor of a joke shop, with 'Norman the Doorman' Collier as the handyman, and one of our guests was David Seaman, England goalkeeper at the time, who kept dropping everything he was handed (well I thought it was funny).

The executive who ordered the pilot left the Beeb, and her successor decided Ricky's character would have weakened the appeal of his award-winning performances as Jim Royle.

My arse!

For a couple of years I worked closely with Alan Zafer, a London-based expert organiser of high-powered conferences and promotions. Noel Edmonds was one of his regularly employed presenters, and along with Alan I came up with a 'Noel Edmonds Road Show' project to launch a new high-tech Sony television. This was all before Noel took off with his Saturday Road Show on BBCtv.

Noel was one of the few broadcasters I found in the class of Eamonn Andrews for professionalism and passion for his work, and we shared the ignominy of being dismissed halfway through a corporate assignment.

During rehearsals, one of the edit-suite crew had, for a laugh, slipped in a video of a spoof commercial showing half a dozen beautiful ladies bouncing on rubber space hoppers fixed with vibrators, and the one who had the longest orgasm revealed that she was using Duracell batteries.

We all had a good laugh and then got on with the rehearsal.

That evening, to our horror, we found that the vibrator video had been left in the running order featuring the client's wares and was well on its way to its, uh, climax before Alan Zafer was able to get it switched off.

The chairman of the company was an American with a strict Bible Belt background, and he sacked Alan Zafer and Associates – including the presenter and the scriptwriter – during the show's interval. We were told we would never work for his company again.

As we left the hotel a witty DJ had slipped the Beach Boys on to the turntable, singing Good Vibrations. Not a happy ending.

Imaginative Fleet Street executive Tom Clarke was always coming up with bright ideas, and once – when George Best was hitting the headlines during one of his drink-driven adventures – he gave me an *Evening Standard* assignment, which to this day makes me tremble at the memory.

He fixed up for me to interview a professor of psychology at one of our most prominent universities. The premise was that we would set up four casebooks of troubled sportsmen, and come to a conclusion as to how they could be helped to overcome their problems.

The professor turned out to be one of those intellectuals who never used a two-syllable word when a five-syllable word would do. He answered my questions with replies that were so deep and philosophical that I was relieved I was recording our two-hour interview. I did not take a note because I was so busy trying to understand what the prof was saying.

When later that day I got back home to my study to write the 3,000-word double-page feature, I turned on the tape recorder and started listening to nothing. The tape had jammed in the opening seconds and all I heard was: "Tell me, professor, what would you advise George Best to do if..?"

Gripped by panic, I quickly jotted down anything and everything I could remember from the interview. I then wrote the feature and dictated it to one of those copytakers who said, typically: "Much more of this …?" after the first couple of hundred words. That was all I needed, a bored copytaker who could shoot down an adlib from 10 paces.

My feature ran through the six editions of the Standard and brought a herogram from Tom, praising me for a "profound and compelling feature."

At round about the same time, I got a telephone call from a mad professor threatening legal action for "misrepresenting me and putting phrases into my mouth that I have never uttered in my life."

I threw myself on his mercy and explained, like a stuttering schoolboy, about the tape recorder. He reluctantly accepted my explanation, and made it clear he never ever wanted to speak to me again. I was going to write a book about it: Planet of the Tapes (I'll get my coat).

I am to technology what Albert Einstein was to ladies' hairdressing, but I was determined to be aboard the computer revolution, which started for me with the launch of the Microwriter, a six-key word processor. When it was first advertised by scriptwriting legend Denis Norden I talked Jimmy Greaves into coming with me to test it at a shop in Holborn. He is left handed, and within minutes of having the machine in his palm he threw it across the counter in frustration.

I bought one for £450, the equivalent of around £1500 today, and persevered with it to the extent that I got up to typing speeds that matched that on a conventional typewriter. I had it hooked to my television, and could write direct to the screen and then print it out on a daisywheel printer, restricted to a 10pt pica typeface.

The Microwriter had a single line LCD display, and you entered text by pushing combinations of buttons, almost like playing chords on a piano, and as a natural master of the piano keyboard it came easily to me (all those who have heard me play the piano will know this is a self-mocking joke).

I wrote the first half of a Greavsie novel on the Microwriter, and just as I had got used to it, Apple came along with the revolutionary ApplePlus, and the Microwriter was, for me, suddenly redundant.

I got myself a normangiller@telecomgold.com email address, but gave it up after a year because there were so few people to email. I was talking to myself. The computer explosion was around the corner, and I have been an Apple disciple for more than 40 years. Yes, right at the core of the revolution.

I have always had a comedy writer fighting to get out (yes, I know, I failed to release him), and along with the Eric Morecambe columns I ghosted special articles featuring several of the masters, including Tommy Cooper and Benny Hill, who were among the few in Eric's league.

I got as close as anybody could to Benny, an intensely private man, with football as our common ground. He had no interest in the English game, but was fascinated by European clubs and he used to send me postcards of Europe's major grounds from his lone Continental trips, during which he gathered material for his hilarious but (now) non-PC shows.

Benny lived alone in an apartment virtually next door to the Teddington Studios, where I worked extensively in television and video production, and I used to call in for coffee and a chat about football. He showed me a script in which he had created a comic goalkeeper who saved everything with his backside, and was called Hugh Jarse. Well I thought it was funny.

The contrast between Benny and Eric Morecambe was startling. Eric buried himself in the warmth of family love and life, while Benny liked his own company and was painfully shy until adopting comedy characters within whose personalities he could hide his complexes. He would have given Sigmund Freud a field day.

Tommy Cooper on the other hand was larger than life, and sadly often drunk when I used to interview him for a series of 'laugh-along' columns. He knew he could make me break up with just a shrug of his wide shoulders, and I rarely got a second's sense out of him.

He was once an amateur boxer when in the Welsh Guards, and I brought him together with namesake Henry Cooper for a comedy crosstalk. One line I recall: "I decided to retire after shadow boxing. My shadow knocked me out in the second, just like that."

Because of my newspaper background, Tommy was suspicious of me, paranoid about it becoming public property that he was involved in a long-running affair. He used to pretend to frisk me like a customs officer when I was leaving him.

"Just want to make sure you're not taking any secrets with you," he'd say with that trademark laugh. But it was a warning not to tell any tales out of school. I obeyed, just like that.

One of the best gigs I had during my headline and deadline chasing days was a back to back scriptwriting assignment at the annual Laureus Sports Awards ceremonies when they were staged in Monaco in 2003 and 2004. If you are fed up with my name dropping on the previous pages, just wait until you see the upcoming selection of celebrities with whom I worked.

Let's start with Sean Connery, who to my mind remains the best and most believable 007 James Bond. Sir Sean was in Monte Carlo making a presentation in honour of the memory of Kiwi yachting legend Sir Peter Blake, who had been murdered by pirates while leading an environmental expedition on the Amazon in 2001.

I tested Sir Sean's trademark Edinburgh-hewn lisp by giving him John Masefield's *Sea Fever* to narrate. Read it aloud with a lisp:

I must go down to the sea again, to the lonely sea and the sky
And all I ask is a tall ship and a star to steer her by;
And the wheel's kick and the wind's song and the white sail's shaking,
And a grey mist on the sea's face, and a grey dawn breaking.

Sir Sean delivered it beautifully, and there was not a dry eye in the glitzy Grimaldi Forum. The lisp made it even more memorable.

During rehearsals I reminded him of the visit of England's World Cup footballers to the Pinewood set when he was filming his James Bond role in *You Only Live Twice*;

This was when Alf Ramsey referred to him as Seen, and Bobby Moore said it was the "funniest thing I've ever shawn or heard."

Sir Sean had a good laugh at the recollection and insisted on sharing the story with former All Blacks captain Sean Fitzpatrick, who was in the theatre with us. They spent the rest of the day calling each other Seen.

Laureus is the premier sporting charity organisation in the world, and their Academy is made up of 52 of the greatest sporting champions in history. Over the course of the two awards ceremonies I put the words into the mouths of such sporting icons as John McEnroe, Bobby Charlton, Gary Player, Ian Botham, Ed Moses, Dawn Fraser, Seb Coe, Tanni Grey-Thompson, Olga Korbut, Nadia Comaneci and Franz Beckenbauer.

Each award was presented by a combination of sports star and show business celebrity, and the likes of Michael Douglas, Morgan Freeman, David Hasselhoff, and Rod Stewart all read my Autocued words.

For the rehearsal in 2004, Rod Stewart came on stage with his soon-to-be-wife Penny Lancaster. Just to complicate matters his previous wife, Rachel Hunter, was also making a presentation, and I was charged by the show producer, Paul Kirrage, with keeping the two stunning ladies apart.

With this in mind, I was not giving total concentration when Penny introduced me to her father while the rehearsals were in full swing.

I was quite a sight to behold. On the first day in the theatre I had managed to fall through the stage and had damaged my size 8 right foot so badly that I had to borrow a size 13 sports shoe to cover the swelling. I was hobbling around like Quasimodo, and got no sympathy whatsoever from Ian Botham, who inspected my wound in front of the Laureus members and announced: "Think it may need an amputation. You certainly won't be fit for Saturday."

Three days later and still hobbling on my size 13 shoe, I was at Nice Airport ready for the flight home when I spotted producer/director Paul Kirrage talking to, so I thought, Penny Lancaster's father.

Now Penny just happens to have the most gorgeous legs that go on and on for ever, and I limped up to the side of Paul and took an exaggerated long view of what I thought was her quite short father.

"Well," I declared like an old-time music hall comedian, "I see she doesn't get her legs from you."

Two stony faces turned to me, with no hint of even a smile. I was obviously not welcome and so limped heavily away. I presumed I had interrupted a business conversation.

Five minutes later I was grabbed by Paul Kirrage and pushed into a corner. He never usually swears, but for this occasion dropped his standards.

"What the f***ing hell were you thinking of, saying that?"

"Saying what?" I asked, innocently.

"About her legs. Who d'you think you were talking to?"

"Penny Lancaster's dad," I replied.

"That," said Paul, about to deliver one of those sentences that remain etched into your memory for life, "is Tanni Grey-Thompson's manager."

Oh dear. What a plonker. I can now never look at wheelchaired Paralympic legend Dame Tanni (or Penny Stewart) without getting a red tide creeping up my face. And I feel a pain in my foot.

Footnote: I sued the hugely wealthy owners of the Laureus concept for my injury, but after lots of side stepping I found myself in a legal showdown with a pair of freelance British stage builders. I tried to pull out but was told by my legal team that if I did I would have to pay the £14,000 costs accrued to date. I finished up settling out of court for £6,000, with the solicitor's bill somewhere up around the £25,000 mark.

Next time around, I'm going to be a lawyer. A profession with legs.

After staying Press Box neutral for all my years writing about football, I was at last able to come out of the closet as a Tottenham disciple once I stopped live match reporting. In harness with A1 Sporting Speakers CEO Terry Baker, I produced a string of Spurs-themed books and we also worked together on memoirs with Pelé and Gordon Banks, and Sir Geoff Hurst, Sir Trevor Brooking and dear old Ron 'Chopper' Harris.

What disturbed me as I moved into the autumn years is how many of my sporting heroes have suffered for the fame they enjoyed. Just take Tottenham, for example. Arthur Rowe, Alf Ramsey, Tommy Harmer, Peter Baker, Ron Henry, Danny Blanchflower, Dave Mackay and Terry Venables all ended up not knowing their names, or having any recall of what they had achieved during their distinguished careers. .

Many of my old boxing buddies suffered pugilistic dementia and as I write former foes Joe Bugner and Richard Dunn are both struggling. The thought of middle-aged women stumbling around appals me as more of them become attracted to the brutal sport.

Alzheimer's is a terrible illness and we must do everything to combat it, which is why I got behind the campaign of Jeff Astle's devoted daughters to raise awareness of how it affects former sportsmen. Much of it, of course, is down to heading those old leather, laced footballs that weighed the same as today's 'beach balls' at kick-off (llb, 16oz, 0.45kg), but they were not water resistant and often weighed twice as much at the end of games.

I feel I have to try to put something back for all the pleasure those footballers gave me in the days before the game was swimming in money, and so all the profits from my Spurs-themed books go to the Tottenham Tribute Trust that quietly does an incredible job helping our old heroes who have hit difficult times. Reporting on their deeds was a privilege, and I believe they all deserve our support. The wealthiest clubs, picking up millions from their television contracts, should set up funds for all those veteran footballers who missed the gravy train.

I appear to have dodged the dementia curse (more famous last words), and keep my writing hand in with Fleet Street nostalgia thoughts for Mike Berry's *BackPass* magazine, and weekly blogs on all things Tottenham on Paul Smith's informative *Spurs Odyssey* website.

Now over to my new wife, who is blessed with all her faculties, for some final thoughts. But she has never headed a ball in her life ...

Chapter Twenty:
Palace of Dreams

F EW people could have had experiences to match those that Joyce enjoyed as she approached her 90th birthday. I will let her tell her tales of the unexpected as we come towards the close of our joint adventure since both starting out in London's East End back in the day when the world seemed young and we had our lives before us. The day before yesterday ...

"Anglia Batteries had been my life for 50 years. After down sizing to a smaller premises facing our London Road shop our manager Rob Lambourne expressed interest in running the company. This suited Steven and Michael. So I sold the business while retaining the properties and got on with my whirlwind of committees and keeping busy at the Iveagh Club.

"Then Norman Giller was introduced into my life. Suddenly all my plans for a slow descent into old age as a dedicated widow went up in the air.

"It all started with Norman's out-of-the-blue proposal in front of the statue of Sir David Amess on Westcliff-on-Sea beach on September 3 2024. I could not understand why he was so keen to get me in front of the memorial to a great man we had both admired. I still didn't twig as he handed his iPhone to a passing lady and asked her to take a photograph. It was an awful afternoon, with a gale-force wind whipping across the front and when he dramatically went down on one knee I thought he'd been blown over.

"Looking back it was hilarious, but confusing at the time. I do not have the best hearing and I could just make out what he was saying, and he repeated what I thought he'd said, 'I want us to spend our sunset years together. Will you marry me ...?'

"I bent forward and kissed him, and the lady holding the mobile telephone shouted, 'Congratulations' Goodness me, we had stumbled on somebody who was so with-it that she had videoed the moment (which Norman has posted on YouTube),

"I was completely numbed by what was happening. Here I was, a month short of my 90th birthday and this gorgeous man was down on one knee proposing to me. Was I dreaming?

"My kiss was a sign of my acceptance. The stranger who had witnessed it all while using Norman's mobile, hugged us both and then wandered off without us asking her name. We have not seen her since and are desperate to thank her. If you know who she is, please, please get in touch. Norman's email is normangiller@gmail.com

"At the time of Norman's proposal, we were on our way to see my two sons, Steven and Michael, at the Roslin Beach Hotel in Thorpe Bay to discuss plans for my 90th birthday party in November. I was still in a state of shock when we told them what had just happened. I think they were as surprised as me.

"The Roslin's managing director is Jacqui Dallimore, a fantastic girl (ok, lady) I have known since she was born and who calls me Auntie Joyce. She happily reacted to news of the marriage proposal with instant schemes for the ceremony, planning it on a grand scale as if I was Jackie Kennedy/ Onassis. We finally brought her down to earth and settled for a small family wedding at the Roslin.

"Norman wanted to marry me on my 90th birthday, but this cut across a party already being planned by Steven and Michael and their wives Lucy and Alison. So we settled for an October 15 wedding at the Roslin and then a brief honeymoon in London, our favourite city.

"I was in a complete daze as we walked hand in hand from the Roslin after announcing we were getting married. Norman turned to me and said quietly, 'You know this is a special day in history.'

"I squeezed his hand, How romantic, I thought.

"Then he added: 'It's September 3, the anniversary of Britain declaring war on Germany in 1939.'

"Yes, how romantic.

"The next few weeks went by in a rush, and I felt as if I was in an Alice in Wonderland *fantasy. We had a wonderful wedding at the Roslin Beach Hotel, overseen by Registrars Tracey Holloway and Nicola Rogerson. Norman gave a Powerpoint presentation showing the history of how we had been born 400 yards apart and then being brought together as octogenarians by our 'children'. He finished it, just as my first Norman Lambert would have done, with a cheerful singalong, accompanied by his piano playing. It was*

moving and marvellous, and I was a very happy Mrs Norman Lambert Giller.

"My five-year-old great grandson Harrison overheard my granddaughter Rachel telling her husband Peter about our wedding plans, and piped up: 'But grandmas don't get married. They die.' Out of the mouths of babes.

"We had first pledged our love for each other when queuing for 14 hours to pay our respects to the Queen as she lay in State in Westminster in September 2022. It was freezing cold as we shuffled along the Thames Embankment, and as we huddled together to keep warm we kissed and expressed our mutual love. Barbara Cartland could not have made it up.

"After our memorable and intimate wedding ceremony at the Roslin, we had a whirlwind honeymoon in London, fitting in three West End shows all watched from front row Royal circle seats at Six, Operation Mincemeat and Les Miserables. We stayed in the honeymoon suite at the posh Chelsea Harbour hotel, and the highlight was a visit by Uber Boat to the ancient Battersea Power Station that has a brilliantly refurbished interior. If you are fortunate enough to go, please make sure you take the Lift 109 ride to the top of one of the huge chimneys. You get a whole new perspective of the city's skyline and have far-reaching views towards the South Coast. It is truly awe inspiring. Norman tells me he has already mentioned this, but I promise it is worth repeating!

"Our honeymoon was nicely interrupted by interest from scores of journalists and broadcasters, and we made appearances on Good Morning Britain, Anglia Television and Meridian TV. There were half a dozen national newspaper and magazine interviews and I got a taste of the studio life that Norman knew so well. During our GMB interview, he was delighted to be reunited with Sir Geoff Hurst and I learned first hand how close they used to be in the days when England ruled the football world. We later visited Irene, the widow of Jimmy Greaves, and she gave us her blessing. What a delightful lady with an East End background not unlike mine.

"When we returned home, we split our time between my Tower Court bungalow and Norman's coachhouse woodland hideaway in Daws Heath where he has set up home in the grounds of his son-in-law John and daughter Lisa's beautiful house.

"Next it was my fabulous 90th birthday party back at the Roslin Beach

It was an extraordinary feat to get the choir headlining there.

"Secretly, Sir David and my husband-to-be had been working on a song to boost his Southend-as-a-City campaign He was going to stand up in the House during Prime Minister Questions Time and sing the chorus:

> *'Good old Southend on Sea*
> *It's a lovely place to be*
> *So much to do, so much to see*
> *At Good old Southend on Sea'*

"The plan was to eventually involve the hugely talented David Stanley and his inspirational choir, The Music Man Project. But Sir David's chilling murder brought a halt to all the bold plans.

"The bubbly Anna Firth, replacing Sir David as our Southend MP, quietly took up the baton to lead the campaign for me to get the MBE. I understand that the Mayor, Stephen Habermel and the tireless Gill Lee were among those who got involved in pushing my nomination. It honestly makes me feel very humble and appreciative.

"We proudly announced my award of the MBE on New Year's Day 2025 at the superb Belfairs Golf course restaurant where we had first met. Norman organised a wonderful brunch attended by my dearest and closest family and friends. Norman had sent them all an invitation card, pointing out that – despite rumours – it was not a baby shower!

"I felt so privileged to be able to reveal that I was being decorated in the King's New Year's Honours List. At last I was able to talk about the award after being gagged for six weeks.

"This was how on-the-ball journalist George Pizani reported it in the Southend Echo:

A FORMER Conservative councillor and lifelong charity worker has been recognised for her services after Sir David Amess began her nomination before his tragic death.

Joyce Lambert Giller, 90, served as a councillor for Southend's Milton Ward in the late 1990s and was a close confidant of local MP for Southend

West, Sir David Amess, a fellow East Londoner..

Sir David put her forward for an MBE in the months before his death and former Southend West MP Anna Firth picked up the campaign to ensure Joyce was recognised for decades of hard work.

Now, Joyce has been appointed an MBE in the New Year Honours.

She is currently the chair of the Iveagh Conservative Club in Leigh, and the honorary treasurer of the Southend-on-Sea Society - a group working to protect the city's heritage.

"I feel so honoured and humble to receive this MBE," said Joyce."It takes a lot to make me speechless but I honestly did not know what to say when I opened the letter from the Cabinet

"To think it has happened to this little East End girl fills me with so much pride. I think of it as a belated prize for my dear old dad, John Palmer, who was a brave fire fighter in London during the Blitz and an unsung hero.

"I have always been community minded and it's been a privilege to be involved in so many ventures aimed at making Southend a better place. I've loved living in the Southend area since back in the immediate post-war years and when I first came here from East London to settle with my mum, dad and four Palmer sisters in 1945 there was still barbed wire along the front.

"Sir David Amess was, I understand, initially behind this recognition, and I so wish he was here to enjoy the moment with me.

"His murder was without doubt the lowest point. It was just one of those freak things that I was not with him helping organise his MP's clinic on that dreadful day when he was senselessly stabbed.

"There has never been such a man who wanted to help everybody regardless of their creed, colour or politics. I feel so desperately sorry for his widow Lady Julia. Nobody deserves what she has had to go through."

Joyce, who recently married her 85-year-old fiancé, Norman Giller, has spent decades volunteering with various community groups and for Conservative causes. In addition to her work in politics and charity, Joyce also had a successful career as a director of Leigh-based Anglia Battery and Filter Company.

Husband Norman said: "I deliberately made my marriage proposal to

Joyce in front of the Sir David Amess statue because I knew how important he was to Joyce. Both of them were East Enders and had a special bond.

"I am so grateful his successor as MP, Anna Firth, and the then mayor Stephen Habermel took up the campaign to get her this honour. I can think of nobody more deserving of this recognition from her peers.

"Since cruelly losing her first husband – another Norman – after 23 years of marriage she has devoted her life to others, particularly her two sons and her Anglia Battery business that has been prominent in Leigh for many years. She is a remarkable lady with boundless energy and I am struggling to keep up with her. I am so proud of what she has achieved and this MBE is thoroughly deserved. I think there's a book in it. Let's rejoice with Joyce!"

Ms Firth added: "I am so delighted Joyce's immense contribution to making Southend the best seaside City in the Country has been recognised by the King.

"Joyce is the most wonderful person, a uniquely talented entrepreneur who has helped so many people, myself included. The very best of Essex and Southend, and it was a huge privilege to support her award."

I could not have put it better myself about my 'child bride'.

Chapter Twenty-one:
The Music Man Project

AND so we come to the third part of this three-in-one book – *The Music Man Project*. Joyce and I were inspired by Sir David Amess to get behind one of the most dedicated and uplifting choirs we have ever seen and heard, and we know there are a lot of people out there who share our assessment.

It was Sir David who first nagged and cajoled Joyce into following the choir, and she quickly picked up the vibe as to why they were well worth not only her ear but her time. Then Joyce took me to see them in full voice and I instantly became a disciple of a choir that pleased your ears while tearing at your heartstrings. If you have not seen them, please make a date to rectify that as soon as possible. You cannot fail but be inspired as well as being thoroughly entertained. For your diary: They are back at the Royal Albert Hall with Michael Ball on May 25 2026.

Sir David was not content just to listen to to the Choir. He became their champion and enthusiastic cheer leader and eventually their President, a role he described as the "most satisfying of my life." It was largely because of his drive and contacts that the Choir got to perform in such prime venues as the London Palladium and the Royal Albert Hall.

When he was cruelly taken from us, the two Davids – Amess and Stanley – were working on bold plans to get the *Music Man Project* to New York and an appearance on Broadway. It was an unbalanced terrorist with a knife who delayed but did not kill off the dream.

Following is *The Music Man Project* Story, starting from scratch and eventually receiving the King's Award for Voluntary Service in 2024 (the equivalent of an MBE for groups) .

This is their inspiring story ...

•Founded by the UK's Disability and Access Ambassador for Arts and Culture and Churchill Fellow, David Stanley BEM, *The Music Man Project* is a multi-award-winning, world record-breaking international music education charity for people with learning disabilities.

The Project provides accessible music tuition leading to inspirational performances, gives grants for accessible arts education, promotes equal access to performance, carries out research and raises awareness of the achievements of disadvantaged people in the arts.

Led by their world famous Global Ambassadors, *The Music Man Project* performed critically acclaimed original productions at the West End's London Palladium and the iconic Royal Albert Hall.

They entertained members of the Royal Family, opened a national TV advert, appeared on the BBC, ITV and Sky TV, and recorded with His Majesty's Bands of the Royal Marines.

They hold the world record for the largest triangle ensemble, delivered a music workshop at 10 Downing Street for the Prime Minister, danced with Mr Speaker at the House of Commons and received a standing ovation from His Majesty The King.

In April 2024 *The Music Man Project* returned to the Royal Albert Hall for their most spectacular concert yet, supported by the Band of His Majesty's Royal Marines and featuring musical theatre legend and *Music Man Project* patron, Michael Ball.

In June they stole the show at the Royal Nova Scotia International Tattoo in front of 20,000 people and in September they performed alongside Italian charity *AllegroModerato* in Milan.

The charity oversees a network of regional teaching hubs in counties across England and has reached every nation of the UK. It has also impacted communities thousands of miles away in South Africa, India, Nepal, USA and the Philippines.

Regional *Music Man Projects* are officially licenced for free, enabling them to access exclusive music, teaching resources and performance opportunities specifically created for musicians with learning disabilities.

The Music Man Project is proud to work in partnership with global marketing company Team Lewis, His Majesty's Bands of the Royal Marines and the Salvation Army.⁹

We went to the multi-talented David Stanley BEM for these remarkable background facts on the man who has voluntarily breathed life and delight into *The Music Man Project:*

•In 1999, I taught music to a young man called Tony, who had Downs Syndrome. I did it out of compassion for one individual and it felt wonderful.

The transformative effect of my music on Tony led me to teach a small group of people with learning disabilities.

I promised them that one day they would play the Royal Albert Hall. It was a joke that became a dream that became an ambition and obsession. Remarkably, 20 years later, I presented 200 children and adults with learning disabilities from across the UK in a groundbreaking concert at the Royal Albert Hall. I taught the students, produced the show and composed the music.

It was the UK's largest ever celebration of accessible music-making, featuring orchestra, massed choirs and celebrity guests, and played to an audience of over 3000 people. It took two decades to fulfil my promise and I battled prejudice, ignorance and barriers to opportunity on behalf of this once-forgotten society.

After my initial, small group sessions, I started a weekly music school with local charity Southend Mencap and then, in 2012, I gave up my job as a Deputy Head Teacher in a mainstream secondary school to start a full-time accessible music education and performance service. The decision was enormously risky for the security of my young family, but I felt called to make this my life's work.

I knew that I would be solely responsible for either my failure or my success and this felt incredibly empowering. I read a testimonial from the mother of a severely autistic child who said,

"Without David, my daughter would still be sitting in the corner of the lounge getting more fearful and frustrated with life, leading me into a deeper and darker place wondering if there was ever going to be any good come into hers or my life". [Saturday Music School Parent]

Inspired by these words, I founded *The Music Man Project*, a new charity dedicated to sharing my work around the world.

Concerts at the London Palladium, a Guinness World Record, performances to members of the Royal Family, a National Lottery TV advert appearance, multiple awards and our Royal Albert Hall debut all followed within eight years. With no ongoing, private or state funding, our achievements all came from my single act of compassion with Tony in 1999.

Now I spend my time finding new ways to reach more people with my music, with plans to launch a *Music Man Project* in every county in England, in every country in the UK and in every country in the world.

I began this journey by helping other people set up their own versions of my accessible music education and performance service across the UK as well as in South Africa, India, Nepal, the Philippines and the USA.

I share my music, my teaching resources, my brand and concert opportunities for free. In doing so, my original act of compassion gets multiplied infinitely every day. I am passionate about using my music to free the constraints placed on people with a learning disability across the world, joining this remarkable community together through song, country by country.

My compassion has given me more that I could ever have imagined. I have the best job in the world and my students have created more opportunities for me to make a difference in this world than they will ever know. For example, I am a Hate Crime Ambassador, helping disabled victims report crimes to the Police.

I am a Global Peace Ambassador for People with Disabilities (Global Peace Challenge 2020), a trustee for individuals with no living relatives, an advocate for families and a campaigner for equal opportunities for people with disabilities. I speak to people impacted by these issues every day and tell their stories through my music (such as my musical 'From the Asylum to the Palladium' at London Palladium in 2015), on my monthly radio show, my podcasts, my blogs and in published articles.

At the heart of my compassion is my love for my students. I think they are the best of humanity because they are incapable of hate. My late grandfather worked in mental hospitals in the 1940s and 50s. These were places where anyone that society deemed to be different would be treated as medically sick patients.

My grandfather would have witnessed the administration of mind-numbing drugs, electric shock therapy and even lobotomy to people with learning disabilities constrained in straitjackets. They didn't have any personal possessions or even their own clothes. Many of these people needed nothing more than kindness and the opportunity to express who they were. I am told that my grandfather showed extraordinary compassion for his patients despite such awful circumstances. Ever since my own act of compassion with Tony, I have been professionally and emotionally immersed within this community. I am extremely close to my students and their families trust me with their lives. I have a deep understanding of the challenges they face just to exist (isolation and loneliness, poverty, physical and mental health problems, dementia, Hate Crime, prejudice, inequality and ignorance) and I feel a responsibility to use my music to help them thrive.

The COVID-19 pandemic reversed years of progress, effectively forcing people with disabilities to return to institutional isolation, to medicalisation rather than the community engagement which our disability reformers fought for decades to achieve.

During the pandemic, I created an online platform to entertain and engage people with learning disabilities around the world and even visited my students to sing and play on their doorsteps. With emergency Government funding, my charity delivered £6000 worth of musical instruments to isolated families and devices for the most difficult-to-reach people to access the internet.

Compassion must be shared in order to spread throughout the world, and I feel a deep responsibility to share my story with as many people as possible. In 2019, I was awarded a Churchill Fellowship which enabled me to learn from world-leading examples of accessible music education in New York. I was also recognised in the 2021 Queen's New Honours List for services to people with Special Needs. My belief, supported by ground-breaking, empirical research at the world's top music conservatoire, is that the challenges faced by most vulnerable communities can be addressed through creative expression, self-worth and a sense of purpose.

This is why my approach is educational, creative and performance-based rather than clinical or corrective Music Therapy. In 2016, I gave a performance and lecture at the Royal College of Music and my work is now the subject of a PhD at this world-famous conservatoire.

I want the amazing achievements of my students to give hope to new parents who feel such despair when they first gaze upon their disabled children. I want to share their stories and show how my music transforms lives for the better. With musical opportunity, parents not only witness their children becoming stars of the Royal Albert Hall, but they also witness them becoming more confident, disciplined and balanced individuals capable of inspiring us all.

I also want to empower and enable musicians like me to use their talents for the greater good, showing them how to achieve success in this field and why it is so important to do so.

Too often, musicians who don't reach the elite level give up on the Arts and tragically waste their gifts and years of training. I have shown that there are many ways to scale a mountain, and sometimes the biggest reward comes when you carve your own path. I have demonstrated a way to unlock the inner compassion that lies within us all.

Voluntary service has always been at the heart of my campaign for more inclusive music education and performance. From helpers at regional teaching sessions, to technicians and performers at our concerts, to our charity directors and trustees, we owe so much to the kindness of individuals who give their time and expertise for the greater good. They improve the world for a community that was once overlooked, and in return, we all gain valuable lessons from individuals with learning disabilities.

I proudly lead the national Music Man Project charity as founder and CEO on an entirely voluntary basis. It's a commitment which has become part of my everyday life. It's the only way I could duplicate my approach across the country and around the world with a zero budget. I'm therefore delighted that The Music Man Project has been acknowledged for its dedication to volunteering thanks to the exceptional and unique work of our highly-regarded Music Man Project Global Ambassadors.

Every ambassador has a learning disability, but far from them receiving voluntary service, they are the volunteers. They've worked tirelessly to increase musical opportunities for disabled people, supporting our charity objectives of promoting equal access to performance and raising awareness of the achievements of disadvantaged people in the arts.

I've known some of these musicians for 25 years. During this time I've witnessed them transform from vulnerable children into powerful musical role models who educate and inspire everyone they meet. Over the last four years they've also supported me in my voluntary role as the UK's Disability and Access Ambassador for Arts and Culture. They've helped the UK become a global beacon for inclusive music.

The life of a *Music Man Project* volunteer ambassador is demanding to say the least! They're expected to tour the UK to launch regional Projects, build national partnerships and professional musical collaborations, teach accessible music workshops to mainstream and Special School pupils, deliver disability awareness training and team building for the corporate sector, lead performances, assist other students, help shape the future direction of the charity and promote *The Music Man Projec*t in the media!

The ambassador's record of impact is extraordinary. They've taught over 16,000 children at their inspirational music workshops across Essex schools. They travel thousands of miles every year to bring the magic of our music to communities across the UK and around the world - thanks to their efforts, we now oversee a network of 14 regional *Music Man Projects*. They've played the London Palladium twice and the Royal Albert Hall four times, most recently leading 300 of their fellow musicians in *The Music Man Project's* massed concert at the Royal Albert Hall in April 2024.

They even received a standing ovation from His Majesty, The King with their rendition of Music is Magic for the Royal Marines' Mountbatten Festival of Music at the Royal Albert Hall.

The ambassadors have also opened a national TV advert, performed with musical theatre legend, Michael Ball and featured on the BBC, ITV and Sky TV. They regularly appear with His Majesty's Bands of the Royal Marines and recorded a Christmas single with their friends which reached the top 10 in the iTunes chart in 2022.

In Canada, they stole the show at the Royal Nova Scotia International Tattoo in front of 20,000 people. And they recently performed alongside an Italian disability charity at a concert in Milan.

These activities helped raise awareness of our charity, inspired new communities to emulate Southend's original service and generated tens of thousands of pounds for our cause. Without *The Music Man Project* Ambassadors, there would be no Royal Albert Hall concerts for our regional projects. There would be no Royal Marines partnership, no Michael Ball patronage and no start-up funding for new centres. For more information about The Music Man Project Global Ambassadors, visit www.themusicmanproject. com/ambassadors.

My next ambitions are to enable my students to perform a concert tour in New York, to present at the UN, to write a book and to give our charity a home in a purpose-built headquarters.

I want to complete my mission to expand my musical family in the UK and overseas so that I connect this remarkable community through song. I have no way of funding any of this, but I had no way of funding any of what I have achieved thus far in my life. I have found compassion to be the greatest currency on earth.'

This is how the Southend *Evening Echo* reported that incredible concert at the London Palladium when a new world record was set for the number of people playing the triangle ...

THE Prime Minister Theresa May has championed a record-breaking Southend charity that supports people with learning difficulties. She congratulated the *Music Man Project*, run by the Southend Mencap charity, after it broke the Guinness World Record for the largest ever ensemble of musicians playing the triangle.

The group performed Concerto for Trumpet, Trombone and 1,521 Triangles by *Music Man Project* founder, David Stanley, live at the London Palladium.

After their No 1 supporter Sir David Amess, MP for Southend West, congratulated the group for the record-breaking performance, Theresa May also showed her support by tweeting about the project.

She said: "Sir David is right to be a proud supporter of the excellent Music Man Project, based in his constituency.

"It is a wonderful music education service specifically for children and adults with learning difficulties."

Sir David expressed his pride for the group after breaking the record. He said: "I am proud to have witnessed the award-winning Music Man Project's world record triumph at the London Palladium. It has taken an enormous effort by David Stanley and his team to pull it all together. I am privileged to have played a part ... including striking one of the triangles. You could describe me as 'tingling'"

The record was created by 200 musicians from Essex, Suffolk, Sussex and London, plus a sell-out audience at the famous London Palladium - smashing the previous record of 876 triangles.

Speaking about the achievement, Mr Stanley said: "They are all world record holders!

"It was such a thrilling night at the Palladium, and to break the world record was a fantastic achievement."

The record attempt was audited by Leigh chartered accountants Francis James & Partners LLP, who provided 50 stewards for the official count.

The performance was conducted by Music Man regional directors, Jenny Hitchcock and Natalie Bradford, featuring Jemma Andrews on trumpet and Leisa Jones on trombone.

The piece was performed before a packed out Palladium with Sophie, Countess of Wessex, in attendance.

At the Palladium, Mr Stanley also announced project's debut concert at the Royal Albert Hall in April 2019.

The concert has been a dream for Mr Stanley and his team since 2001 when he promised his students they would one day perform at there.

Mr Stanley added: "At the current rate of expansion, the Royal Albert Hall concert will feature our Music Man Project students from across the country.

"It will be the world's greatest celebration of accessible music-making ever."

In anticipation of the next performance, Sir David said: "I am thrilled that they will now be performing at the Royal Albert Hall in April 2019. Everybody whoever sees and hears this choir is immediately converted to becoming not only a supporter but an advocate of everything they stand for. It gives me untold pleasure to be involved with them as Pfresident . I consider it an honour and a privilege.

"I cannot give David Stanley enough praise for the tireless work he carries out to make the choir what it is. The Music Man Project is his concept and it provides educational services to children and adults with learning difficulties.

"Everybody's heart fills with joy when they listen to them perform. If we could spread the enthusiasm and sheer joy they convey the world would be a much better place."

Now meet the hero who was Sir David Amess ... and our army of Philanthropists. The tributes to Sir David by a procession of distinguished Lords and Ladies are well worth reading. They will give you an insight into just how special he was ...

Appendix
Remembering Sir David Amess

WE turned to *Hansard*, the record of what is said in Parliament, to capture how respected Sir David Amess was by his fellow Politicians. This is a cross-section of the tributes paid to him in a moving and emotional House of Lords debate :.

The first contribution came from the Lord Speaker, **Lord McFall of Alcluith**

•My Lords, before I call the Leader of the House to begin the tributes to the late Sir David Amess MP, I would like to make some brief remarks of my own: Sir David was not a Member of this House, but he was one of us. He was a true Parliamentarian. He was also an exemplar of decency and courtesy. When I entered Parliament in 1987, Sir David had already served in the Commons for four years. I quickly found myself working with him on cross-party and international issues, as well as on social campaigns and causes that promoted the common good. David relished working across the party divides. He was not tribal. As an example to the society we live in, he embraced minorities and was tolerant, not intolerant. His willingness to reach out and engage with those he represented went to the heart of what he considered to be his vocation in life. He could never have been accused of being remote or detached.

He championed Private Members' Bills on animal welfare and fuel poverty, always speaking up for his constituents and placing their concerns at the heart of his work here in Westminster. He was well known in his local area and was keen to engage the local press in his many campaigns; his frequent engagement with the sub-editors obviously paid off when, following a trip to Rome, one headline read "Pope Francis meets David Amess".

His character was well known. At the weekend, I heard one TV commentator refer to him as a little eccentric. Well, if that was the case, I declare: long live eccentrics. Not once did I meet him in these corridors over the 34 years we served together without being met with an enormous smile as he bounded toward me with a spring in his step. He had an ability to make every encounter bright, something which reminded me time and again of the inherent goodness of humanity.

Today, Parliament mourns. We join with his family, his friends, his staff and those who knew him and worked with him. It is right that we conclude our proceedings today by joining together with the House of Commons to pray for him, remember him and celebrate all that he was and all that he gave to this place and to the nation.❥

The Lord Privy Seal
(Baroness Evans of Bowes Park (Con)

❧Like all noble Lords, I was shocked, shaken and saddened by the tragic death of Sir David Amess on Friday. He was killed while holding a constituency surgery in a place of sanctuary, serving the residents of Southend West as he had done proudly since 1997. As the Lord Speaker said, Sir David was a veteran Parliamentarian of almost four decades who was admired and respected across both Houses of Parliament. Only three other sitting MPs have served the House of Commons and their constituents longer than Sir David had.

A working-class boy from the East End of London, Sir David was first elected in Basildon, in 1983. It was a bellwether seat for the 1992 general election which he held on to with the backing of Essex men—and women— providing the pivotal moment of the night that Sir John Major won an unexpected majority.

At the 1997 general election, Sir David moved to the neighbouring constituency of Southend West, and our very own Lady Smith followed him as the MP for Basildon. She tells me that she soon discovered that one of Sir David's traditions was giving students a spelling test on primary school visits. Apparently, he had a preoccupation with two words in particular, and the local schools had posters of them plastered all over the walls to ensure that their students were ready to impress their visiting MP. I understand that there is a certain cohort, educated in south Essex, who has Sir David to thank for being able to spell "yacht" and "unnecessary" correctly.

In his new seat, Sir David continued his tradition of campaigning in a motorhome, playing his song, which I assure noble Lords I will not attempt to sing but which went:

> *"Vote, vote, vote, for David Amess,*
> *David is the man for you.*
> *If you want to be true blue, and to air your points of view,*
> *Then David Amess is the only man for you."*

Although his campaign style was compared to that of an ice-cream vendor, it was authentically Sir David, and it worked.

Throughout his Parliamentary career, he was well known as a dedicated Brexiteer, a doughty animal rights campaigner, a devout Roman Catholic and a devoted constituency champion. It is true to say that he achieved more on the Beck Benches than many Ministers manage to achieve in government; he piloted numerous Private Member's Bills into law, such as those on cruel tethering and warm homes, helped to ensure that the bravery of Raoul Wallenberg was recognised with a memorial statue, and organised 200 inspirational students from the Music Man Project to perform at the Royal Albert Hall and again at the London Palladium.

There cannot be anyone in this House who is not aware of Sir David's campaign to make Southend a city, a campaign that he pursued doggedly and determinedly, but with the humour and warmth that characterised his approach, because above all, he was a kind, generous and decent human being. I am delighted to tell the House that the Prime Minister has confirmed that Her Majesty the Queen has agreed that Southend will be accorded the city status that it so clearly deserves and a suitable memorial for an outstanding man of Essex.'

Baroness Smith of Basildon (Lab)

'My Lords, As the news unfolded on Friday that Sir David had been attacked, our hope that he had not been seriously hurt was mixed with that dreadful feeling we had in the pit of our stomachs that something deeply shocking and terrible had happened. When it was confirmed that he had not survived, it was hard to find the words to convey our feelings about this act of devastating horror.

We send our deepest and heartfelt condolences to Sir David's wife Julia, their children, their wider family, and his many friends and colleagues. Their loss is profound and overwhelming. We also feel for the staff who were with him at the time; the emotional shock that they suffered will be deeply felt for a long time.

I first met Sir David Amess in 1983, when he famously achieved that remarkable victory that many thought impossible: winning the newly drawn parliamentary constituency of Basildon, where there was not a single Conservative councillor.

At the time, I was living in Southend and working for the League Against Cruel Sports. David was one of the then small group from his party strongly supporting our campaign to ban fox hunting and hare-coursing. He remained passionately committed to the welfare of animals; indeed, his recent, final comments in Parliament were to urge for debate on animal welfare.

Over the years, our paths criss-crossed in Basildon, Southend and Westminster—and, just occasionally, on the same side of an issue. Leaving Basildon for Southend was both painful and an opportunity for him. As with everything else, he embraced his new constituency with enthusiasm, commitment and genuine affection, which, as has been clear from the responses of his constituents, was warmly reciprocated.

Throughout his nearly 40 years in Parliament, he was a formidable campaigner on a range of issues, usually triggered by a constituent who had come to him for help.

At the end of term in the House of Commons, Sir David would always be there until the very end, making the most of an opportunity to speak in the Adjournment debate on the constituency issues closest to his heart. There were often a lot of them. His last opportunity to do so was on 22 July this year. You have to smile and admire the fact that, with just a three-minute time limit, he managed to raise the issues of care home costs, building regulations and accessibility, zero-carbon emissions, energy costs, gas boilers, tidal power, jet skis, single-use plastic, sewage discharge, the Queen's Platinum Jubilee, trees in Southend, the export of live animals, the Pensions Ombudsman, charity raising by a constituent, vulnerable children, the Olympics and Paralympics, the Royal British Legion and a memorial to Dame Vera Lynn. He finished by saying that, "we must make Southend a city."

Some made the mistake of not initially taking his Southend campaign seriously, but he was totally committed. A few weeks ago, he formally launched the bid for city status. In typical Sir David style, it was quite an occasion, with the town crier and local dignitaries all there in Southend in support. The council leader, Ian Gilbert, told me that Sir David arranged everything, saying of the event: "It had a serious purpose but also a great sense of fun, which was the hallmark of Sir David's work".

As the whole House heard, we greatly enjoy the fact that the Queen has now given permission for Southend to become a city. What a great tribute, which will be well received not just in Southend but across the whole of Essex.

To those who knew him best, it comes as no surprise that so many shared their experiences of acts of kindness and support from David when they needed it most. A good friend of mine, Southend Labour Councillor Julian Ware-Lane, was David's opponent in the 2015 and 2017 general elections. Julian tragically died before his 60th birthday. David's thoughtfulness and kindness, including visiting Julian in hospital, was not something that most people knew about, but it meant so much to Julian and his friends and family.

It is clear from accounts over the weekend that this was not a random act but part and parcel of how Sir David lived his life. The Mayor of Southend, Councillor Margaret Borton, spoke for the whole town and wider when saying:"To have him taken away in this manner is a tragedy for our community".

This is the third time since 2016 that this House has paid tribute to a dedicated public servant colleague killed in the line of duty—Jo Cox MP in 2016, PC Keith Palmer in 2017, and today Sir David Amess. They were killed because they embodied the best of selfless public service.

On behalf of these Benches, I pay tribute to the life and work of Sir David Amess and offer our condolences to those who knew and loved him.**

The Archbishop of York

**My Lords, on behalf of the most reverend Primate the Archbishop of Canterbury, the bishops of the Church of England and, I am sure, all Christian people and all people of good will, I am here to offer the family of Sir David Amess and the constituents of Southend West my condolences and the assurance of the prayers of the Church. I am very grateful for all that has been said thus far, and, certainly, we on these Benches wish to associate ourselves with those comments.

I considered David Amess a friend. Leigh-on-Sea is my home town. Southend—now the city of Southend—is where I grew up. This appalling murder happened in streets I know well, just around the corner from where my mum lives. It was characteristic of David, whom I got to know during my time as Bishop of Chelmsford, that, when I was appointed, he was one of the first people to congratulate me. When I was translated to York, it was the same. He thought this was another way of putting Southend on the map: a boy who went to a secondary modern school in Southend was now the 98th Archbishop of York. He was so pleased. Last time I saw him, he asked to have his photograph taken with me.

I reckon that, now Southend has been declared a city today, forget about a statue of Vera Lynn at Dover; we are going to put a statue of David Amess at the end of Southend pier. He was—and I know this from the work I did with him—a deeply committed constituency MP. He exemplified what that means. He knew the people he served, and in the constituency he was completely colour blind to political difference. He just served the people he had been elected to serve.

189

I will conclude with some words that I wrote in a newspaper yesterday about his faith:"David Amess didn't wear his faith on his sleeve. He wore it in his heart."

That is the best place for faith because, when you wear it in your heart, it shapes everything.⁹

Lord Howard of Lympne (Con)

⁶My Lords, David Amess and I entered the House of Commons together at the 1983 general election. He was my colleague and friend for nearly 40 years. He was, as so many others have said, a really lovely man. He was one of that select band of people who are truly life-enhancing. When you left a meeting with David, you felt happier and better than you had felt before.

He was one of those rare human beings who looked for the best in others and, in doing so, brought out the best in them. He was a living antidote to the cynicism with which so many regard politics and politicians, and I join so many others in expressing my heartfelt sympathy to his family.

David was, of course, a Conservative, and his beliefs were deeply held and truly felt. However, as so many have said this afternoon, they did not in any way prove an impediment to his working with others across parties for the causes in which he believed.

This appalling tragedy has focused attention on the constituency role that was the core of David's parliamentary life. It is one of the great strengths of our parliamentary democracy that every Member of the House of Commons represents a constituency. In my opinion and on the basis of my 27 years in that House, the constituency surgery plays a key role in the bond between a Member of Parliament and his or her constituents. I

t ensures that whatever our failings—and heaven knows there are many of them—it is quite difficult for a Member of Parliament to be out of touch

Many years ago, not long after President George Bush senior had failed in his bid to be re-elected, I was visited by a Presidential contender from the United States. He asked what plans I had for the weekend and I explained that I would be in my constituency, holding my surgeries.

He asked what they were. He was very puzzled. When I explained, he expressed his surprise that a Cabinet Minister—which I was at the time— would be spending his weekend on this kind of activity. If George Bush's Cabinet had held surgeries, he said, he would still be President.

Although I have no doubt that measures can be taken to improve the security and safety of Members of Parliament, I hope that nothing will be done to weaken the links between Members and their constituents, in which surgeries play such an important part. That would be the very opposite of the legacy which David Amess so richly deserves.'

Baroness Harris of Richmond (LD)

'My Lords, we never discussed politics: David knew mine and I his, and it was always like that over the years we worked together. He succeeded me as chair of the Industry and Parliament Trust in 2014, having been a board member himself for a number of years previously. I always valued his contributions, if not always the way he put them.

I well recall him saying to me before one meeting, with that lovely crinkly smile on his face and his eyes twinkling, "Now, Angela, this isn't going to take too long, is it?" The agenda was huge.

Nick Maher, the trust's chief executive, told me a lovely story which epitomised David. He was introducing the Lord Mayor of London at an event and said, "I would like to introduce the Lord Mayor. Of course, none of us can aspire to be Lord Mayor because we don't have enough money and didn't go to the right school." The room went very quiet. That was so David. You never really knew what he might say next.

I know that Nick would also want me to say that David would always go that extra mile for the IPT, was adored by the staff there and worked enormously hard for the trust, which he continued to chair until 2017.

We also worked together on the British Parliamentary Committee for Iran Freedom. David was passionate about the Iranian resistance movement, and we shared many platforms together over the years. His commitment to everything he campaigned for was inspiring.

He was a kind, funny and thoughtful man, dedicated to his beloved Southend, which I often teased him about as I had worked at the airport there in my younger days. He was totally without malice or nastiness and always charmed everyone with whom he came into contact. It is almost impossible to believe that anyone would want to harm him, let alone attack him so brutally and fatally. He was a true Parliamentarian, who lived for his family and for his constituency—in that order—and his loss to us is deeply felt and incredibly painful.'

Lord Clarke of Nottingham (Con)

'My Lords, I knew David Amess when he first came in because I was elected before him. For nearly 40 years, I was on good and friendly terms with him as a Parliamentary colleague. I am as shocked as anybody in this House that such a man should come to such a terrible end. I cannot believe that a man like that ever had an enemy and that applied to his political life as much as to his private life. People from across the other side of the aisle from him, people from different parties who disagreed profoundly with him, have said these things. I, too, was a Conservative but it cannot be said that David and I were on the same wing of the broad coalition—as it is with all political parties in this country—that is the Conservative Party. He was a very fierce Eurosceptic. He was a great supporter of capital punishment. These are opinions which, to put it lightly, I do not share.

He was one of that group—the majority of British politicians—who would never have dreamed of allowing political disagreement to interfere with personal friendship. He respected the true right of free speech in a free society, which is that you respect the integrity and the sincerity of the person with whom you are having an argument and you maintain civilised dialogue. David was also an enthusiast—a hard-working, enthusiastic Back-Bencher who never betrayed the slightest interest in being such a keen party man that he was seeking preferment.

As parliamentarians, we all have to maintain the standards, as we undoubtedly do, and mourn the loss of a very great, very nice and hard-working parliamentarian.❜

Lord Alton of Liverpool (CB)

❛It was with profound and aching sorrow that I heard the shocking news on Friday that Sir David Amess MP had been murdered. Over the past 40 years, David and I had become close friends, and I shared many platforms with him, in his constituency and elsewhere.

We both had our working-class origins in the East End of London and, indeed, were baptised within a year of one another in the same church by the same Franciscan priest. He often joked that there must have been something in the holy water. His faith was in his DNA, and it animated his belief in public service and the principle of duty.

I first met David when he came into the House in 1983. From across the House, we joined forces in taking up the case of Raoul Wallenberg, the Swedish diplomat who saved thousands of Jewish lives from the Nazis. In 1997, thanks to David's assiduous campaign, a statue was erected to Wallenberg outside the Western Marble Arch Synagogue.

There were other campaigns, about Soviet Jewry and the plight of Alexander Ogorodnikov, a Russian Orthodox dissident. We frequently shared platforms to highlight the persecution of people because of their religion or belief or human rights violations, especially—as we have heard from others—the situation in Iran.

David's faith informed his passionate commitment to the very right to life, human dignity and the common good. But it was also rooted in his absolute conviction that an MP's first priority was to their constituents. It was the death of a constituent from hypothermia which led to his successful Private Member's Bill on fuel poverty.

Just a few weeks ago, David asked me to take part in the launch of his memoir, Ayes & Ears. Typical of David's kindness and generosity, as we heard from the Leader of the House, the proceeds of the book were dedicated to three charities: Endometriosis UK, Prost8 and the Leigh-on-Sea-based Music Man Project. David's causes were rooted in the neighbourhoods and people he represented. He was committed to direct face-to-face engagement, which, as the noble Lord Howard, was right to remind us, is at the very heart—the essence—of being a Member of Parliament.

Indeed, the noble Lord contested the constituency I was ultimately elected in in a previous general election, and he knows, as I do, that it is a precious relationship you have with your constituents. But now it has taken David's life, as it took the life of Jo Cox.

But as Mr Speaker, Sir Lindsay Hoyle, has rightly said, heinous crimes must not be allowed to drain the lifeblood from our representative democracy. This was an attack on democracy itself. We would be making a terrible mistake—and I know it is not what David would have wanted—for his death to simply lead to more barriers being put between the people and their representatives.

As David's family said in a statement today, people of faith, from all the great religions, and people of no faith must work much harder to create a more respectful society which honours difference.

His death reminds us of the deep-seated challenges we face. Above all, it will have devastating consequences for his family and loved ones, and my principal thoughts and prayers today are with Julia and their children. May this good man now rest in peace.'

Lord Rogan (UUP)

'On this sad occasion, when we mourn the death of our colleague, I remember a smile—the smile of David Amess. I have known David for some 15 years, and I never saw him without that smile on his face. In those years, I never heard a bad word said about him. How could there have been? He was, in the true sense of the word, a true and perfect Christian gentleman.

I remember fondly an all-party delegation to the Philippines led by David. It was an honour and privilege to be a part of it and to be with him. He moulded a very diverse group of parliamentarians into a very united group. His personality, charm and smile charmed the pants off all the Philippine members we met, both Ministers and parliamentary delegates.

As many have mentioned, Sir David had many interests; one was a keen and abiding interest in Northern Ireland. Each time we met, either the first or second sentence he would say was, "Well, Dennis, how's Northern Ireland? How can I help?".

Julia Amess has lost a husband. David's children have lost a father. We parliamentarians have lost a colleague. Northern Ireland has lost a friend. David, we all miss you.❞

Lord Young of Cookham (Con)

❝My Lords, I will pay a very brief tribute to David, based on 32 years of shared friendship in the other place. As my noble friend Lord Howard said, he was basically loyal to his party. Speaking as a former Chief Whip, of the 876 votes in the 2010 Parliament, David supported the Government 97.6% of the time. No one could complain about that. However, he was a man of strong principle, impervious to the bait of ministerial office, as my noble and learned friend Lord Clarke said.

When he voted against the Government, he did so on a matter of principle. Your Lordships might be interested to hear that he voted against the Government on the House of Lords Reform Bill in 2011. He also voted against military action against Syria, when the Government were defeated, and he opposed the badger cull, animal welfare being one of his special subjects. More recently, he actually voted against the Government on leaseholder compensation post the Grenfell tragedy, on which many of us may share his views.

His sunny optimism, revealed by that broad smile, his basic decency, his generosity and his modesty made him a great colleague. We would see him walking briskly from engagement to engagement with a sheaf of papers under his arm, his timetable fractured both here and in Southend by his willingness to stop and talk to colleagues. The shadow Leader mentioned his insistence that the House of Commons should not adjourn for the Christmas Recess until it had answered 18 issues of great importance to the burghers of Southend. Just pity the Leader of the House replying to that debate.

I mention one other factor about David. He was generous with his time and happy to visit and speak in the constituencies of Conservative MPs—an obligation often overlooked by his more self-important colleagues. He was also capable of mischief. He once came to North West Hampshire, and the convention is that the visiting speaker pays a glowing tribute to the industry and energy of the incumbent, however well founded in truth that may be. But there was none of that from David. "Great to be here in George's patch," he began, "but I don't want to waste time talking about him. I want to tell you about myself."

David's family has expressed the hope that some good should come from this tragedy. He was essentially a generous man, and he would not mind sharing some of the tributes to him more broadly if it helped to change the perception of the profession to which he has selflessly given his life.❜

Lord Blencathra (Con)

❛My Lords, I was also elected in 1983, but I first discovered Sir David's fundamental decency, integrity and courtesy when I was a junior Whip. Later, I was David's Chief Whip for four years. I held him in the highest regard because he was the sort of MP we Chief Whips liked and rated—not because he sycophantically voted for us 96% or 97% of the time, but because he always told us well in advance on the 3% of occasions when he could not because his conscience and constituency priorities prevailed. Chief Whips can live with MPs who have that level of courtesy and decency.

As has been said, he was deeply religious. That clearly influenced his views on political issues, but he was always capable of seeing the other point of view. He always disagreed with the viewpoint, not the person making it; that is a sign of greatness and generosity of spirit.❜

Lord Blunkett (Lab)

❛My Lords, I want to put on the record very briefly some messages that I picked up from Sir David's constituents. Jill Allen-King, aged 82, has written about her guide dog. Most recently, she asked me to write a foreword for her latest book about being blind in lockdown. In that book, she talks about Sir David, and when I phoned her a couple of months ago, she described what a wonderful man he was: attending charitable dos when it would have been a lot easier not to; helping her with fundraising; and being there at the drop of a hat. That was the measure of Sir David Amess.

One thing that I picked up over the last few weeks about Sir David that is very close to my heart was his engagement with young people learning about politics, citizenship and democracy.

If there is one thing that we can carry forward, which I hope will bring comfort to his family and close friends, it is being able to teach our young people how to do democracy, how to be understanding and how to have very strong opinions but express them in a way that is respectful to others as well as to themselves.

If that comes out of this and people can have a dialogue across the country about how we could make that work better, Sir David's life —wonderful as it has been—will also be remembered for making another contribution, like that of Jo Cox, to changing the way in which we do our politics.'

Lord Cormack (Con)

'My Lords, there is one aspect of Sir David's work that is perhaps not widely known. Every year for the last 30 years, he took into his office a young American student from the Catholic University of America. I had the honour of arranging the programmes over those years, so I worked closely with him. He gave those young people a wonderful insight into British parliamentary democracy.

Those young people, who had perhaps met the Senators or Congressmen they had worked for on the Hill only once in a three or four-month period, saw Sir David every day. He took them to his constituency. They saw at first hand what it meant to be personally represented. They all benefited from that experience, and he made an intangible contribution to British-American relations in the process.'

Lord Moynihan (Con)

'My Lords, it is almost 40 years since the first meeting David and I attended on our respective roads to Westminster, entering Parliament for marginal constituencies in 1983. Here was a man who was constructive, committed, amusing and always willing to go the extra mile for you, or indeed for anyone he felt he could help. We stayed close for many decades.

Last week, at his request, I was with him on a delegation to Qatar, where his charm and mischievous sense of humour, deployed in a way only David could get away with in front of the most elevated in society, was put to wonderful effect. It was so good to be with him. On asking the Father Emir how many children he had, and receiving the reply "24", he promptly reached for a small House of Lords picture frame as a gift and challenged him to fit all 24 into the frame.

When he told the Emir, who had just received a copy of David's book, that he could "throw it in the wastepaper basket" that led to more laughter and marked him out as being wonderfully self-deprecating. We flew out sitting together and flew back chatting away. The mission had been one of the most successful we had been on.

His sensitivity and determination to help rehouse the 13 unaccompanied Afghan children with British family connections; his strong Catholic faith; his work as a strong supporter of Israel, yet always welcomed and respected in so many Arab countries; his ability to bring together and unite members of many a parliamentary delegation; and the quips and asides that always raised a smile, were there for all to see.

As co-founders and co-chairs of the All-Party Group for the Olympic and Paralympic Games, we were planning a celebration for our Olympic and Paralympic medallists here in the Lords, an event he was much anticipating. It was no surprise, then, to receive the following tribute from the president of the International Olympic Committee, Thomas Bach, who yesterday wrote:

> *"Sir David fought keenly for sport and for all it could do. He understood that the Olympic Games are the only event this can bring the entire world together in peaceful competition ... He worked tirelessly to keep the games free of politics and dispute."*

David was a true friend. He proved that politics was more than the collective DNA of ministerial ambition. It is, as has been said many times, not least in this House, about public service, about challenging and changing the lives of constituents, even in the smallest possible way; and to make a difference to your constituents and the causes you felt passionately about was everything that David stood for.

He was a decent, uplifting, unstintingly hard-working, kind man with a mischievous sense of humour; an outstanding Parliamentarian and constituency MP; devoted husband to Julia and loving father to their children; and such a loyal friend and colleague to so many of us. At the end, he was doing what he loved best and what he was brilliant at: helping his constituents, and not least realising his long-standing ambition that Southend, for which he long campaigned, should be a city, both on earth and, God willing, in heaven.[9]

The Philanthropists

FOLLOWING is a list of our supporters who, through ordering this book prior to publication, have generously donated to *The Music Man Project* funds. Norman and Joyce Lambert Giller MBE will be paying £5 to the charity for every name mentioned plus a share of future profits from sales after overheads have been cleared. Those who have agreed to donate, please contact me by email at normangiller@gmail.com and I will get the book to you. Overseas donors will receive a PDF file of the book. Thank you.

Ken Adam, California, USA,

Marut Agdeue, Leigh-on-Sea, Essex

Richard Alger, Norwich, Norfolk

Paul Aplin, Basildon, Essex

Patricia Ayres, Chalkwell, Essex

Marie Banks, Bristol, Avon

Bev and Chris Baker, Leigh-on-Sea, Essex

Becky Barritt, Rochford, Essex

Jane Bateman, Wembley,

Richard Beevis, Evesham, Worcestershire

Rob Belcher, Bridport, Dorset

Alexander Bell, Westcliff-on-Sea, Essex

Aubrey and Felix Bell, Westcliff-on-Sea, Essex

Ettie Bell, Westcliff-on-Sea, Essex

Mike Berry, BackPass Editor

Karen Boshier, Southend-on-Sea, Essex

Philip Brady, Birmingham, Warwickshire

Fran and John Bramble, Leigh-on-Sea, Essex

Gary Braybrooke, Oksburg, Gauteng, South Africa

Paddy and Ann Briggs, Orpington, Kent

Maggie and Gary Briley, Leigh-on-Sea, Essex

Katherine Brooks, Hockley, Essex

Peter Brophy, Moscow via Manchester

Ian and Millie Brown, alberttortoise.com

Jean Brown, Facebook friend
Pat Brown, Brighton & Hove
Kevin and Paula Buck, Leigh-on-Sea, Essex
Sarn Burns, Southend-on-sea, Essex
Caroline Burriss,Shoeburyness, Essex
Jackie Camacho, Southend-on-Sea Essex
Owen Cartey, Leigh-on-Sea, Essex
Judith Canham, Leigh-on-Sea, Essex
Steve Casey, Cheltenham, Gloucestershire
Jenny Cast, Leigh-on-Sea, Essex
Lesley and Colin Catterick, Leigh-on-Sea, Essex
Chris Chapman, Great Wakering, Essex
Antionette Cini, Tottennham, N17
Ian Clark, Kingswood, Surrey
Jo Clark, Westcliff-on-Sea, Essex
Tom Clarke, Brentwood, Essex
Tony Corbey, Harrow, Middlesex
Alison Corder, Leigh-on-Sea, Essex
Linda Cornelus, Southend-on-Sea, Essex
Steve Cox, Poole, Dorset, via Billericay, Essex
Lauren Crader, Ilford, Greater London
Alexander Edward Crane, Southend-on-Sea, Essex
Julie Cushion, Belfairs, Essex
Pamela Czuba, Westcliff-on-Sea
Jackie Davidson, Eastwood, Essex
Ivor Davis, California, USA
Ken and Meg Davison, Southchurch, Essex
Colin Dawson, Belfast, Northern Ireland
Paula Dawson, Belfast, Northern Ireland
Sarah Dawson, Belfast, Northern Ireland
Sally Jane Carr Day, Southend-on-Sea, Essex
William Geoffrey Day, Hythe, Kent
Keith Dibble. Aldershot, Hants
Tom Dixon, Edinburh, Scotland
Jacqui Dallimore. Thorpe Bay, Essex

Katy Duddridge, Southend-on-Sea, Essex

Lisa and John East, Daws Heath, Essex

Arthur Evans, Sevenoaks, Kent

Barry Evans, Waltham Cross, Herts

Michael Evans, Coggeshall, Essex

Phil Evans, Bushey, Herts

Graham and Kerry Eyre, New South Wales, Australia

Jonathan Fellows, Shenstone, Shropshire

Anna and Edward Firth, Leigh-on-Sea, Essex

Lesley Folgate, Bournemouth,

Paul Foot, North London

Angelo Foscari, Palermo, Italy

David and Zoe Foxall, Southend-on-Sea, Essex

Marilyn Fowles, Southend-on-Sea, Essex

David Garston, Leigh-on-Sea, Essex

Sarah and Simon, Futcher, Westcliff-on-Sea, Essex

John Garforth, Hockley, Essex

Alice Giller, Poynton, Cheshire

Andrew Giller, Toft Monks, Beccles, Suffolk

James and Daniel, Giller, Ringwood, Hampshire

Sarah Giller, Ringwood, Hampshire

Sue Godwin, Southend-on-Sea

Ted Graham, Cartagena, Murcia (via Belfast and Fleet Street)

David and Jean Guthrie, Wokingham, Berkshire

Clive Hall, Girton, Cambridgeshire

Emily Hadjinicolaou, Reigate, Surrey

Lesley Harris, London

Sally Hayes, Leigh-on-Sea, Essex

Sue Hayter, Canvey Island, Essex

Steve Heywood, Hertfordshire

Colin Hicks, Leigh-on-Sea, Essex

Caroline Hince, Leigh-on-Sea, Essex

Mick How, Chatham, Kent

Hazel Howard, Southend-on-Sea

Craig Ireland, Upper Beeding, West Sussex

Paul Jerrom, London
Ian Jewell, Southend-on-Sea, Essex
Viv Jones, Watford, Herts
Leanne Jupe, Rayleigh, Essex
Andrew Juvan, Elmhurst Ilinois, USA
Christine Kemble, Spalding, Lincolnshire
Laraine Kempster, Bexleyheath, Greater London
Stephen Kester, Croydon, Surrey
Brian and Charmaine Klein, Hampstead, London
Hannah Lambert, Dubai
Lorelei Lambert, Rayleigh, Essex
Lucas Lambert, Brighton, East Sussex
Lula Lambert, Rayleigh, Essex
Ryan Lambert, Rayleigh, Essex
Carol Langton, Facebook friend
Mark Langton, Berro, Murcia, Spain via Somerset
Linds Anita Lawton, Cartura, Italy
Professor Peter Lawton, Haifa, Israel
Gill Lee, Eltham, Greenwich
Liz Liston, Southend-on-Sea, Essex
Jim Logan, Sanderstead, Surrey
Joao Lyle, Facebbok friend
Isobel Mackay, Nottingham
Val Mackay, Nottingham
Jeff Maluske, Nova Scotia, Canada
Lorraine Marash, Westcliff-on-Sea, Essex
Jim Marianski, Florida, USA
Gerry Mason, Bourne, Lincs
Christine Matthews, Chelsea
David Matthews, Cheshunt, Herts
Beverley Miller, Westcliff-on-Sea, Essex
Philip Miller, Southend-on-Sea, Essex
Adam and Lesley Millward, Egham, Surrey
Helen Findlay Morris, Kingston-upon-Hull
Roger Morris, London

Bobby Kevin Munro, Telford, Shropshire

David Nathanson, Hadleigh, Essex

Philip Nyman, Tottenham, N17

Stephen Olley, Southend-on-Sea, Essex

Patricia O'Sullivan Leigh-on-Sea, Essex

David Painter, Southchurch, Essex

Carol Palmer, Thirsk. Yorkshire

Annette Parris. Bishop's Stortford, Herts

Terry Pattinson and Valerie Glassbrook, Maidenhead

Matt Payne, Facebook friend

Kim and Steve Perryman, Wiltshire

Heather Price, Great Wakering, Essex

Janice Price, Prittlewell, Essex

Ann Randall, Walthamstow

Julie Anne Rayment, Belfairs, Essex

Dave Read, Southend West, Essex

Peter Redburn, Southend-on-Sea, Essex

Maureen Rhodes, Facebook friend

Derek Rowe, Beckenham, Kent

Chris Rushton, Morpeth, Northumberland

David Rushton, Australia

Adele Ryntjes, Northwood, Greater London

Valerie Self, Facebook friend

Tim Sexton, Hackney, London E8

Louise Sherman, California, USA

Richard Tango Smith, Reading, Berks

John Spencer, Iveagh Club, Leigh-on-Sea, Essex

Rachael Spicer, Rayleigh, Essex

Harrison Spicer, Rayleigh, Essex

Nancy Spicer, Rayleigh, Essex

Lilian Spicer, Rayleigh, Essex

Joanne Stanley, Leigh-on-Sea, Essex

Roland Stanley, Leyton, London E10

John Stevens, Preston, Lancashire

Judith Suttling and family, Westcliff-on-Sea, Essex

Annette Taylor, Canvey Island, Essex

Carol Thomas, Southend-on-Sea, Essex

Mick Thomas, Camborne, Cornwall

Pauk Thomas, Coltishall, Norfolk

Denis Tilbrook, Rayleigh, Essex

Kim Townsend, Canvey Island, Essex

Deborah J. Tucker, Facebook friend

Katharine and Callum Wallace, Chalkwell, Essex

Martha Wallace, Chalkwell, Essex

David G. Ward, Thorpe Bay, Essex

Ann Watson, Facebook friend

Mark Watson, Cheshunt, Herts

Craig Watt, Leigh-on-Sea, Essex

Sue Webb, Great Cambourne, Cambridgeshire

Debra Joyce Williams,, Southend-on-Sea, Essex

Colin Wilson, Stroud, Gloucestershire

Wanda Wilson, Southend-on-Sea, Essex

Susan Winter, Rayleigh, Essex

Colin and Carole Wood, Leigh-on-Sea, Essex

John David Wood, Wiltshire via Southend

Beryl Worsdale, Dagenham, Essex

Alan Worsdale, Hayes Barton, Essex

Nick Wurr, Ljubljana, Slovenia

The Last Word

JOYCE and I thank you for accompanying us on our long and winding road from the East End to Buckingham Palace. We like to think this is a fairly unique book. It's not too often you will read a story told by two people with a combined age of 175 years, with no ghostwriter involved (despite my family saying I should employ one!).

We counter accusations that we are being egotistical daring to write this book with the argument that we have just one aim in mind, to raise money and appreciation for the thoroughly deserving Music Man Project.

The two Davids – Sir David Amess and music maestro David Stanley – shared the crazy ambition that the choir should appear on Broadway. Can you imagine the astronomical costs plus the sheer logistics of such an enterprise? But the Davids both liked the challenge of the 'impossible'. When Sir David was brutally and senselessly murdered, the 'other' David decided – in Sir David's memory – to take on the challenge alone.

This is why we are donating all profits from this book to the Music Man Project and we thank you from the bottom of our hearts for your support. Please encourage others to buy it for the simple reason of helping the wonderful Music Man Project. Tell anybody who is interested to email normangiller@gmail.com for full details.

If you wish to become a supporter of an inspiring cause, please go on line to the Music Man Project website at:

www.themusicmanproject.com And you can make personal donations to *www.justgiving.com/musicmanproject,* or alternatively to: *www.gofundme.com/f/music-is-magic-on-broadwa*y.

It is a joy to see the choir thoroughly engrossed in making music under David Stanley's supervision. Joyce and I have been prileged guests at choir rehearsals and consider it an experience from the heavens.

People who usually struggle to communicate suddenly find a voice and a purpose, and they give total concentration and a discipline that speaks volumes for the caring way they are taught and encouraged.

It was particularly heartening to see them conquering a song I had written to support Sir David's campaign to have Southend recognised as a city. Here we go with the lyrics for *Good Old Southend-on-Sea.* How's that for a last word! Yes, Life Begins at 90 ... Enjoy every second.

GOOD OLD SOUTHEND ON SEA **For the Music Man Project**

© Norman Giller 2025 Arranged by David P. Stanley

CHORUS
Good old Southend on Sea
Such a lovely place to be
So much to do, so much to see
At Good old Southend on Sea

Verse 1
It's got a pier that's without peer
Where day-trippers appear all through the year
And swooping seagulls you'll always hear
It's a charming place full of good cheer
It's unbeatable for cockles and winkles
The Golden Mile brightly twinkles
The National Jazz Centre piano tinkles
And there's lots to do even when it sprinkles .. at (chorus)…

Verse 2
Roll up your trousers for a bracing paddle
Ride down leafy lanes in a saddle
Whether it's a horse or bike that you straddle
And the Adventure Playground's sure to razzle-dazzle.
You'll find the friendliest people in the land
Enjoy walking on the pebbles and the sand
Where star-struck lovers stroll hand in hand
Come along and listen to the band ..at … (chorus)

Verse 3:
It's the tops as a seaside resort
Where you can eat ice cream and enjoy all sport
Travel the world from the local airport
But to see Southend you don't need a passport
Places like Old Leigh are so pretty
There are great views of the Estuary
We're so very proud of our city
That we'll keep repeating this little ditty … (chorus)

Verse 4:
We've appeared at the Royal Albert Hall
And at the London Palladium, best of all
We've sung for Royalty and with Michael Ball
Now on Broadway we want a curtain call
Please help us get to the Great White Way
And in New York City to sing and play
We promise it will really make our day
If we can appear on old Broadway ... from (chorus)

PREVIOUS BOOKS BY NORMAN GILLER
(www.normangillerbooks.com)

'Sir Bill' (The definitive Bill Nicholson story, with Steve Perryman)
Headlines Deadlines All My Life. My autobiography
The One and Only Jimmy Greaves The authorised biography
The G-Men, Jimmy Greaves and Alan Gilzean partnership
My 70 Years of Spurs   **Bobby Smith, Forgotten Hero**
Eighty at Eighty, with Sir Geoff Hurst
The Man Who Put A Curse on Muhammad Ali
(The amazing story of Richard Dunn's world heavyweight title fight challenge)
Banks of England (with Gordon Banks)
Footballing Fifties
Bobby Moore, The Master
The Glory and the Grief (with George Graham)
Banks v Pelé (with Terry Baker, Pelé and Gordon Banks)
SPURS 67 The gripping story of the first all-London FA Cup final
Lane of Dreams (A full history of 'old' White Hart Lane)
Shooting Spurs, This 100-goals club
The Managing Game It's the book that you play
Bill Nicholson Revisited (Based on 40 years of conversations with Mr Spurs)
Danny Blanchflower This WAS His Life
The Golden Double An Unforgettable Season
 Football And All That (an irreverent history of the game)
The Seventies Revisited (with Kevin Keegan)
The Final Score (with Brian Moore)
ABC of Soccer Sense (Tommy Docherty)
Billy Wright, A Hero for All Seasons (official biography)
Billy Wright, My Dad (with Vicky Wright)
The Rat Race (with Tommy Docherty)
Denis Compton (The Untold Stories)
McFootball, the Scottish Heroes of the English Game
Chopper's Chelsea (with Ron Harris)
Hammers-80 (introduced by Trevor Brooking)
The Book of Rugby Lists (with Gareth Edwards)
The Book of Tennis Lists (with John Newcombe)
The Book of Golf Lists (with Peter Allis)
TV Quiz Trivia Sports Quiz Trivia
Know What I Mean (with Frank Bruno)

Eye of the Tiger (with Frank Bruno)
From Zero to Hero (with Frank Bruno)
The Judge Book of Sports Answers
Watt's My Name (with Jim Watt)
My Most Memorable Fights (with Henry Cooper)
How to Box (with Henry Cooper)
Henry Cooper's 100 Greatest Boxers
Sir Henry Cooper, A Hero for All Time
The Ali Files, Every contest and whatever happened to his opponents
Mike Tyson Biography
Mike Tyson, the Release of Power (with Reg Gutteridge)
Crown of Thorns, the World Heavyweight Title (with Neil Duncanson)
Fighting for Peace (Barry McGuigan biography, with Peter Batt)
The Real Rocky (Dial M for Marciano)
World's Greatest Cricket Matches
World's Greatest Football Matches
Golden Heroes (with Dennis Signy) The FWA Footballer of the Year Award
The Judge (1,001 arguments settled)
The Great Football IQ Quiz Book (The Judge of The Sun)
The Concorde Club (with Col Mathieson)

Children's books:
Tales of Uncle Rhymo
Duncan the Talking Football

Timeframed Great Moments in British History (partwork collection)
The Marathon Kings
The Golden Milers (with Sir Roger Bannister)
Olympic Heroes (with Brendan Foster)
Olympics Handbook 1980 Pre-The Moscow Games
Olympics Handbook 1984 Pre-The Los Angeles Games
Book of Cricket Lists (Tom Graveney)
Top Ten Cricket Book (Tom Graveney)
Cricket Heroes (with Eric Morecambe)
Big Fight Quiz Book (100 rounds of boxing knowledge tests)
TVIQ Puzzle Book
Lucky the Fox (with Barbara Wright)
Gloria Hunniford's TV Challenge
July 30 1966, Football's Longest Day

World Cup 2010 (with Michael Giller)

The Glory-Glory Game (Spurs Writers' Club)

How to Self Publish

Satzenbrau Sports Quiz Book 1 Satzenbrau Sports Quiz Book 2

Comedy novels:

Carry On Doctor Carry On England Carry On Loving What A Carry On

Carry On Up the Khyber Carry On Abroad Carry On Henry

(These were sequel stories to the films)

A Stolen Life (novel)

Mike Baldwin: Mr Heartbreak (novel, introduced by actor Johnny Briggs)

Hitler's Final Victim (unpublished novel)

The Contenders (unpublished novel)

Keys to Paradise (novel) **The Glory and the Greed** (novel)

A Blaze of Lives (novel)

Novels featuring J.C. Campbell, Fleet Street crime reporter turned private eye:

Beyond the Krays   The Fleet Street Murders

The Henley Murders   The Football Murders

Books in collaboration with RICKY TOMLINSON

Football My Arse Celebrities My Arse   Chcers My Arse,

Reading My Arse (The Search for the Rock Island Line)

Books in collaboration with JIMMY GREAVES:

This One's On Me, The Final (novel), **The Ball Game** (novel),

The Boss (novel), **The Second Half** (novel)

Let's Be Honest (with Reg Gutteridge)

Greavsie's Heroes and Entertainers

World Cup History (From Uruguay 1930)

GOALS! Taking Sides (Comparing the greatest sides)

Stop the Game, I Want to Get On (Crazy moments on and off the pitch)

The Book of Football Lists   Funny Old Games (with The Saint)

Sports Quiz Challenge   Sports Quiz Challenge 2

It's A Funny Old Life

Saint & Greavsie's 1990 World Cup Special

Greavsie At Seventy (with Terry Baker and Michael Giller)

The Sixties Revisited

Don't Shoot the Manager (Post-war history of England football managers)